Mastering Stress
in Child Rearing

Mastering Stress in Child Rearing

A Longitudinal Study of Coping and Remission

James E. Teele
Boston University

LexingtonBooks
D.C. Heath and Company
Lexington, Massachusetts
Toronto

Library of Congress Cataloging in Publication Data

Teele, James E
  Mastering stress in child rearing.

  1. Parent and child—Longitudinal studies. 2. Children—Management—Longitudinal studies. 3. Stress (Psychology)—Longitudinal studies. I. Title.
HQ755.85.T43   649'.1   79–48006
ISBN 0–669–03622–6   AACR2

Published simultaneously in Canada

Printed in the United States of America

International Standard Book Number: 0–669–03622–6

Library of Congress Catalog Card Number: 79–48006

For Ann, Lisa, and Teddy

Contents

List of Tables

Foreword

Most civilized societies have abandoned the use of punishment as a means of managing and correcting the difficult and socially undesirable behavior of children. They did so because punishment seemed ineffective or positively counter-productive, and because, whether it worked or not, it was incompatible with contemporary standards of humanity. The notion lingers on, however, and there is frequently a punitive element in otherwise progressive programs of treatment for delinquent or disturbed children. One reason for the occasional but persistently recurrent calls for a stricter discipline, is widespread uncertainty or frank disbelief about the effectiveness of the many alternative forms of treatment that have been tried in recent decades. Most such alternative forms were based on psychiatric theories that saw deviant or delinquent behavior as evidence, not of willful and knowing misconduct, but of an underlying mental or emotional disturbance, to be treated as sickness rather than wickedness. What was required was a skilled diagnosis accompanied by an appropriate course of treatment. Unfortunately, it has not been possible to identify causes with any degree of certainty, nor to demonstrate that treatments have been effective in providing a cure. With many physical diseases treatments are visibly effective, or alternatively, elegant research designs have been developed and applied that demonstrate the positive or negative effect of treatments. With behavioral disturbances such experimental proof has not emerged, partly because of the complexities of the problem and partly because therapists have been resistant to the possibility of proof. Indeed a number of investigators cited in this book, using experimental and control groups, have claimed with some plausibility that patients are no more likely than controls to be "cured," or to cease their neurotic or antisocial behavior. Such studies may have faulty designs or inadequate controls, but they have nevertheless created a hypothesis of "spontaneous remission" that cannot be ignored. The idea has its attractions. If treatment brings no measurable benefits, and if, left alone, most disturbed individuals will spontaneously get well, what is the justification for the continued use, on such a large scale, of highly paid professionals and of long and expensive courses of so-called treatment?

This book questions the idea of spontaneous remission. Using observations at two points in time, separated by thirteen years, Dr. Teele demonstrates convincingly that spontaneous remission of behavioral disturbance in children is a practical and logical impossibility. It is not a defense of psychotherapy. Dr. Teele states firmly that he has no intention of evaluating psychotherapy and that he does not have data capable of being used for evaluation. Taking advantage of a natural experimental opportunity, he documents, across the thirteen-year interval, the help-seeking efforts and, to a lesser extent, the help-receiving experiences, of a cohort of parents whose requests for assistance in 1962 had been turned down by psychiatric and court guidance-clinics. This was a natural opportunity because Dr. Teele had studied this same cohort in 1963, a year after the initial refusal. Impelled by both personal and scientific curiosity, he wondered what had happened to these children and what had been the behavioral outcome in 1975 or 1976, when most of them had become young adults. He is, himself, plainly astonished at the events of the intervening years. There had indeed been remission of a kind. According to the general assessment of the parental respondent only 23 percent of these children referred to psychiatric clinics in 1962 were doing poorly—an assessment broadly in line with their more detailed judgments about their children's job satisfaction, social life and family involvement. This remission was, however, far from being spontaneous. In 11 percent of the cases no external assistance had been received; the remaining 219 respondents reported receiving 602 relevant episodes of assistance from other psychiatric agencies and professionals, from physicians, social workers, clergy, teachers, rehabilitation institutions and (a minority) neighbors and relatives. The extent of help-seeking had obviously been much greater than the help received. Such use of external assistance is one reflection of the coping strategies of parents. External assistance, while important in itself, is only one manifestation of the stream of actions, events, strategies, and concerns occurring within the family milieu and focused upon the child's behavior.

Like many research revelations this research finding, once made, looks simple and self-evident. Yet its implications are far-reaching. It disposes, brutally, of the notion of "spontaneous" remission. Any long-term controlled evaluation of psychotherapy, or of any other form of treatment or management, must face up to the probability that the experimental intervention is only one, and perhaps a minor, occurrence in a stream of influencing events, some of which may support and some which counteract the therapeutic intention. And, of course, these contaminating effects are likely to apply to both the experimental and the control groups. There is a terrible naivety to the crude evaluation of therapeutic intervention, which seems to assume, not only that a particular intervention may be significant, but that life ceases between intervention and evaluation.

This study has important implications for the organization of services. Analysis of the selection procedure that led to the offer or refusal of service suggests that the criteria used had little reference to the intrinsic problem but were more reflective of the therapeutic interests or the financial and administrative practices of the agency and its professional staff. Particularly notable was their preference for accepting younger children and those with neurotic symptoms rather than older children showing antisocial behavior. In one sense this is understandable—why accept children whose problems are not amenable to the theories, skills, and therapeutic practices in which the agency specializes? On the other hand, Dr. Teele's data show how refusal sends concerned parents out into a long and frustrating search for other help through a confusing maze of agencies, using their own coping strategies while still facing the same or an increasingly severe problem. Our understanding of the issues has changed since 1962. We are less prone to regard "disturbed" children as being themselves sick, and we are more ready to seek causes in the child's history and microenvironment. Prolonged individual psychotherapy of unproven efficacy is being complemented or replaced by briefer intervention in which treatment is applied to the environment and particularly to the parents as well as the child. Dr. Teele's perceptive account of the awe-inspiring efforts of parents to obtain help, and the relationship of their own hopes, ideas of blame, frustrations, and coping strategies, to the eventual outcome should reinforce this promising tendency. It is consistent with much other research, in Britain as well as the United States, which has demonstrated the illogicality of treating children for environmentally induced problems while leaving the environment to look after itself.

This book provides an excellent example of the painstaking research invariably needed before we can evaluate the effectiveness, let alone the efficiency, of therapeutic intervention. The simple yes or no of laboratory experiments, where annoying irrelevancies can be excluded by design, and which are often themselves the culmination of much prior research and development, is rarely attainable in social and behavioral affairs. Children refused treatment, and therefore potential controls on one occasion, become patients or clients on later occasions and themselves become potentially the experimental group. Throughout the period from intervention to outcome they are subject to all kinds of obfuscating influences—in this case the coping strategies of parents who probably had a hand in the creation of the problem. Treatment itself is a highly equivocal concept and, as Dr. Teele's study shows, patients appearing with one kind of problem later reappear with another. Formal intervention/outcome evaluation must, in these circumstances, be replaced by successive partial evaluations accompanied by continued observation, analysis, and understanding of all the contextual influences. Evaluation in this sense is no more than the development of understanding and is conceptually inseparable from therapeutic activity itself. In trying to reach that understanding, Dr. Teele reveals the poverty of our knowledge about the dynamic interrelationships between treatment, the continuing environment, and child behavior. One hopes that Dr. Teele will take his analysis of this rich source of data to more detailed levels and that other researchers will follow his lead into this rewarding but difficult research.

One final comment. During my first period of residence in the United

States I was greatly impressed by the mobility of the population. In my community, residents told me, one-eighth of the population leaves and is replaced each year. Longitudinal study was clearly out the question. Dr. Teele traced 98.6 percent of these migratory Americans after a period of thirteen years. This is almost as awe-inspiring as the help-seeking efforts of his respondents. I hope this achievement will encourage research workers and practitioners to indulge in more longitudinal studies. It makes long-term evaluation of therapeutic intervention a realizable possibility.

Raymond Illsley
Institute of Medical Sociology
Aberdeen, Scotland

Preface

There used to be a time when parents' power over their children was relatively total; responsibility was presumed to accompany this authority. In the nineteenth century, similar power relationships are reported for employers and workers, men and women, victor and vanquished, and others. Many of these power relationships have changed in this century, which may stand as the most momentous one in history in this regard.

This century has seen child labor laws emerge, then expand into a demand for children's rights—one of the major themes of the 1970 White House Conference on Children. But in spite of these changes, parents are still responsible for rearing their children, and most parents willingly accept that responsibility. They know that their relationship with their children is precious but at the same time fragile, even perilous. Most survive the journey. This book is about parent and child—the quintessential relationship—and some of the problems they share.

This book reports on research that was begun in late 1962. At that time I was a Russell Sage Resident in sociology assigned to the Judge Baker Guidance Center in Boston (1961–1963). My fellowship was given in order to permit me to gain research experience in an applied field. The Judge Baker was chosen because it encouraged evaluative research and also because its director at that time, Dr. George Gardner, wished to have a sociologist who could work collaboratively with members of clinical disciplines.

The fellowship permitted me the luxury of listening, reading, inquiring, and talking about clinical and research practices with a number of the professionals on the clinic staff. After a while, these activities led me to focus on the type of problems that people brought to child psychiatric clinics and the nature of clinic-selection practices. Thus, I decided to include a number of psychiatric clinics in a study of intake and selection practices and also to undertake follow-up interviews with parents whose children were not accepted for treatment. I envisioned only a short-term study and had made no plans for a long-term follow-up. My early goals were reached during 1963–1964, when I analyzed and reported on the data I had gathered.

It was not until early 1974 that I decided to carry out a longitudinal study, using the first-stage data primarily as a baseline. My interest this time was spurred by my continuing concern with the problem-solving behavior of parents and of their relationships to the adult adjustment of the children. This interest appeared reasonable given my own selection procedures in 1963; that is, I had included only those parents whose children had not been accepted for service by the clinics in 1962. I thus proposed and carried out, in 1975–1976, a study that focused on the coping activities of parents during the period between interviews and the adjustment of the children, then averaging approximately twenty-three years of age, as adults.

Given the declining birthrate and the changing features of the family, it seems more urgent than ever to study and enhance the development of children. I hope that this study will contribute to that development.

Acknowledgments

A very large number of people and organizations have contributed to the research reported on in this book. Although it is not possible to acknowledge or even to know all the people who made this research possible, I wish to mention some of them.

My greatest debt is to the respondents who graciously participated in our study. They shared their problems and experiences with us in order that others might benefit. I thank them for their sincerity and their generosity.

The major funding for this research was provided by a research grant (MH26419-01-03) from the Juvenile Problems Office, Applied Research Branch of the National Institute of Mental Health. This grant supported the long-term stage of the project beginning in 1975, and I am extremely grateful for this support. The earlier stage of the research in 1962–1963 was supported, in part, by a grant from the President's Committee on Juvenile Delinquency. In addition, a grant from the Maurice Falk Medical Fund of Pittsburgh aided in the analysis of second-stage data.

Many other institutions provided research support during the course of this study. They include the Russell Sage Foundation, which provided me with a postdoctoral fellowship in 1961–1963, the Judge Baker Guidance Center, which appointed me as staff sociologist between 1961 and 1965, the Harvard School of Public Health, with which I was associated during the early research stage, and Boston University, which appointed me to its faculty in 1970 and gave support during the later stage of the project. During a sabbatical year, I was employed for a period by the Medical Research Council of London (United Kingdom) and was assigned to the Institute of Medical Sociology at the University of Aberdeen in Scotland. I am extremely grateful for the chance to discuss problems and exchange ideas with colleagues in each of these settings. In addition, I am indebted to the five child psychiatric clinics that cooperated in the study and to the American Association of Psychiatric Clinics for Children, which lent its support to the study. I am grateful also to the Office of the Commissioner of Probation in Massachusetts for permitting me access to some of its records.

I am indebted to a number of people who assisted me in various ways during the long history of the project. I owe a great debt to Sol Levine, then a Harvard colleague, who collaborated with me during the first-stage study. I am also indebted to the Faculty Seminar organized at Harvard by Stan Wheeler, which involved a number of Boston-area researchers in delinquency who came together once a month over a two-year period in order to exchange ideas. George Gardner, the director of the Judge Baker Guidance Center, gave strong support during the first stage of this project. Louise Corman was my research assistant, and Mary New, then the director of the computer center at the Harvard School of Public Health, was my computer consultant during the first-stage study. Raymond Illsley, director of the Institute of Medical Sociology at the University of Aberdeen, has contributed wise counsel in connection with this project, through the many years of our friendship. I am grateful also to Marge Roy of the Probation Department for her assistance in obtaining needed records. I thank Teri Levitin and Ed Flynn of NIMH who were most cooperative and supportive in administering our research grant.

My valued associates during the arduous second stage of the project included Gina Abeles, who was the project field director and troubleshooter and who was most valuable in helping to relocate the respondents. This study could not have been completed without the careful attention she directed at a wide range of conceptual and technical issues in the second stage. Dr. Abeles was supported during part of her association with the project through a postdoctoral training program (No. 5 T 32 MH14629-01-02) Social Science Section, Research Manpower Development Branch of the Alcohol, Drug Abuse, and Mental Health Administration. Phyllis Blake and Martin Sawzin were my research assistants, and they performed beyond the call of duty during the difficult relocation effort, as did Heidi Little, the project secretary. Steve Cohen, Barbara Hannon, and Dr. Abeles were the computer consultants on this project. Steve Cohen also served as statistical consultant. I am indebted to them for their sensitive responses to the project's requirements. Marian Hughes supervised the preparation of the final manuscript; I can never repay her dedication.

I am grateful also to Margaret Zusky, my editor at Lexington Books, for the support and encouragement she gave me.

My wife, Dr. Ann Skendall Teele, a clinical psychologist, was my closest collaborator and a patient companion throughout the final stage of the project; I could not have completed this book without her. That is why the book is dedicated to her and to our children, Theodore Scott and Lisa Margaret, who never let me forget that I was a father.

**Mastering Stress
in Child Rearing**

1 Background

Much has been written about various outcomes for mentally or emotionally disturbed people, and much more in recent years, it seems. The helping professions often have been critized for not helping enough or for not knowing the consequences of their help. The recent growth of evaluation research derives from a growing impatience by many, professional and lay alike, regarding the absence of concrete evidence concerning the effects of their work. And the growth of alternatives to the professional cultures presented by psychiatrists, psychologists, social workers, and others in the mental health field is another result of the current impatience with the traditional work style and with the results produced by these professionals. These alternatives are speeded along by researchers who claim that for certain categories of mental disturbance (such as adult and child neurosis) and juvenile delinquency, there is evidence that those exposed to psychotherapy improve at a rate barely equal to that of control-group members. Thus we have seen some growth of nontraditional approaches and of self-help groups recently for adults seeking to improve their mental health. Novel alternatives for problem children appear to be developing more slowly.

In this book I argue that it is time to take stock of the ways in which people go about solving their problems—our problems—of life. Mental and emotional disturbances confront many families, whether or not the rates of psychoses and of neuroses are increasing, remaining stationary, or declining in society as a whole. The research reported here addresses the problem-solving behavior of parents and/or parent surrogates when they are confronted with a special problem of child-rearing—an emotional problem in a family child that apparently resists parental solution, at least in the view of the concerned parent.

In the view of many such parents, and many professionals too, one of the first problem-solving steps is to consult a child psychiatric agency or professional. However, were parents aware of the large reservoir of social science research and resulting skepticism concerning the effectiveness of psychotherapy, they might not be so strongly inclined to seek the assistance and advice of the clinicians. The skepticism about treatment effectiveness covers a variety of childhood problems, although here I will address only two general categories of childhood problems, childhood neuroses and antisocial behavior. Social science research bearing on these two categories has produced fairly disappointing reports of results on the effectiveness of psychotherapy or of professional counseling. This has been true both of rigorous experimental studies and of less-rigorous studies that have utilized comparison groups. Indeed nearly all of the studies reporting results of delinquency-prevention experiments, whether employing professional counseling or a treatment model based on sociological premises, have concluded that the treatment made little difference. And the most recent of these, by McCord, who reported on a thirty-year follow-up of boys in the Cambridge-Somerville Study, suggests that the treatment may have been damaging.[1]

There seem to have been fewer experimental studies of children in treatment at child psychiatric agencies, perhaps because of the psychiatric professionals' reluctance to set up control groups, who receive no treatment. Perhaps for this reason, there is great debate over the efficacy of psychotherapy with children. Since the focus of this study is the child psychiatric agency, I begin by examining this long controversy over the effects of intervention by mental health professionals. The core of this controversy centers on whether and to what extent changes among persons undergoing psychotherapy is greater than that experienced among comparable persons not in psychotherapy. Put another way, the debate focuses on the issue of spontaneous remission.

Spontaneous Remission

The controversy over psychiatric intervention has taken a variety of forms. Some researchers, like Maher and Kathovsky, suggest that, in general, cases untreated by clinics are less likely to improve than treated cases.[2] Levitt, on the other hand, in his much-cited analyses of treatment and defector cases, found clinic treatment unrelated to improvement.[3] In this, Levitt's results closely parallel those reported by Eysenck.[4] Many of these intense arguments concerning the effectiveness of psychotherapy for adult neurotics have been repeated in the literature bearing on children. Researchers studying the effects of treatment for children continue their debate when attention is focused on the type of childhood problem under consideration. Thus, Maher and Kathovsky found that learning problems were unimproved whether treated or untreated, whereas problems of aggression improved only under treatment. In contrast, Levitt found the lowest (short-term) improvement rate among acting-out and delinquent children and the highest improvement rate among children with neurotic behavioral symptoms such as enuresis and school phobia.

Another form of the debate focuses on long-term consequences of intervention with emotionally disturbed or antisocial juveniles. Robins, in a thirty-year follow-up of problem children seen at the St. Louis Municipal

Psychiatric Clinic, found that antisocial behavior in childhood is predictive of sociopathic behavior in adults.[5] More specifically, Robins found that adult schizophrenics and alcoholics had been referred, as children, principally for antisocial behavior, while adult neurotics had been initially indistinguishable as children from those children later classified as well adults. Nervousness, irritability, shyness, tantrums, insomnia, fears, speech defects, hypersensitivity, and tics in childhood were unrelated to poor psychiatric status later in life. Such findings question the practice of guidance clinics that typically give preference to children with quiet symptoms because of the apparent belief that internalizing styles have dangerous long-term consequences in contrast to acting-out problems.

In apparent contrast to the assumption held by many that processes and principles of socialization and of learning apply mainly to the young, Robins found that the age range during which the largest proportion of her study group showed improvement was between thirty and forty years.

Yet another form of the debate centers on the nature of treatment, more specifically on the relationship among form of treatment and type of problem, and nature of outcome. This includes therapist interpersonal skills under treatment.[6] This debate begins but does not end with the issue of diagnostic clarity, a matter that both Rosenhan and Lambert have dealt with recently.[7]

Such an extensive list of competing hypotheses suggests the need for further research into issues bearing on the evaluation of psychotherapy for children. One would certainly think that the resort to spontaneous remission as an explanation would not be very appealing. However, Levitt, in 1957 and in 1963, concluded that the rate of spontaneous remission (improvement) among defector groups in studies evaluating psychotherapy was between 60 and 70 percent, or the same as the improvement rate for treated groups. In his most recent review of evaluation research on psychotherapy with children (1971), Levitt indicates that studies in the United States and Britain suggest that the so-called spontaneous remission rate was somewhere between 60 and 70 percent, about the same as that found for treated cases.[8] Like Eysenck, Levitt laments the fact that psychotherapy has not been proven effective but hastens to add that this conclusion is based on sparse research; he blames, unfortunately, antiresearch forces who control child-guidance clinics.

Levitt utilized defector cases in estimating the spontaneous remission rate. Although this is a sensible research approach given the difficulties associated with obtaining control groups, there are problems associated with their use. Levitt apparently assumes that the diagnostic process that led to acceptance for treatment had no therapeutic benefits for those who defected. Recent research suggests that this assumption may be unwarranted.[9] Second, Levitt apparently also assumes that there is an end to problem-solving behavior among defectors. He believes the defector groups provide a sound basis for estimating spontaneous remission if in addition to having been subjected to the same diagnostic procedures as treated cases and having been accepted into treatment, they have also never had any formal therapy sessions. I suggest that the absence of formal therapy does not mean that the families involved have ceased their problem-solving activities and that such activities may include contacts with various professional and nonprofessional sources of assistance. To our knowledge, no one has ever documented this probability for either treated or defector cases. Finally, Levitt presents no evidence rejecting the possibility of selection bias, which may characterize his defector groups. Eysenck, in fact, noted this problem in a review of Levitt's research.[10] I, too, question the use of defectors. Indeed, in using defectors, Levitt is employing dropouts from treatment, thus confounding selection with mortality. In effect, Levitt is comparing those who stayed in treatment with those who dropped out. But the clinic's procedures could have been involved in some parents' decision to withhold the child from treatment. (A substantial sociological literature on organizational behavior and on decision making supports this notion.) Second, the decision to withdraw from a clinic does not necessarily mean that the parents will cease problem-solving activities. Thus the possibility that such activities continue after defection should be considered. The assumption that defectors represent a no-treatment control group is questionable.

A number of other social scientists conducted research on psychotherapy in situ and came to conclusions similar to those of Levitt and Eysenck around that time. This failure of studies conducted by social scientists and clinicians to show clear-cut positive effects of clinical treatment programs should have alerted more psychologists and sociologists to the possibility that there were limitations inherent in their research designs. Perhaps we were more concerned with rebutting the clinicians' claims that they were helping their clients than in questioning the truth of our own research assumptions. Thus in the case of repeated findings that defectors or controls fared as well as treated cases, researchers often arbitrarily stated a negative case: that X does not make a difference. In fact, perhaps they should have wondered why Y made the same difference as X.[11] Defectors, in fact, might not have been treatment defectors but, rather, defectors from a certain kind of treatment. Perhaps too narrow a view of treatment has been taken.

Instead of considering the possibility that defectors or controls had some kinds of effective but nonpsychiatric, nonprofessional treatment experience, researchers almost invariably took the position that the treatment was useless or ineffective. Although they might consider that the treated and controls were not drawn from the same population—for example, that defectors or controls were less sick than the treated groups—they were unlikely to consider the possibility that the controls or defectors received treatment.

Social scientists engaging in such evaluative research return often to two notions: spontaneous remission is a possible explanation of no difference, and research in this field needs improvement. Eysenck has received due recognition for his contribution leading to the call for conceptual and methodological rigor in the evaluation of psychotherapy for adult neurotics, and Levitt has performed a similar service in the children's field with similar rewards. Lambert has lately joined Bergin, however, in lamenting the preoccupation with the notion of spontaneous remission. Indeed continued preoccupation itself is untimely since the appearance of Bergin's well-drawn conclusion that "the concept has retarded scientific progress by seeming to make remission a consequence of events that are unresearchable."[12] Among many other stimulating ideas, Bergin suggests that we ought to stop deluding ourselves that changes occur spontaneously in disturbed persons and begin to examine why they occur. He reminds us that much evidence from both sociological and psychological udies show that many of the persons who seek psychotherapy also seek elp from nonpsychiatric sources. Thus, we need to know why the 70 percent of defector cases (if 70 percent is the correct figure) improve. Perhaps equally important, we need to know why the remaining 30 percent do not improve.

A number of researchers have suggested that good experimental design is the direction our research should take. But although such research is highly useful, I do not think it can respond to some of the most pressing questions. We do not know whether Bergin is correct in asserting that "psychotherapy is such a heterogeneous collection of diverse and conflicting events that any attempt to definitively test its effect by virtue of classical pre-post control group designs is doomed to failure."[13] Certainly more rigorous designs are needed. Thus, Kiesler and others have clearly stated the need to untangle the effects of therapists, kinds of patients, and types of outcome. Historical events should be added to this list.

This problem of history, in longitudinal, in-situ research featuring comparison or control groups, has never received proper attention. Historical procedures may be taking place that could account for similar outcomes for experimental and control groups. The lack of experimental isolation in the face of important historical experiences, including alternative treatment resources employed by control-group members and their families, could account for the failure to find differences between controls and experiments in in-situ projects employing psychotherapy or counseling as the experimental variable. Perhaps the most unrealistic research expectation of all takes place in studies assessing the effects of psychotherapy on children, where it is assumed that the control group of children will have a history of nontreatment or of noncomparable treatment. But parents of control-group children cannot be expected to stand by and see their children go without treatment. They can be counted on to do their best to enhance their children's lives, no matter what the assumptions and needs of experimenters may be. Indeed numerous researchers on psychotherapy have noted that many members of control groups find assistance elsewhere for their problems. The questions thus are, What is the nature of this assistance, and what are its effects? Because it is so difficult to control for the effects of history in longitudinal, in-situ research, researchers have tended to avoid considering this avenue. We need to confront it now.

In his review on the effects of psychotherapy for children, Levitt has called attention to the need to consider maturational or developmental effects; we now call attention to the need to consider the effects of history. Research on the effects of selection, of history, and of maturation may go far toward helping to dampen enthusiasm for spontaneous remission as an explanation for changes. The remainder of this book will focus on the process of history, which I prefer to refer to as problem-solving behavior.

We are only beginning to realize the importance of the conceptual journey from spontaneous remission to problem-solving behavior. Since the appearance of the classic *Handbook of Psychotherapy and Behavior Change* by Bergin and Garfield in 1971, scholars have begun to reassess the issue of spontaneous remission. A search of the psychological and sociological literature since 1971 produced sixteen references to spontaneous remission; of these, only thirteen dealt with psychiatric or psychological works. And of these thirteen, only three (Lambert, Strupp, and Malan and his colleagues) stated the need to study the history of our clients, especially the therapeutic mechanisms (problem-solving behavior) of everyday life.[14] Of these, only one study actually presented data bearing on the importance of these therapeutic mechanisms. This single study of history (by Malan and his associates), involving follow-up on forty-five adult neurotic patients who were seen for consultation but never formally treated, took place in Great Britain. But there has been no similar study concerning children.

A New Direction: Research on History

Issues of this type led to the type of study that I conducted in 1963. I was particularly concerned with focusing on family reactions and short-term consequences for problem children who were not accepted for services. (I made this study only after satisfying myself that the clinic's decision to treat apparently was not related to the kind or intensity of problems.)

In 1963–1964, I directed an intensive study of five child psychiatric clinics (three child-guidance and two court psychiatric clinics) in the Boston-

Worcester, Massachusetts, area. The first part of the earlier study consisted of an analysis of the disposition of all intake applications to the five clinics during 1962. Disposition was carefully defined by the researchers and then dichotomized into "received service" and "did not receive service." Only 28 percent of all applicants received service according to the classification system. (This proportion is similar to that found in other studies.) Relationships between disposition and child's age, sex, type of presenting problem, father's occupation, and referral agent were then analyzed; the results showed that only two of these variables—child's age and source of referral—were related to case disposition. It was somewhat disconcerting to find that the measure of problem severity was unrelated to acceptance for service.

In the second part of this study, an interview was held with a parent (mother was the preferred respondent) in 352 families where the child did not receive service, the parents were agreeable to an interview, and a parent was the referring agent. Interviews, conducted in 1963, were held approximately a year after the parent applied for help. Eighty-five percent of the target group (352 of 415 cases) were successfully interviewed to obtain data on the child's earlier problems, on the family's problem-solving activities, and on the family's experience with the clinic during application; in addition, short-term consequences or sequellae of being turned away by the clinics were assessed.

In connection with this earlier study it is instructive to observe diagrammatically (table 1-1) the potential population from which the study group was derived and ways in which subject-selection strategy differed from studies of clinics that commonly focused on treatment outcome or involved evaluation. In so doing it may facilitate the issue that Thomas Kuhn illuminates in his work: the nature of the new questions that may be stimulated by nontraditional approaches.[15] The paradigm presented below includes at least three variables that apparently exhaust the contingencies determining the potential population of child psychiatric clinics; the decision concerning whether one needs help, the decision concerning whether to apply for help, and the clinic's decision concerning whether to accept for service.[16] (The fourth variable in the paradigm concerns outcome and will enter into my discussion of subsequent research.) These contingencies are seldom the object of research or are seldom considered problematic, yet they are extremely relevant to the outcome that concerns researchers.

Cells 3 and 5 in the table represent the people accepted into service among those who applied. The extent to which clients feel help is needed is often an unknown, although this is a proper research concern. Clinical researchers typically have no interest in persons in cells 1 and 2 since these persons, regardless of the extent to which they may feel in need of help, do not come to the attention of clinicians and are forgotten. They represent a

Table 1–1
Selection Contingencies in Typical Studies

	A1: Uncertain or Not Sure of Needing Help		A2: Need Help	
B1: Did not apply	(1)		(2)	
B2: Applied for help	C1: Clinic accepts (3)	C2: Clinic rejects (4)	C3: Clinic accepts (5)	C4: Clinic rejects (6)
D: Outcome studies	D1: Defector study Follow-up studies Experimental studies (7)	D2: Follow-up studies (8)	D3: Defector study Follow-up studies Experimental studies (9)	D4: Follow-up studies (10)

majority of the population of potential help-seekers and have been of concern primarily to researchers interested in the etiology and/or incidence of a disease or problem.[17] Regarding cells 3, 4, 5, and 6, the clinic has made a judgment based on a cluster of factors operating differently for various clinics at various times as to whether to accept for service. The factors entering this decision may include diagnostic judgment, the clinic case-load limits, training needs, research needs, parental influence, source of referral, and professional satisfactions. Thus the clinic's decision is problematic.

At this point, the clinic, in terms of cells 3 and 5, has selected its case load. Of more importance to researchers, the clinic typically has selected the researcher's study group (cells 7 and 9). Perhaps of even greater importance in terms of discovery, the clinic, because of its monopoly of the decision concerning case load and study group, has restricted the range of questions that can be asked. The questions typically asked are, What are the short-term effects of treatment, and what are the long-term effects of treatment? Both questions are asked of volunteers for help—those applying and accepted. These are important questions, which should be asked and answered. Clinicians, academicians, school officials, court officials, parents, and the general public all wish to know if treatment makes a difference. However, this past research has been bounded by selection processes, diagnostic processes, and a narrow conception of treatment (ignoring history) regardless of variety: treatment-defector study, evaluation study employing comparison or control groups, or follow-up study. In effect, ignorance of the pretreatment and/or in-treatment problem-solving processes acutely hinders efforts to ask and answer the important research questions concerning why treatment works and does not work.

The questions that could be asked of persons in cells 4 and 6 are different. One cannot ask of people who are turned down by a clinic, What difference did the treatment make? Yet, many of the people turned away by one service facility go on to a second or third facility until they find the desired assistance. Or they may turn to nonprofessional sources of help. These, then, are other questions that could be asked of those in cells 4 and 6: What do people do who seek help and do not find it? What stress-relieving steps can they now take? Do their problem-solving mechanisms wind down or wind up?[18] What determines or influences the subsequent course of action? These questions could guide the research considered in cells 8 and 10. Such issues are oriented to problem-solving as well as developmental processes in the family.

In a modest way, I began to look at some of these family problem-solving processes among persons in cells 4 and 6 fourteen years ago. I wanted to find out how the clinic went about selecting its clients and identifying those who were turned away. And I conducted an interview with the mother approximately one year after the clinic had turned the family away. Thus, some of the questions posed focused on the family's problem-solving behavior but only in the short run.

Extending this earlier study in recent years (1975–1976), I pursued some of the issues raised by my earlier studies, this time examining long-range changes. Although, the questions raised may not be directly relevant to the treatment issues raised with respect to persons in cells 3 and 5, indirectly this inquiry about the postclinic contact behavior and experiences of families not accepted in 1962 should enlighten the problems that bedevil researchers concerned about the treatment effects. More specifically, many of the subsequent experiences and behavior of those not accepted parallel the ensuing behavior and experiences of those in defector, control, and other comparison groups commonly utilized in research on treatment effects. These family processes, revolving around problem-solving behavior, may also be taking place among persons in psychiatric treatment and could be as important as professional treatment in their effects. Just as the study by Rosenthal and Jacobson suggests that experiments and experimenters both have effects, so too may the behavior of persons encountered in the process of seeking help for one's child have an important and little-noticed effect.[19]

A Tentative Formulation of the Mastery of Stress

The discussion of research on treatment effects focused on two concerns: the stress-coping behavior of parents facing child-rearing problems and the long-term outcome for the child. Although the major focus here is on the coping behavior of parents, this study is also attentive to many other conditions and life events that I believe to be important to long-term outcome. Table 1-2 summarizes the contingencies that I believe will affect the long-term problem outcome. My second stage research proposal employed this framework in the development of three general hypotheses.

First, the parents' earlier cognition of their child's problem, seriousness of the problem, attribution of blame, attitude to the child, degree of frustration and future expectations will be more strongly related to the child's adult outcome than will be the type of problem presented initially. In support of this notion, a number of social scientists have commented repeatedly on the power of expectations. Stouffer and his colleagues, Rosenthal and Jacobson, Freeman and Simmons, and Rosenhan are just a few whose work has documented this phenomenon with respect to soldiers, schoolteachers, the relatives of released mental patients, and psychiatric professionals.[20] Although the nature of the child's problem is important, I assumed that the parents' definition or cognition of the problem is of greater consequence.

The second hypothesis is that the extent of resources available to parents (income, family strength, external sources of emotional support, intelligence, and social class) is directly related to the outcome of the problem. This hypothesis has been suggested earlier by the work of the Dohrenwends, Scott and Howard, Teele, Croog, and more recently, Pearlin and Schooler.[21] Barbara Dohrenwend and Bruce Dohrenwend have consistently emphasized the complexity of the relationship among social status, stress, and mediating factors, invariably cautioning about a facile assumption that status is inversely related to experienced stress. Still they suggest that resources such as stable families and strong command of goods and services

Table 1-2
Long-Term Outcome Contingencies

I. Problem cognition in 1962–1963
   Includes definition of problem, extent of concern, attribution of blame

II. Advice received
   In 1962 at application
   Between 1962 clinic response to application and 1963 interview by researcher

III. Potential evaluation of early advice or assistance

IV. Parent's coping response, 1963–1976
   Includes definition or redefinition of problem, seeking and receiving assistance, use of assistance

IV. Outcome, 1976

Note: Circumstance and conditions that could affect each contingency include internal mediators (such as personality), available material resources (such as money), life events (such as death), and developmental features of the child (such as age and sex).

are less common among lower-status people. Similarly I hypothesized that high intelligence (indexed by a word test) and other personal traits would prove to be valuable resources for many parents in the study. Coping behavior in particular would seem to benefit from a willingness and an ability to communicate one's concerns to others. Pearlin and Schooler, like many other students of stress, also make the distinction between personal and social resources in their recent work.

The third hypothesis is that the nature of parental response to the child's presenting problem (searching for resources, reinterpretation of the problem, and utilization of available resources, whether professional or lay) will be directly related to adult outcome. This hypothesis focuses on the concrete steps parents take in dealing with the problem. It is tied to the first two general hypotheses in that it related to the uses made of available resources based on cognition. Thus, for example, I expect that higher-status parents will be more persistent than lower-status parents in their search for help and that this persistence more often will result in finding help for the child's problem.

Although my strategy included hypothesis testing, my strongest interest was in ascertaining the processes occurring in those families during the twelve to thirteen years prior to my 1975–1976 interview.

Notes

1. See, for example, Richard Powers and Helen Witmer, *An Experiment in the Prevention of Juvenile Delinquency* (New York: Columbia University Press, 1951); Henry Meyer, E.F. Borgatta, and Wyatt Jones, *Girls of Vocational High* (New York: Russell Sage Foundation, 1965); Lamar Empy and Maynard L. Ericson, *The Provo Experiment: Evaluating Community Control of Delinquency* (Lexington, Mass.: Lexington Books, D.C. Heath and Company, 1972); and Joan McCord, "A Thirty Year Follow-up of Treatment Effects," *American Psychologist* 33 (March 1978): 284–289.

2. Brendon Maher and Walter Kathovsky, "The Efficacy of Brief Clinical Procedures in Alleviating Children's Behavior Problems," *Journal of Individual Psychology* 17 (November 1961):205–211.

3. E.E. Levitt, "The Results of Psychotherapy with Children: An Evaluation," *Journal of Consulting Psychology* 2 (1957):189–196, and "Psychotherapy with Children: A Further Evaluation," *Behavior Research and Therapy* 1 (May 1963):45–51.

4. H.J. Eysenck, "The Effects of Psychotherapy: An Evaluation," *Journal of Consulting Psychology* 16 (1952):319–324, and "The Effects of Psychotherapy," in Eysenck, ed., *Handbook of Abnormal Psychology* (New York: Basic Books, 1961), pp. 697–725.

5. Lee Robins, *Deviant Children Grown Up* (Baltimore: William and Wilkins, 1966).

6. See Donald Kiesler, "Experimental Designs in Psychotherapy Research," in Allen Bergin and Sol Garfield, eds., *Handbook of Psychotherapy and Behavior Change* (New York: Wiley, 1971), pp. 36–74. Also see James Teele and Maxwell Schleifer, "Treatability, Treatment and Outcome: The Judge Baker Pilot Project," *Community Mental Health Journal* (Winter 1965):369–374; C. Rudolf and J. Cumming, "Where Are Additional Psychiatric Services Most Needed," *Social Work* 7 (1962):15–20; and Charles Truax and Kevin Mitchell, "Research on Certain Interpersonal Skills in Relation to Process and Outcome," in Bergin and Garfield, *Handbook,* pp. 299–344.

7. See D.L. Rosenhan, "On Being Sane in Insane Places," *Science* 179, pp. 250–258, and Michael Lambert, "Spontaneous Remission in Adult Neurotic Disorders: A Revision and Summary," *Psychological Bulletin* 83 (1976):107–119.

8. E.E. Levitt, "Research on Psychotherapy with Children," in Bergin and Garfield, *Handbook,* pp. 474–494.

9. See Stanley Kissel, "Mothers and Therapists Evaluate Long-term and Short-term Child Therapy," *Journal of Clinical Psychology* 30 (July 1974):296–299; Harold Stewart, "Six Months, Fixed Term, Once Weekly Psychotherapy: A Report on 20 Cases with Follow-Ups," *British Journal of Psychiatry* 121 (October 1972):425–435; and David Malan, Sheldon Heath, Howard Bacal, and Frederick Balfour, "Psychodynamic Changes in Untreated Neurotic Patients: II. Apparently Genuine Improvements," *Archives of General Psychiatry* 32 (January 1975):110–126.

10. H.J. Eysenck, "Effects of Psychotherapy," p. 715.

11. Perhaps the Hawthorne effect was not taken seriously enough by such researchers.

12. Allen Bergin, "The Evaluation of Therapeutic Outcomes," in Bergin and Garfield, *Handbook,* p. 242.

13. Ibid., p. 253.

14. See Lambert, "Spontaneous Remission," pp. 117–118; see also Malan et al., "Psychodynamic Changes"; and Hans Strupp, "Spontaneous Remission and the Nature of the Therapeutic Influence," *Psychotherapy and Psychosomatics* 74 (1974):4–6, 389–393.

15. Thomas Kuhn, *The Structure of Scientific Revolutions* (Chicago: University of Chicago Press, 1962).

16. The paradigm is similar to that of Charles Kadushin, "Individual Decisions to Undertake Psychotherapy," *Administrative Science Quarterly* 3 (1958):379–411, but Kadushin's paradigm does not include the important variable of acceptance-rejection by the treatment facility.

17. See L. Srole, T. Langner, S. Michael, M. Opler, and T. Rennie, *Mental Health in the Metropolis: Midtown Manhattan Study* (New York: McGraw-Hill, 1962).

18. See S. Levine and N. Scotch, eds., *Social Stress* (Chicago: Aldine, 1970).

19. R. Rosenthal and L. Jacobson, *Pygmalion in the Classroom* (New York: Holt, Rinehart and Winston, 1968).

20. S. Stouffer, E. Suchman, L. De Vinney, S. Star, and R. Williams Jr., *The American Soldier: Adjustment during Army Life* (Princeton, N.J.: Princeton University Press, 1949), vol. 1; Rosenthal and Jacobson, *Pygmalion;* O. Simmons and H.E. Freeman, "Familial Expectations and Post-hospital Performance of Mental Patients," *Human Relations* 12 (1959):223–242; Rosenhan, "On Being Sane."

21. See Barbara S. Dohrenwend and Bruce P. Dohrenwend, "Class and Race as Status Related Sources of Stress," pp. 111–140; Robert Scott and Alan Howard, "Models of Stress," pp. 259–278; James E. Teele, "Social Pathology and Stress," pp. 228–256; and Sydney Croog, "Family as a Source of Stress," pp. 19–53, all appearing in Levine and Scotch, *Social Stress.* Also see Leonard Pearlin and Carmi Schooler, "The Structure of Coping," *Journal of Health and Social Behavior* 19 (March 1978):2–21.

2

Outline of the Book and the Research to Be Reported

Beginning in early 1963, when I was a staff sociologist at a child-guidance clinic in New England, I directed a study of families seeking help for an emotionally disturbed family child at one of five child psychiatric clinics in Massachusetts. I included a representative set of guidance and court clinics in the study and was permitted to examine, for calendar year 1962, all applications to these five clinics. I was interested in examining the type of presenting problem, the disposition of each of the 1,381 applicants to the clinics, and factors related to case disposition insofar as the clinic record of contact permitted. Chapter 3, in part, presents the results of this first-stage study. Additionally, it presents some results from a nationwide study conducted in 1964 that was designed to see if the findings from the study of the five clinics were supported. In short, chapter 3 is about the rather neglected issue of selection. The problem of definition, including classification, is an integral feature of selection procedures and, as such, is discussed in this chapter. It also considers the role of referral agents, the social characteristics of applicants, and the stated needs of the agency as selection factors.

In 1963, using the results of the case disposition study, I designed and carried out an interview study of all parents, meeting the selection criteria, who had not received the help they sought a year earlier. This study involved interviews with 352 parents who had contacted the clinic in 1962. These interviews, semistructured and conducted by psychiatric social workers, focused on the child's earlier problems; parents' help-seeking behavior and experiences, prior to as well as during the year subsequent to contacting the clinic; and the child's condition at the time of the interview in 1963. Chapter 4 reports on the first of these issues—the child's problems, including those appearing before and at the time of clinic contact—and also presents data on the factors related to the problem behavior of the children.

Chapter 5 continues the analysis of the data from the 1963 interview. It focuses on the parents' problem-solving behavior, both before the 1962 clinic contact and during the period between the 1962 contact and the 1963 interview. Factors related to coping behavior are also examined.

Chapter 6 considers the child's short-term outcome as indexed by the child's behavior at the time of the interview. The main task here was to analyze changes that took place in the child's behavior between the time of application to the clinic in 1962 and the interview in 1963. The mean interval between application at the clinic and our research interview was 10.8 months. (My use of the phrase *short-term outcome* is necessitated by the fact that later I report on changes taking place over a twelve to thirteen-year interval. In some studies, eleven or twelve months might represent long term and three to six months might be considered short term.) The factors discussed and related to short-term changes in the child's behavior include the parent's problem-solving behavior, children's and parents' social characteristics, parents' attitudes, parents' personality, and parents' perceptions of both the child and of the experience with the clinic.

Chapter 7 introduces the second stage of the study and describes procedures. The long-term problem-solving behavior of the parents is the focus of chapter 8. The stage II data for this chapter come from a follow-up interview, conducted in 1975–1976, with over 80 percent of informants from the 1963 interview. This second interview, again conducted primarily by psychiatric social workers, was unstructured (in the survey sense). The questions posed were open-ended, designed to obtain respondents' views in their own words. Clinicians' views were solicited during the preparation of the interview questions.

I was particularly interested in the various tactics and strategies parents employed over a long period of time in their attempt to cope with and resolve their children's problems. The major thrust of chapter 8 is an analysis of the relationships of parents' social and psychological characteristics, collected during the first interview (referred to here as time I), to my indexes of parental long-term problem-solving behavior. Social-psychological variables include parent perception of the cause of the child's problems (parent attribution of blame) and parent expectations for the child's future.

Chapter 9 examines the child's long-term outcome, data for which were collected during the second interview with the parents in 1975–1976 (referred to as time II data). In 1963 when I conducted the first interview, the mean age of the children for whom help had been sought was approximately ten and one-half years; thus, their mean age in late 1975 was twenty-three years. The time II data draw, in part, on the informant's recall of events subsequent to the first interview in 1963. (Some data were collected in order to test the strength of the parent's recall of events reported earlier, and such data are presented, where appropriate.) The child's long-term outcome used three different measures: a direct statement of outcome given by the concerned parent, a measure of the child's extent of involvement with the family, and a measure of the child's current social functioning. Among the analyses presented in chapter 9, one of the more important ones looks at the relationship between the parents' problem-solving behavior and the child's long-term outcome. In addition, characteristics of children (such as, sex and age) and of parents (for example, marital history, marital adjustment, expectations, social class, and personality measures) will be presented as they relate to long-term outcome measures. Most of these social and psychological variables are based on time I data; however, a few, such as marital history and experience of stressful life events, are based on data collected during time II.

Chapter 9 also presents the results of my analysis of higher-order relationships. I begin by controlling some key variables in the attempt to pin down a few of the crucial factors related to problem-solving behavior and to long-term outcome. Regression analysis is then undertaken in the attempt to predict long-term outcome.

Conclusions are presented in chapter 10, which summarizes the main findings and attempts to draw out the meanings and implications of findings.

Chapter 8, 9, and 10 focus only on the guidance-clinic cases because the first-stage analysis convincingly demonstrated that the framework for the analysis of these cases was not appropriate for the court-clinic cases. I discuss this matter further in chapter 7 and also present some preliminary long-term outcome data (criminal record data) for the court-clinic cases in appendix A.

3

Client Selection by Child Psychiatric Clinics

The child-guidance clinic has long been a symbol of help to troubled parents whose children exhibit behavior deemed by them to be a sign of an emotional problem.[1] Among those parents who call or come to such a clinic, which of them are accepted by those agencies for service? That is, whom do agencies select as clients and why? How do those chosen differ from those not chosen?

Our data on these questions come from two sources. First, we examined the clinics' records of contact with all persons applying to them during calendar year 1962. The bulk of the analysis presented in this chapter is based on these clinic records and was conducted in 1963. Second, at the completion of this initial analysis of these intake records for five child psychiatric clinics, we undertook, in 1964, a nationwide survey of all member clinics of the American Association of Psychiatric Clinics for Children in order to ascertain if some of our findings on the selection decisions of the clinics studied in Massachusetts appeared to be generalizable to the United States as a whole.

Hypotheses

In designing the intake study, we assumed that factors other than the applicant's symptoms might affect acceptance by the clinic. More specifically, the clinic's decision to accept or reject might be related to the source of referral, the social status of the applicant, and the stated needs and goals of the agency.

We assumed that individuals referred by professionals would be more likely to be accepted for service than those referred by laypersons. This assumption is based on a delineation by Mishler and Waxler of the successive selection decisions made by hospitals regarding patients seeking psychiatric treatment.[2] We also took into account the fact that professionals have access to both the formal and the informal channels of communication in the child clinic system and that they also may apply sanctions to one

Portions of this chapter are reprinted from James E. Teele and Sol Levine, "The Acceptance of Emotionally Disturbed Children by Psychiatric Agencies," chapter 5 in S. Wheeler, ed., *Controlling Delinquents* (New York: John Wiley, 1968). Reprinted with permission.

another by withholding further referrals. Laypersons, especially members of the client's family, generally have access only to the formal channels and rarely are able to retaliate if the clinic renders an unfavorable decision.

Further, we posited that middle- and upper-class individuals would be accepted as clients more often than those from the working class. Since most child clinics can barely keep up with operating costs, they either have to warn the prospective client of the fees or make some judgment about the client's ability to pay. Moreover, in the psychiatric world, a belief is prevalent that lower-class people are more resistant to treatment than those from the middle and upper classes.[3]

Finally, we assumed that a child-guidance agency will more often admit the type of case useful to it for reasons of its own. However, since we were not able to study the organization of each clinic intensively, we shall present only tentative formulations of this point.

Method

The institutions cooperating in this study were in the Boston-Worcester, Massachusetts, area and included three child-guidance clinics and two court clinics. The child-guidance clinics are referred to as A, B, C. Clinic A is an old, established clinic founded over a quarter of a century ago. A relatively small institution, it receives no state funds but obtains enough money from the community fund to cover one-fourth of its operating expenses. Its policy is to serve no children who live outside the metropolitan area or who are over twelve years of age. In 1962, it had a professional staff of eighteen; in addition, the clinic trained twelve specialists in child care.

Clinic C is a large organization consisting of about eighty professionals. It receives no state funds and only enough from the community fund to cover approximately 4 percent of its operating expenses. It does not confine its services to local children, and it accepts children from five to seventeen years of age. Like clinic A it depends on clients' fees to a substantial degree.

The size of the staff of clinic B is in between those of A and C; it employs approximately fifty professionals and trainees. Clinic B receives three-fifths of its funds from the state and is the only one of the three with a well-developed service of consultation to the schools and other local agencies. It confines its attention to local children but will accept any children up to and including those seventeen years old. Clinic B is the only one of the three that grants every eligible applicant a personal interview, except during the summer when new cases are not accepted.

The two court clinics are referred to here as D and E. A well-established clinic, D works closely with the court's probation department. Clinic E, a newer establishment, is located in an urban community with higher rates of crime and delinquency than clinic D must contend with.

Intake data were collected on all applicants for service at each of the five clinics during calendar year 1962. In that time, there were 1,241 applicants for service at the three guidance clinics and 140 referrals to the two court clinics.[4] The kinds of data collected and recorded at the five clinics necessarily restrict the study of the correlates of acceptance for service. We delayed collecting data until February or March 1963 in order to allow sufficient time for action on applications made in the preceding December.

Reporting the results and analyzing the relationships between case disposition and other variables is difficult because of gaps in the information recorded by the clinics. The gaps are especially great in periods during which intake is closed.

Coverage of the major variables in the three guidance clinics is as follows: source of referrals (86 percent), presenting problems or symptoms (84 percent), disposition (99 percent), sex (98 percent), age (86 percent), and father's occupation (59 percent). Coverage at the court clinics is offense (96 percent), sex (100 percent), age (94 percent), father's occupation (72 percent), and disposition (99 percent). The least information available is on the occupation of the father; it is known in only 60 percent of the total cases at all five clinics. Although the agencies do manage to record most items of information adequately, there is certainly need to have more complete coverage of the occupational data. In general, it would help considerably in carrying out evaluation studies of child psychiatric agencies if basic information on clients were collected uniformly and systematically.

Characteristics of the Guidance Clinics'
Population

The basic frequency distributions in each of the three child-guidance clinics and the two court clinics indicate the composition of the population that comes to or is sent to each clinic in the course of the year. The breakdown of the 1,381 applications made at the five clinics during the year 1962 was as follows: A, 198; B, 528; C, 515; D, 46; and E, 94.[5] Clinic B, with a much smaller professional staff than clinic C, had the highest number of applicants for service during the year. That severe pressures for service are exerted on clinic B's staff undoubtedly reflects the fact that it is the only recognized guidance clinic in its area and is dependent on public support.

At each of the guidance clinics there were many more boy applicants than girl applicants; the proportions of male applicants at clinics A, B, and C, respectively, were 76 percent, 67 percent, and 73 percent. Thus, approximately seven out of every ten applications are made on behalf of boys. That girls are much less likely than boys to apply or be referred to psychiatric clinics is a repeated finding in studies of delinquency in the United States.[6] The average age of applicants at clinic A was eight and one-half years, at clinic B it was nine and one-half years, and at clinic C it was ten and one-half years. These age differences reflect the different policies of the clinics.

Child-guidance agencies rarely do case finding; they obtain most of their client by referrals, which link recipients, social agencies, and health professionals in the community. A number of different professionals clearly play a part, but the mother figures most frequently in directing the child to the clinic; this is to be expected because usually she is the person closest to the child (table 3-1)[7] We do not know to what extent the mother's involvement in the referral process actually reflects what Raphael terms the "acceptance of the social innovation of seeking psychiatric help."[8] The findings probably reflect the current policy of clinics to focus on the family instead of on the child alone as the unit of treatment. Members of the family are encouraged to call the clinic directly; in fact, if a professional should call on behalf of the family, the clinic usually asks that person to have the child's parent, preferably the mother, get in touch with it.

Although the classification of children's problems has been of considerable interest to clinicians, to our knowledge no systematic effort has been made to determine what specific problems are presented to guidance clinics at intake. One reason is that clinicians usually find it necessary to do considerable testing and interviewing of the child and his family before

Table 3-1
Major Sources of Referral to Child-Guidance Clinics

Source of Referral	N	Percent
Mother	478	44.1
Father	77	7.1
Other relative	44	4.1
Mother and professional	77	7.1
Minister	24	2.2
Physician	95	8.8
School personnel	80	7.4
Child guidance clinic	86	7.9
Friend	15	1.4
Family service	44	4.1
Hospital	63	5.8
Total	1,083[a]	100.0

[a]No data for 158 cases.

making a diagnosis. However, in our study, most of the calls to a clinic involved discussion of the child's problem or his symptoms, so these data were available, and we were able to classify and enumerate all presenting complaints in the three guidance clinics.

Table 3-2 reports the total frequency with which each complaint was presented to clinics during intake. Problems of learning rank first and those of delinquency or near-delinquency (for instance, stealing or aggression) rank second. Together these account for approximately one-half of all complaints. By contrast, psychosis, suicidal behavior, and other extreme manifestations of child pathology rarely come to the attention of child-guidance clinics. These general findings are also specific to each of the three clinics.

A basic assumption of our intake study was that conditions other than the applicant's symptoms affected his acceptance by the clinic. The testing of this assumption required a classification of symptoms, which in turn could be used as an independent and control variable in the study. Since one of the objects of this study was to obtain information that would be helpful in developing curricula for the control of delinquency, we classified the thirty presenting symptoms according to whether they manifestly constituted a social threat or were in violation of the law.

We did not try to categorize symptoms in terms of psychodynamic formulations or clinical criteria of amenability to treatment but according to how seriously the child's behavior appeared to be inimical to others or how much it was in conflict with the law. From a psychoanalytic viewpoint, a child who is afraid or inhibited, for example, may be judged to be suffering from more severe intrapsychic problems than a boy who steals; from a sociological point of view, however, the one who steals may appear to merit more concern since he is not only violating the mores but also the law. Our classification scheme was modeled partly after that of sociologists Robins and O'Neal and consists of two general types or classes of presenting symptoms.[9] With the exception of psychosis, all of the symptoms or presenting complaints that we have categorized as type I are often violations of the law:

Type I: Stealing, homosexuality, setting fires, sexual aggression, aggression or fighting, running away or truancy, psychoses, and attempted suicide.

Type II: Poor peer relations; poor family relations; lying; inhibitions; temper tantrums; obscene language; depression; problems of separation; daydreaming; masturbation; problems of learning, speech, or hearing; retardation; school phobias; night terrors; tics and nervousness; psychosomatic complaints; enuresis, soiling; obesity; medical problems; effeminacy; and immaturity.

Table 3–2
Presenting Complaints in Guidance Clinics

General Problem	Specific Presenting Complaint	Number of Children with Specific Complaint	Total
Relations in school or difficulties in learning	Learning problem	370	
	School phobia	36	
	Speech or hearing	30	436
Delinquency or near-delinquency	Aggression, fighting	172	
	Stealing	71	
	Running away or truancy	28	271
Behavior and medical problems	Medical and other Behavior problems (non-specific)	142 121	
	Obesity	5	268
Neurosis	Night terrors, nervousness	118	
	Enuresis	28	
	Soiling	20	166
Relations with authority	Temper tantrums	58	
	Poor family relations	56	
	Lying	33	
	Obscene language	4	151
Autism	Inhibition or shyness	70	
	Daydreaming	14	84
Relations with peers	Poor peer relations	73	73
Retardation	Retardation	44	44
Depression	Depression	41	41
Sex	Sexual aggressiveness	21	
	Homosexuality	9	
	Masturbation	6	36
Setting fires	Setting fires	25	25
Psychosomatic difficulty	Psychosomatic complaint	23	23
Psychosis	Psychosis or near-psychosis	17	17
Suicidal threat or attempt	Threatened or attempted suicide	14	14
Separation	Separation problem	8	8

Note: Number of complaints is larger than the number of cases (1,241) as some children had more than one complaint. In addition, there were a few cases without any information on type of presenting problem. It seems likely that intake workers may not have inquired about the reasons for the call in some cases. This may have occurred, for example, if intake were closed.

At one point in our analysis, we classified all symptoms into three levels of severity, with the most severe symptoms consisting of those at present included in type I and the intermediate and least-severe cases consisting of those included in type II. The criterion for determining severity was the degree to which the symptom or behavior was judged to be socially inimical or in violation of the law. However, we could not agree on whether a few specific symptoms should be classified as moderately severe or least severe. Even more important, the term *severity* had some undesirable connotations, which tended to confuse our discussion. Accordingly, we collapsed the thirty presenting symptoms into type I and type II.

On the basis of these criteria, 31 percent of the population were classified as having type I symptoms and 69 percent as having type II. A child who presented more than one symptom was classified as type I if he manifested any of the symptoms included in this general category. Clinic C received more applications from the type I cases, relatively and absolutely, than did the other two clinics, with clinic A receiving the smallest proportion of these. This finding may reflect age differences in the applicant populations of the three clinics, for, in each clinic, type I symptoms occurred most frequently in the older age groups.

We were able to obtain occupational data on only 60 percent of the fathers of applicants. Of these, we discovered that approximately 32 percent were employed as professionals, proprietors, or businessmen, 20 percent as clerical workers, 43 percent as manual or service workers, and 5 percent were unemployed and/or the family was on welfare. This suggests that the middle and upper classes may be overrepresented in the population seeking help at child-guidance clinics.[10] This finding, however, must be viewed tentatively because of the lack of complete data and also because we were unable to make age-controlled comparisons between our study group and the local population. Perhaps because it is a community clinic and well publicized as such locally, clinic B had a greater proportion of applicants whose fathers were in lower-status occupations.

The specification and measurement of the dependent variable of our study—case disposition—required considerable effort and deliberation.[11] It was necessary to develop a range of categories that would cover the diverse fates of those applying to the child-guidance agencies for service. On the basis of our analysis of clinic records and interviews with clinic personnel, case disposition was finally categorized as follows:

Rejected: Includes applications marked as either "rejected" or "told intake was closed." Those marked as "referred out" were also included in this category when the place was not specified. These applicants were not granted interviews.

Withdrew, no personal contact: Includes cases marked as "withdrew" but in which there was no indication of an interview with the applicant. This category included applicants who were asked or told to call back but did not.

Held: Includes cases marked "hold" and open cases on which no disposition had been indicated as of February 15, 1963. Most of them had no interview.

Referred: Includes cases in which the applicant was referred to another clinic or person. Ninety percent of them did not receive a personal interview at the clinic.

Consultation: Includes cases where parents sought and received either a testing service or advice from the clinic's intake personnel.

Withdrew, after personal contact: Includes cases who, after at least one interview, failed to appear for the last scheduled contact with clinic personnel. This category does not include applicants who withdrew after diagnosis was begun.

Diagnosis: Includes applicants for whom diagnosis was begun, whether or not completed.

Treatment: Includes applicants accepted for treatment, whether or not begun.

During calendar year 1962, the largest proportion of cases (30 percent) was disposed of by referral elsewhere (table 3-3). Surprisingly, however, fewer than 12 percent of all cases were in treatment by the time the study took place, although an additional 12 percent were in process of being diagnosed and a good proportion of them were likely to obtain treatment eventually. Only 28 percent of all applicants received what might be termed complete service.[12]

The evidence suggests that there may be upper limits of service beyond which these specific child-guidance clinics cannot go in view of their existing orientation, techniques, personnel, and modes of operation. One interesting finding is that when the two major service categories (diagnosis and treatment) are added together, the clinics were quite similar. The proportions of all cases in these two categories are: clinic A, 25.2 percent; clinic B, 25.4 percent; and clinic C, 22.4 percent.

Of greater concern is the ratio of professional staff (full- or part-time personnel or trainees) to the number of applicants who were diagnosed or treated during the study year. A superficial computation of this ratio in the three clinics is as follows: clinic A, 1 to 2; clinic B, 1 to 2.5; and clinic C, 1 to 1.4. Our purpose is not to compare the clinics with respect to this variable

Table 3–3
Disposition of Cases at Child-Guidance Clinics

Disposition	N	%
Rejected[a]	185	14.9
Withdrew, no personal contact	158	12.7
Held	163	13.1
Referred	372	30.0
Consultation	11	0.9
Withdrew, after personal contact	39	3.2
Diagnosis	154	12.4
Treatment	145	11.7
No information	14	1.1
Total	1,241	100.0

[a]Included were forty-nine cases who were told that intake was closed

but to point up the relatively few diagnostic and treatment services rendered to new cases per professional person in all three clinics. Of course, many patients may be receiving very intensive care and may also be obtaining services from several different professionals at the clinic. In addition, a large number of professionals have other case loads from previous years.

Through research and training, these clinics may have been making a profound contribution to the control of delinquency and the treatment of emotional problems of children; however, in 1962 they appeared to be rendering only a few of the number of new services that were needed. Even with the addition of a large number of professional personnel, it is hard to see how the problem could be met without the introduction of some innovations.

Relationships among Variables at
Guidance Clinics

The three clinics did not differ significantly from one another in the proportion of boys and girls accepted for service, nor did boy and girl applicants differ in the kinds of problems they presented. Clinics did give more service to younger than to older children, a difference that may reflect their belief in the importance of early intervention (table 3–4). The older children, however, manifest delinquent behavior more frequently than do younger children. Since the data from other studies reveal that delinquent behavior reaches a peak at about fourteen years of age, the gap in services for the eleven-year-olds to fourteen-year-olds may be a serious shortcoming, a fact

Table 3-4
Age and Disposition of Cases at Child-Guidance Clinics

	Service Incomplete		Service Complete		
Developmental Age	N	%	N	%	100% =
Preschool (to 5)	67	62.0	41	38.0	108
Latency (6–10)	280	62.1	171	37.9	451
Pre- and early adolescence (11–14)	236	71.1	96	28.9	332
Middle and late adolescence (15–18)	123	74.1	43	25.9	166
$X = 12.36$, 3 df; $p < .01$					

Note: N = 1,057. There were insufficient data in 184 cases.

that should be of prime interest to those concerned with the prevention and control of delinquency.[13]

Furthermore, that children with delinquency symptoms do not necessarily receive service more readily than others without these symptoms is suggested by the disposition of applications as presented for each specific category or complaint (table 3–5). Complaints of psychosis, homosexuality, suicidal behavior, and truancy are among those least likely to receive full service, while enuresis, soiling, setting fires, poor peer relations, night terrors, and other forms of phobic and nervous disorders are among those most likely to receive full service. These general findings remain fairly stable within each clinic. Thus, by service given, enuresis, soiling, learning problems, and poor peer relations hold about the same rank among the thirty presenting complaints in each clinic.

When all of the symptoms are classified into type I or type II, the absence of any discernible relationship between general class of symptom and the disposition of the case is even more apparent. In other words, the delinquent or near-delinquent cases were not more likely to receive service at the clinic than were the nondelinquent cases (table 3–6). Indeed there was even a slight tendency for the nondelinquent to receive more complete service, a finding that holds true for all three clinics.

Since there is a direct relationship between age and type of symptom and since we also found that older children were given service less frequently, we examined the relationship between type of symptom and disposition while controlling age. We classified children up to ten years of age in one category and those eleven years of age and above in a second category. This analysis failed to reveal a relationship between symptom and

Table 3–5
Presenting Complaints and Disposition of Cases at Child-Guidance
Clinics

General Complaint	Presenting Complaint	Receiving Service		Total
		N	%	
Relations in school or	Learning problem	360	36.1	
difficulties in learning	School phobia	36	30.6	
	Speech or hearing	30	30.0	426
Delinquency or	Aggression, fighting	168	35.1	
near-delinquency	Stealing	69	39.1	
	Running away or truancy	27	22.2	264
Behavior and medical	Medical and other	131	29.0	
problems	Behavior problems			
	(nonspecific)	119	30.2	
	Obesity	5	40.0	255
Neurosis	Night terrors, nervousness	117	42.7	
	Enuresis	28	50.0	
	Soiling	20	55.0	165
Relations with authority	Temper tantrums	56	37.5	
	Poor family relations	56	32.1	
	Lying	31	38.7	
	Obscene language	4	25.0	147
Autism	Inhibition or shyness	70	35.7	
	Daydreaming	12	41.7	82
Relations with peers	Poor peer relations	73	42.5	73
Retardation	Retardation	43	41.9	43
Depression	Depression	40	32.5	40
Sex	Sexual aggressiveness	21	38.1	
	Homosexuality	9	11.1	
	Masturbation	6	50.0	36
Setting fires	Setting fires	25	44.0	25
Psychosomatic difficulty	Psychosomatic complaint	22	36.4	22
Psychosis	Psychosis or near psychosis	16	18.7	16
Suicidal threat or attempt	Threatened or attempted suicide	14	28.6	14
Separation	Separation problem	8	50.0	8

Note: Differences between number in table 3–2 and 3–5 due to incomplete information on case disposition.

disposition in either age group. In other words, among children of each age group, those manifesting delinquent or near-delinquent behavior were not more likely to receive service than those without these types of problems.

Table 3-6
Presenting Symptom and Disposition of Cases at Child-Guidance Clinics

	Disposition				
	Service Incomplete		*Service Complete*		
	N	*%*	*N*	*%*	*100% =*
Type I	199	72.4	76	27.6	275
Type II	439	68.7	200	31.3	639
$X^2 = 1.23$; 1 df; n.s.					

Note: $N = 914$. Incomplete data in 327 cases.

Source of Referral and Disposition

One of our major hypotheses was that referrals made with the intercession of professional personnel, in contrast to those that were not, would receive more services from the guidance clinics.[14]

There is significant support for our hypothesis regarding the role of professionals in the disposition of cases (table 3-7), and the relationship persists when the categories of disposition are not collapsed. Because it was possible that professionals were referring the more-delinquent types of cases, we inspected the relationship between source of referral and disposition within each general class of symptoms (table 3-8). The type of complaint, it turns out, does not account for the relationship between the sources of referral and the disposition of the case. Nor does the occupational variable explain these differences. When the occupational variable is controlled, the relationship between source of referral and disposition remains significant (table 3-9).

Since it was possible that the combined effect of occupation and type of symptom might obscure the relationship between source of referral and case disposition, we examined the relationship while controlling these two variables simultaneously. This analysis confirmed our previous finding that the source of referral was related to case disposition; the father's occupation, like the type of problem, does not account for the relationship.

Possibly professionals make good use of the formal and the informal channels that link personnel in a network of communication and that are less accessible to laypersons. To be sure, the professionals often need one another, and it may be this mutual dependence upon services that results in the greater attention given professional referrals. Another explanation, is

Table 3–7

Source of Referral and Disposition of Cases at Child-Guidance Clinics

	Disposition				
	Service Incomplete		Service Complete		
Source of Referral	N	%	N	%	100% =
Nonprofessional	468	75.5	152	24.5	620
Professional	301	66.6	151	33.4	452
$X^2 = 10.19$; 1 df; $p < .01$					

Note: $N = 1,072$. Incomplete data in 169 cases.

Table 3–8

Source of Referral and Disposition of Cases at Child-Guidance Clinics, by Type of Symptoms

	Service Incomplete		Service Complete		
	N	%	N	%	100% =
Type I					
Nonprofessional	123	77.4	36	22.6	159
Professional	76	65.5	40	34.5	116
$X^2 = 4.70$; 1 df; $p < .05$					
Type II					
Nonprofessional	248	72.3	95	27.7	343
Professional	191	64.5	105	35.5	296
$X^2 = 4.47$; 1 df; $p < .05$					

Note: $N = 914$. Incomplete data in 327 cases.

that intake personnel often arrive at the decision to provide service on the basis of a telephone call and are influenced by professionals who are more articulate and may summarize the child's symptoms more clearly than a parent would, for instance. Thus it seems that Mishler and Waxler's conclusion about the bearing of source of referral on the disposition of the case in a mental hospital applies equally well to child-guidance clinics.

Occupation of Applicant's Father and Case Disposition

The second hypothesis of our study was that applicants with fathers in middle- or upper-status occupations are more often accorded complete ser-

Table 3-9
**Source of Referrals and Disposition of Cases at Child-Guidance
Clinics, by Father's Occupation**

	Service Incomplete		Service Complete		
	N	%	N	%	100% =
Middle class					
Nonprofessional	120	64.5	66	35.5	186
Professional	62	48.8	65	51.2	127
X^2 = 7.64; 1 df; $p < .01$					
Lower class					
Nonprofessional	123	71.1	50	28.9	173
Professional	42	40.4	62	59.6	104
X^2 = 25.43; 1 df; $p < .001$					

Note: N = 590.

vice than are their lower-placed counterparts. Unfortunately it was impossible to submit this hypothesis to a fair test since information on occupation was available for only 60 percent of the fathers in the study population. An examination of those cases in which we do have occupational data fails to lend any support to this hypothesis and does not reveal any relationship between the occupational status of the father and the acceptance of the child.

In view of the limitations of the intake data in general and of the occupational data in particular, we are on tenuous grounds in attempting to draw any firm conclusions from the finding of no relationship between occupation and disposition. It may well be a special finding stemming from the incompleteness of our data. On the other hand, it might reflect a real departure from the apparently prevailing practice in the psychiatric world of giving more treatment to applicants of higher-social status. It does appear that although the professional and white-collar class is overrepresented in the population of applicants to guidance clinic (within the agencies we studied, at least), clinic personnel do not show favoritism to them as opposed to working-class applicants.

Organizational Needs and Case Disposition

We were not able to study organizational characteristics with any thoroughness, and although we did not attempt to test our assumption that organizational needs affect case disposition, in the course of the study we did obtain information suggesting that there may be a basis for this hypothesis. For example, complaints of psychosis and truancy were less likely to receive service in each clinic, whereas soiling and learning problems were more likely to do so, and in terms of service given, enuresis, soiling, learning problems, and poor peer relations hold approximately the same rank among the thirty presenting complaints in each clinic.

At least two interesting exceptions appear to reflect the role of organizational needs and interests: clinic A gave complete service to 27 percent of all school phobia cases and clinic C to 35 percent, but clinic B gave full service to none. What may explain these findings is that clinic C recently undertook research on school phobia and needed cases of this sort. By the same token, clinic B, which was coordinating a study of runaways, gave more service to them and to truants than did either of the other two clinics. The fact that clinic A accepted a number of school phobia cases is probably attributable, in part, to its relative physical proximity to clinic C and interaction with it.[15] These are, of course, ex-post-facto explanations. What is required is a study in which the agencies' specific orgaizational needs would be identified systematically and then predictions made as to which categories of clients they would accept in view of these needs.

Thus our findings reveal that organizational needs and requirements did affect, to some degree at least, the kind of applicants accepted. It is no criticism of an individual agency with more applicants than it can handle that it selects certain applicants who thereby help the agency realize other objectives as well (for instance, research). However, for the community as a whole, the cumulative consequences of this kind of selection may require serious appraisal.

Characteristics of the Court Clinic's Population

The court psychiatric clinic is a relative newcomer to the geographic area covered by our study, having made its appearance as recently as 1948. At that time, many clinicians feared that the authoritarian setting of the court clinic would prevent the development of an effective therapeutic program. However, virtually every clinician whom we interviewed in the course of our study expressed confidence in the court clinics.

Because the court and child-guidance clinics had different modes of operation (for example, the process of referral to the clinic), we analyzed their data separately. Indeed the differences between the two types of clinic made it difficult to extend our hypotheses to the court clinics. Since almost all referrals to the court clinics were directed from the court or the probation department, our hypothesis about source of referral became irrelevant in the study of these clinics. Our hypothesis about occupation and disposition could not be tested adequately since referrals to the court clinics mainly involved youths from the working and lower classes. However, because of our general interest in circumstances bearing on case disposition in the court clinics, as well as our desire to ascertain the fate of children not accepted for treatment by them, we decided to include the court clinics in our study.

With respect to the sex distribution of referrals, the court clinics were very much like the guidance clinics: approximately seven of every ten referrals were made on behalf of boys. However, community differences are apparent in the sex distributions. In clinic D, nine of every ten referrals were male, whereas in clinic E it was six of every ten. An obvius explanation was the proportion of boys to girls brought to each of the courts. Although we were unable to obtain the data for 1962, we secured information on the cases in the two courts during 1960; about 12 percent of all juvenile cases brought into court D were female, while in court E girls accounted for 20 percent of the total.[16] Moreover, at court D about 10 percent of all juvenile probationers were female as compared with 22 percent in court E. One question that naturally arises is whether these communities respond differentially to boys and girls who commit offenses.

The mean age of children in the two clinics was fairly close; in clinic D it was approximately fifteen and one-half years as compared with fourteen and one-half years at clinic E. In the court clinics, problems of unmanageability (truancy, running away, and stubbornness) and offenses against property (auto theft, larceny, robbery, and arson) appear more frequently than do sex offenses or cases of assault (table 3-10).

Table 3-10
Major Offenses Reported at Court Clinics

Offense	N	%
Use of car without authority	17	12.1
Open and gross lewdness	4	2.9
Larceny, robbery, and breaking and entering	27	19.3
Obscene language	4	2.9
Prostitution, fornication, and homosexuality	8	5.6
Drug violations	2	1.4
Stubbornness	26	18.6
Running away or truancy	35	25.0
Assault and battery	11	7.8
Arson	3	2.2
Other	3	2.2
Total	140	100.0

In marked contrast to the substantial representation (52 percent) of upper- or middle-class persons among referrals to guidance clinics, the court clinics had only a small proportion of them (10 percent) among their referrals. The population of court-clinic cases clearly came predominantly from the working and lower classes (table 3–11). We can only wonder whether child-guidance clinics and other agencies for the control of delinquency could appreciably reduce the official delinquency rate by focusing their preventive efforts on children from the lower class who give evidence of antisocial or near-delinquent behavior.

The central interest of our study, case disposition, had a different meaning in the court clinic than in the guidance clinic. In the court clinic, all cases referred by the judge or probation department received a diagnostic evaluation, on the basis of which the clinic may have recommended in-clinic treatment or placement or simply returned the case to its source and advised that it would not benefit from in-clinic treatment. Thus, in the court clinics, there were generally no holding operations, no referrals elsewhere, and no long waiting lists. When court clinics and child-guidance clinics are compared (table 3–12), their differing case-disposal procedures should be kept in mind. With respect to the disposition of cases in court clinics, "incomplete service" simply denotes the clinic's decision not to treat the case, while in child-guidance cases, "incomplete service" may denote "rejected," "held," "referred," or "withdrawn before a personal interview."

There is a rather impressive similarity between the two types of clinic with respect to the proportion of cases accepted for service (table 3–12). The guidance clinics paralleled each other in the proportion of cases for treat-

Table 3–11
Occupation of Fathers of Referrals to Child-Guidance and Court Clinics

	Guidance Clinics		Court Clinics	
	N	%	N	%
Professionals, proprietors, managers	231	31.7	6	5.8
Clerical	144	19.8	5	4.8
Manual and service	314	43.2	50	48.1
Unemployed, welfare, or absent from the home	39	5.3	43	41.3
Total	728[a]	100.0	104[b]	100.0

[a]No data for 513 cases.
[b]No data for 36 cases.

Table 3–12
Disposition of Referrals at Child-Guidance and Court Clinics

	Guidance Clinics		Court Clinics	
	N	%	N	%
Service incomplete	878	71.6	911	65.0
Service complete	349	28.4	49	35.0
Total	1,227[a]	100.0	140	100.0

[a]No data on fourteen cases.

ment (39 percent and 33 percent respectively). These strikingly similar proportions encourage speculation as to the relative role of psychiatric technique, organizational arrangements, professional culture, and other social conditions in producing these case-load limits or ceilings.

Relationships among Variables at Court Clinics

Although younger children were more often given service in the guidance clinics, neither sex nor age was found to be related to disposition in the court clinics. Exactly as in the guidance clinics, the father's occupation was also found to be unrelated to disposition in court-clinic cases. The professional-managerial, clerical, and manual-service-unemployed groups showed virtually the same proportions in the "complete service" category: 36 percent, 34 percent, and 33 percent. In view of the very small number of middle- and upper-status occupations in our court-clinic population, this finding must be viewed cautiously. However, on the basis of available data on the court-clinic cases, none of the demographic variables is related to disposition, a finding that also held when data on the two individual clinics were analyzed separately.

In our analysis of the relationship between offenses and disposition, we combined the various types of offenses into the following main categories:

Offenses against property: Use of car without authority, larceny, robbery, breaking and entering, and arson.

Unmanageability: Stubbornness, running away from home, and truancy.

Morals charges: Open and gross lewdness, prostitution, fornication, homosexuality, and obscene language.

Assault and battery.

Juveniles charged with offenses against property or with assault and battery were much more likely to be assigned to treatment by the court clinics than were those charged with unmanageability or with offenses against morals (table 3–13).

Because the two clinics differed considerably with respect to the kinds of offenses charged against the children referred to them, we examined separately the relationship between offenses and disposition in each court clinic. The two clinics differed notably: clinic E assigned for treatment more children charged with offenses against property than did clinic D. On the other hand, clinic D assigned for treatment more unmanageable children and offenders against morals.

In interviewing court personnel, we found a greater interest in sex offenses evinced by the judge and probation department in clinic D. We must note here, as in the guidance-clinic findings, the apparent operation on case disposition of a factor other than type of severity of behavior. We are not making judgments about the degree of influence of organizational interests on case disposition but are simply calling attention to the f t that organizations are affected by their needs.

The Nationwide Survey

Because we wondered about the generalizability of the findings presented so far, which are based on a rather intensive study of five clinics, we undertook a national survey, which focused on selection activities of a large number of child psychiatric clinics. Since it was not possible for us to study directly the selection procedures at each of the clinics in our national sample, we relied

Table 3–13
Offense and Disposition of Cases at Court Clinics

	Not Accepted for Treatment		Accepted for Treatment		
	N	%	N	%	100% =
Unmanageability	46	75.4	15	24.6	61
Offenses against property	25	53.2	22	46.8	47
Morals charges	11	68.7	5	31.3	16
Assault and battery	6	54.6	5	45.4	11

Note: $N = 135$. Five cases could not be logically placed in these categories of offense.

on questions to administrative personnel, which we assumed, would indirectly provide data on selection procedures.

In the summer of 1964, a mail questionnaire was sent to the directors of
all 132 child-guidance agencies accredited by the American Association of
Psychiatric Clinics for Children along with a supporting letter from Dr.
George Gardner, the director of the Judge Baker Guidance Center and
former editor of *Orthopsychiatry*. After appropriate follow-up procedures,
87 percent of the clinics completed and returned their questionnaires.
Three-fourths of those who filled out the questionnaires were clinic directors; the others included chief psychiatrists, clinical directors, chief social
workers and other professionals. Only 2 percent of the respondents were
not professionals.

One-third of the clinics operated in cities with a population of 300,000
or less, about one-third in cities from 300,000 to 1 million, and the remaining one-third in cities of more than 1 million. As expected, the number of
full-time professionals in each clinic showed considerable variation: 22 percent of the clinics had five or fewer full-time professionals, 40 percent had
six to ten, 30 percent from twenty-one to thirty, and about 8 percent more
than thirty.

Approximately 60 percent of the clinics in the study group were af-
filiated with a hospital. Almost all served children up to seventeen years of
age. The average patient load showed considerable variations ranging from
fewer than fifty to more than six hundred. Slightly less than one-third of the
clinics had an average patient load of fewer than one hundred. The patient
load for another third of the clinics was between one hundred and two hundred, and the remaining third of the clinics generally handled more than two
hundred cases.

Clinic administrators were asked to indicate what percentage of applicants were made up of children with different types of problems. Of nine
different types of symptoms, learning problems ranked highest, followed by
delinquent problems and neuroses, the latter two almost equal in
magnitude. Although these categories did not coincide precisely with those
presented earlier, nevertheless there is a good deal of similarity between the
two schemes. It appears that this ordering compares favorably with that
shown in table 3–2, where learning problems and delinquency problems
hold the first two ranks of problems presented to clinics. Further similarity
emerges in examining case disposition in both studies. In each case, the indications are that the clinics are more likely to accept neurotic cases for
treatment. Indeed the major discrepancy concerns volume, not acceptance.
That is, clinics report themselves as ''referring elsewhere'' less frequently
than we found in our intensive study.

Although generalizations about all child psychiatric clinics must be
made with caution, we feel confident that the clinic applicant population

reported on in this book are representative of people generally applying to child psychiatric clinics at the time our study was undertaken.

Conclusions

Perhaps the most startling finding presented here is the apparent absence of symptomatic differences between those accepted for service and those who were not. Equally disconcerting is the finding that most applicants for help apparently were not given the assistance they sought, a finding that should warrant the concern of those who care about children and their parents. On its own, such a finding called for the kind of study reported on in this book. The first finding (that there are few, if any, symptomatic differences between those accepted and those not accepted) extends the generalizing potential of the follow-up studies reported here, for it suggests that our study group has the advantage of resembling a no-treatment control group for the children typically accepted in psychotherapy programs in child psychiatric clinics. As such, our study should prove useful to clinicians, because many of them have long wondered what happened to those who are not given prompt assistance, and to researchers, who have often made untested assumptions about the comparability of their control and treatment groups with respect to treatment during the duration of quasi-experimental studies. Such assumptions in part have given rise to the acceptance of the estimate that 65 to 70 percent of untreated children improve or show spontaneous remission. Our study of the selection process, we think, has now set the stage for the consideration of history.

Notes

1. By emotionally disturbed, we mean any child in the study group for whom help was sought.

2. Elliot G. Mishler and Nancy E. Waxler, "Decision Processes in Psychiatric Hospitalization: Patients Referred, Accepted, and Admitted to a Psychiatric Hospital," *American Sociological Review* 28 (August 1963):576-587.

3. For a study that deals with the relationship between social class and the treatment of mental illness, see August B. Hollingshead and Frederick C. Redlich, *Social Class and Mental Illness* (New York: John Wiley, 1959).

4. Case disposition is defined differently for the guidance and court clinics.

5. In this study an application is an inquiry made to the clinic. This usage is at variance with that of one of the clinics where the first call is an inquiry and the interview, if granted, is the application.

6. Elio Monachesi, for example, notes that boys have more opportunities than girls to engage in antisocial behavior. See "Some Personality Characteristics of Delinquents and Non-Delinquents," *Journal of Criminal Law and Criminology* 38 (January–February 1948):487–500.

7. Social workers involved in intake at the three clinics were asked about procedures used in recording the source of referral. The clinics' intake workers all used a brief form, which contained a line or a box entitled "source of referral." Their procedure was to record the name and status (mother, doctor, and so forth) of the first person to call, write, or otherwise contact the clinic about the child. Thus, if a mother called at the suggestion of a doctor, the worker recorded the mother as the source of referral, although mention was also made of the doctor's suggestion on the intake form. In such an event, we recorded the mother and the doctor as the referral source.

8. Edna E. Raphael, "Community Structure and Acceptance of Psychiatric Aid," *American Journal of Sociology* 69 (January 1964):340–358. Some other studies that discuss the referral process are George S. Stevenson and Geddes Smith, *Child Guidance Clinics: A Quarter Century of Development* (New York: Commonwealth Fund, 1934); Helen L. Witmer, *Psychiatric Clinics for Children* (New York: Commonwealth Fund, 1940); Mishler and Waxler, "Decision Processes"; Earl Lomon Koos, *Families in Trouble* (New York: King's Crown Press, 1946).

9. Lee N. Robins and Patricia O'Neal, "Mortality, Mobility, and Crime: Problem Children Thirty Years Later," *American Sociological Review* 23 (June 1958):162–171.

10. For the occupational distribution of males in the United States, see Lawrence Thomas, *The Occupational Structure and Education* (Englewood Cliffs, N.J.: Prentice-Hall, 1959).

11. When information on disposition was not available, we reported it to the intake personnel, and an effort was made to obtain it. We were especially attentive to this matter not only because disposition was the major dependent variable but because case disposition determined whom we were to interview; we wished to interview those who had not received what we termed full service, and we did not want to interview those who had.

12. In our analysis of relationships between the independent variables and case disposition, the latter was classified as "complete service" or "incomplete service." "Complete service" included cases categorized as "consultation," "withdrew after contact," "diagnosis," and "treatment." All others were classified as "incomplete service."

13. See, for example, Leslie T. Wilkins, "Delinquent Generations," in Marvin Wolfgang, Leonard Savitz, and Norman Johnston, eds., *The Sociology of Crime and Delinquency* (New York: John Wiley, 1962). See

also Milton Barron, *The Juvenile in Delinquent Society* (New York: Alfred A. Knopf, 1960), p. 54.

14. When analyzing the relationship between sources of referral and disposition, we collapsed the categories of source of referral as follows: professional referrals include those from physicians, school personnel, clinics, family-service agencies, and hospitals, as well as joint referrals involving the mother and a professional person; nonprofessional referrals include those from mothers only, fathers, other relatives, friends, and ministers.

15. See W. Miller, R. Baum, and R. McNeil, "Delinquence Prevention and Organizational Relations," in S. Wheeler, ed., *Controlling Delinquents* (New York: John Wiley, 1968), chap. 4.

16. We are indebted to the State Office of Probation in Massachusetts for supplying us with the statistics on which these percentages are based.

4 History of Symptoms

This chapter begins our investigation of history and is largely based on interviews with parents in 1963 who applied for help unsuccessfully in 1962 or, in court-clinic cases, were not accepted for treatment though the court referred them. Two facets of history will be considered in our study, and they constitute the emphasis of this book. The first concerns the history of the problem or symptomatic behavior that induced the parents to contact a clinic, and the second concerns the problem-solving or coping efforts undertaken by the child's parents as a result of the child's behavior.

Any discussion of symptoms must start with the admission of their limitation as data. These include the arbitrariness of the assumptions of their beginning, the inadequacy of their descriptive efficiency, and their frequent transience. Although volumes have been written on the investigation of symptoms and the attendant problems, we will offer no such thorough analysis here. Instead we will attempt only to clarify our major assumptions concerning the children's symptomatic behavior, present an analysis of symptoms based on several sources, and examine relationships between selected background factors and symptomatic behavior.

Selection of the Interview Study Group

Our study of the clinic selection process, subsequently informed our own selection behavior for our interview study in 1963. During calendar year 1962, 878 of 1,241 applicants to the guidance clinics received less than full service, and another 39 applicants withdrew voluntarily after a face-to-face interview. In the court clinics, we found that 91 of 140 referrals were not accepted for in-clinic treatment. Thus there were 1,008 cases from which we drew our target population for interviewing. The study group was delimited further in that cases were included only if they satisfied all of the following conditions.

1. The mother or another member of the immediate family was involved in the call to the source agency.
2. Residence outside the agency's territory was not the reason for incomplete service.

3. The disposition was "rejected," "referred," or "withdrew" in guid-
    ance-clinic cases and "not recommended for treatment" in court-clinic
    cases.
4. The family was locatable (that is, an address or telephone number was
    found in one of the directories).

The reason for including only cases in which a member of the family
had called was that we wished to avoid the possibility of interviewing a relative who was unaware that someone outside the family had contacted the
clinic. The reason for our second condition was that two of the three
guidance clinics served a specific territory and rarely made exceptions. As to
the third principle of selection, the reader will recall (chapter 3) that we
included the following in the category "incomplete service": "hold,"
"rejected," "withdrew, no personal contact," and "referred." From the
target population, we omitted now, all cases where the disposition was
designated as "held" since it was quite possible that the source agency
might be in touch with them by the time we requested the interview. In such
cases, requests for interview might interfere with the clinics' efforts to help
and might lead the applicants into mistaking the interviews for part of the
diagnostic process. However, we did conduct interviews with applicants
whose disposition was "withdrew after a personal contact," a category
including 10 percent of those in the reduced target population. On the
whole, then, most of those with whom field interviews were sought had not
been seen at the clinic.

These principles of selection yielded a target population of 415 parents
to whom letters were sent requesting interviews; of these, 352 (85 percent)
were completed. There were 297 interviews with applicants to guidance
clinics and 55 interviews with referrals to court clinics. Approximately
three-quarters of the children on whom information was gathered were
males. Of the informants, 80 percent were mothers, 87 percent were white,
approximately 60 percent had completed high school or had had further
schooling, and 59 percent were non-Catholic. Structured interview
schedules were administered by professional social workers, the average
interview requiring approximately one and one-half hours. All interviews
were conducted at least 4 months, but not more than 18 months, after the
contact with the clinics; the mean interval was 10.8 months and in only
twenty-seven instances (8 percent) was it less than 6 months. All interviews
took place in the spring of 1963. (See appendix C for this interview schedule.)

The interviews covered a wide range of data, including the paths to
earlier sources of aid, experiences with the clinics, the informant's reactions
to the experience with the clinic and the child's behavior before and after
the contact with it, sociocultural characteristics of the family, type and

extent of the informant's social participation, parental aspirations, attitudes toward the neighborhood, and various aspects of personality. We found no significant differences among the families interviewed and the remainder of the target population with respect to child's age and sex, type of symptom, disposition of case, and type of clinic. The relative scantiness of our data on clinic intake, however, precluded a fuller inquiry into possible differences between those interviewed and the remainder of the target population.

Symptoms to be Examined

The child's presenting problems, though recorded in agency records, were probably the joint product of the parent's description of the child's behavior (usually over the telephone) and the clinic intake worker's translation of the parent's description. Because of our uncertainty concerning how the clinic record of the problem was produced, we inquired directly about the child's symptoms during our interview with the parents in 1963. At that time we asked about the child's symptoms at three points in time: prior to 1962, around the time the clinic was called in 1962, and at the time of our first interview in 1963. Although the first two of these required the respondent's recall of earlier events, we believed that because of their importance to them, the parents would be likely to have a fairly accurate recall of their child's behavior.

Table 4-1 presents a summary of the symptoms data and their designations. The third item (1962 symptoms is somewhat repetitious of item 2 (presenting problems in 1962). Although both items pertain to the same point in time, item 3 is taken from the interview and item 2 from the clinic record. We did not wish to rely completely on the clinic record, so we directly queried our respondents on the child's behavior. Employing symptoms checklists, we asked our respondents in 1963 to indicate the type and extent of the child's symptoms at both the time of the 1962 application and at the time of the interview in 1963. Only the checklist pertaining to the period of the 1962 application will be presented in this chapter. Later the data from both checklists will be utilized in the development of indexes of short-term change in the child's behavior during the year between the 1962 application and the 1963 interview.

Theoretical Assumptions about Symptoms Data

The primary assumption we made here is that symptoms are indicative of a set or sets of interaction processes going on between and among individuals

Table 4-1
Symptoms Data and Designations

Symptom	Source
Early symptoms, prior to 1962	1963 interview (open-ended question)
Presenting problem at 1962 application	1962 clinic intake record
Symptoms at 1962 application	1963 interview (checklist)

in social systems. We agree with many students of interaction analysis who hold that symptoms arise in relation to specific, and observable, behaviors performed by others in the individual's significant social world (including but not restricted to the family). These symptoms and the related behavior of others are then seen to continue in mutual support of one another, comprising a feedback loop within the social system.[1]

This approach proposes that symptoms are not indicative of individual disease, although this view was in vogue at many child psychiatric clinics at the time our study was initiated. Our view of symptoms is compatible with the following positions: that symptoms represent "problems in living"[2] and that symptomatic behavior may be seen as "meaningful interpersonal communication."[3]

The point to emphasize is that the child's symptomatic behavior is primarily, though not exclusively, an aspect of family interaction. This view incorporates many of the distinctive positions taken by interactionists, including labeling theorists, gestalt therapists, symbolic interactionists, and systems theorists.

The Earlier Problems

During our interviews with parents in 1963, we attempted to ascertain whether they had sought help for their child earlier than the time at which they called the clinic. We asked, "Before the _____ [source] clinic was contacted, were any of the following persons or agencies contacted about (his) (her) problem: Clergymen, psychiatrists, social workers, probation or police officers, teachers, child guidance center, family service agencies, or other?" If the respondent answered "yes" for any of these persons or agencies, they were then asked "how long ago" such persons or agencies were contacted and why (what the child's problems or symptoms were). These earlier symptoms were roughly distributed or categorized into the eight major subdivisions shown in table 4-2.

Table 4-2
Distribution of Earlier Problems

Type of Early Problem Manifestation	Guidance Clinic		Court Clinic	
	N	%	N	%
Peer and adult relations	65	29.0	10	27.8
Learning	63	28.1	4	11.1
Behavioral (nonlaw violation)	32	14.3	8	22.2
Delinquency (law violation)	25	11.2	12	33.3
Physical or medical	24	10.7	0	0
School phobia	6	2.7	1	2.8
Suicidal behavior or depression	6	2.7	1	2.8
Sex problem	3	1.3	0	0
Total	224[a]	100.0	36[a]	100.0

[a]No earlier problem was reported in seventy-three guidance-clinic cases and nineteen court-clinic cases.

For guidance-clinic cases, early problems in relations with peers and adults and learning problems show the highest frequencies. However, delinquency and other behavioral (nonlaw violation) problems were also frequently cited. The apparently serious early problems have considerable implications when paired with findings presented in chapter 3 and showing the absence of a relationship between severity of the problem presented at application and the clinic's decision to accept or reject. In the court-clinic cases, delinquency problems were most often reported as having arisen earlier, with peer and adult relations appearing next in reports of earlier problems. Learning problems were seldom mentioned, and physical or medical problems were never mentioned as earlier problems by court-clinic respondents. Neither sex nor age was related to the type of earlier problem for both guidance and court clinic cases.

An issue that is closely related to the type of earlier problems for which help was sought by parents concerns some indication of length of time that elapsed between help-seeking events. Thus, we focused our attention on the length of time respondents had waited between the time when they had sought earlier help for the child and the time in 1962 when they applied for help at guidance clinics or were required to appear at a court clinic. Table 4-3 presents the distribution of the number of years our respondents waited

Table 4-3
Distribution of Cases by Number of Years Parent Waited between Seeking Help for Earlier Problems and Contact with Clinic

	Guidance Clinics		Court Clinics	
	N	%	N	%
Less than 1 year	78	36.4	21	63.6
Between 1 and 2 years	49	22.9	8	24.2
Between 2 and 3 years	28	13.1	4	12.2
Between 3 and 4 years	19	8.9		
Between 4 and 5 years	17	7.9		
Between 5 and 6 years	6	2.8		
Between 6 and 7 years	9	4.2		
8 or more	8	3.8		
Total	214	100.0	33	100.0

[a]No earlier problem in seventy-three cases and no information on time waited in ten cases for guidance clinics; no earlier reported problem in nineteen cases and no information on "waiting" time in three cases for court-clinic cases.

after their earlier help-seeking efforts before seeking help at guidance clinics or appearing at court clinics. The guidance- and court-clinic cases are not strictly comparable, however; all that can be said is that most of the court-clinic cases were in court less than a year after the parents-respondents had sought help on their own. This may simply mean that help-seeking appearances to the contrary, the court-clinic respondents waited much too long before seeking the earlier help. This is mere speculation, however, since we do not have more data on the earlier history of each family's help-seeking efforts.

Over 60 percent of the guidance-clinic respondents reported waiting more than a year between their earlier help-seeking and the application to the clinic. As in the case of court clinics, appearances may be deceiving; the guidance-clinic respondents started looking for help earlier than did the court-clinic respondents although the initial impression of table 4-3 may be that they waited longer. The problem for guidance-clinic respondents would be magnified, however, upon being unable to find the sought-for help when they did apply. Perhaps it would be safe to say that parents who had not sought help for two or three years would be more frustrated than those who had sought help more recently. Thus researchers will have to consider other waiting periods beyond mere waiting time at an agency when conducting research on help-seeking behavior and its attendant problems.

The Presenting Problems

We wondered if the early problems would appear to be the same ones presented in 1963. We pursued this comparison differently for the two types of clinics since all of the court cases were charged with some legal offense in 1962 and would require a different classificatory scheme. For guidance-clinic cases, table 4-4 presents a cross-tabulation of the earlier problems reported during the interview, by the presenting problem, taken from guidance-clinic records; although an effort was made to categorize the presenting problems in ways similar to categories of earlier problems, there are differences in the two classifications. Thus table 4-4 does not accurately reflect change of symptoms over time, although there is at least some justification in viewing the relationship as being suggestive of change and persistence.

Table 4-4 suggests strongly that the presenting problems were much more serious than the earlier ones. When we asked the question about earlier problems, we intended to ascertain the extent of the parent's concern as indexed by the extent of their help-seeking behavior. Almost as an afterthought we then asked why they had sought earlier help. We thus expected to find a good deal of overlap—more than is presented in table 4-4—between those two time periods. The fact that a good deal of time had passed between the two help-seeking events lends some weight to the idea that the child's problems often changed over time. We do not wish to attach too much weight to the comparison presented in this table, but we do wish to emphasize the great possibility that many of the children's behavior either changed over time or was perceived differently, by someone, at the time the clinic was called. Of course, some of this behavior was newly perceived as a problem at the time the clinic was called since seventy-three respondents reported "no earlier problems"; however, this does not account for all of the rather extensive changes noticeable in table 4-4. Thus substantial numbers of children reported to have relational or learning problems earlier are described in the clinic record as having delinquency-type problems at the time of application. Perhaps the major reason why these respondents called a guidance clinic in 1962 was not because the children were in desperate straits but because the parents perceived that their child was "getting worse." Reinforcing this notion is the fact that in the past these parents had overwhelmingly relied on nonprofessional and informal sources of aid, while in 1962 they all applied to child psychiatric agencies for help.

In an effort to simplify the data presented in table 4-4, we classified the presenting complaints as type I (either in conflict with the law or inimical to self or others) and type II (less antisocial and not law violative). (See table 4-5.) We did not attempt to categorize symptoms in terms of psychody-

Table 4–4
Earlier Problems and Presenting Problems in Guidance Clinics

Earlier Problem	Delinquent Behavior and Firesetting	Poor Peer or Family Relations	Physical or Medical Problems	Learning Problems	School Problems and Separation Problems	Depression or Suicidal Problems	Sex Problem	Psychiatric or Autistic	Other	No Information	Total
Delinquent behavior	15	1	1	4	1	—	—	—	2	1	25
Poor peer and adult relations	24	16	1	8	2	1	—	3	3	7	65
Physical or medical problems	2	1	7	8	—	1	—	1	—	4	24
Learning problems	11	7	1	31	2	3	—	3	—	5	63
School phobia or separating problem	—	—	—	3	2	—	—	1	—	—	6
Depression, suicidal behavior	—	3	1	1	—	—	—	—	1	—	6
Sex problem	—	2	—	—	—	—	1	—	—	—	3
Other behavior problem	6	1	3	7	5	1	—	5	2	2	32
No earlier problem	19	11	—	13	5	2	3	2	7	11	73
Total	77	42	14	75	17	8	4	15	15	30	297

Table 4–5
Persistence of Symptoms for Guidance-Clinic Cases

| | Presenting Problems | | | |
Earlier Problems	Type I	Type II	No Information	Total
Type I	16	12	—	28
Type II	52	125	19	196
No earlier problems	23	39	11	73
Total	91	176	30	297

namics or clinical formulations of amenability to treatment. This table shows that there were proportionately and absolutely more severe problems (type I) at the time of application than there were at the earlier time when more informal help was typically sought.

Regarding court-clinic cases, charges of law violations rather than presenting problems were involved; in addition, the court cases were not voluntary applicants but had been referred by the court for evaluation. In spite of these differences, we still wished to obtain some historical data related to the earlier recognition of problems by respondents of the children sent to court clinics and to compare the severity of such problems with the legal offenses. Thus, we asked court-clinic respondents the same questions put to guidance-clinic respondents about the presence of earlier problems, seeking help for such problems, and the time span between seeking earlier help and the child's appearance at the court clinic.

Earlier problems for court-clinic cases also were categorized into type I and type II problems. The categories of offenses listed by the court just prior to the appearance of these children at the court clinic were (frequency is given in parentheses): use of car without authority (five), larceny (eight), sex-related offenses, such as prostitution or fornication (two), stubborn child (fourteen), runaway or truancy (seventeen), obscene language (two), drug use (one) and assault (six). In our attempt to rate the severity of these offenses, we categorized them in a way similar to our clustering of the presenting problems for guidance-clinic cases. We were not entirely satisfied with the results of this effort since court-clinic offenses seemed to reflect more-severe problems than those of guidance-clinic cases, and the presenting problems of guidance-clinic cases and the offenses of court-clinic cases were not congruent. Thus, we divided the offenses into two categories of "more severe" and "less severe." Into the less-severe category were placed charges that appeared to reflect unmanageability at home or school, such as stubbornness, running away, truancy, and use of obscene language. The remaining cases—those who committed offenses against property, persons, or moral standards—were placed in the more-severe category. Our purpose was to see whether there was any apparent relationship between the severity of the earlier problems and the severity of the offenses later charged against court-clinic cases. The results, presented in table 4–6, show no relationship between type of earlier problems and severity of offenses for court-clinic cases, although as in the case of guidance-clinic cases, there was an increase in the number of severe cases. The increase in the number of more severe cases from thirteen to twenty-two is due to offsetting shifts for earlier type I and type II problems and to the appearance of more-severe charges for nine court cases for whom no earlier problems were reported.

As far as the history of all cases is concerned, there was an apparent increase in the severity of the children's problems over the period of months or years preceding the parent's call to or appearance at a psychiatric clinic in 1962. Furthermore, there seems to have been a greater worsening over time of the guidance cases when compared with court cases. Thus, the increase of more-severe problems for court-clinic cases was from 25 percent for earlier problems to 40 percent with respect to offenses, while the increase for guid-ance-clinic cases was from slightly less than 10 percent for more-severe earlier problems to 31 percent at the time of application in 1962. Admittedly the categories of symptoms employed for the two types of clinics differ to some extent; moreover, the two groups differed in demographic characteristics, with the court clinic cases having a higher average age, a higher proportion of males, and a larger proportion of lower-class families. Nevertheless, there seems to have been an increasing similarity in the symptomatic behavior of the two groups as time elapsed prior to the 1962 clinic contact. This apparent similarity, however, rests primarily on the comparison of two sets of data—presenting problems and court-charged offenses—that were taken from clinic records.

The Symptoms Checklists

In our 1963 interview, both guidance-clinic and court-clinic respondents were presented with a list of twenty-three symptoms and asked to indicate how frequently—"never," "rarely," "sometimes," or "often"—their children did these things around the time of the 1962 clinic contact and around the time of our 1963 interview. The frequency with which each study population manifested different symptoms around 1962 appears in table 4–7. In addition, we ranked the frequency of symptoms in each study population. Although the results are generally consistent with expectations, based on known demographic differences between the two groups, there are also some interesting similarities.

Approximately half of the court-clinic cases were playing truant at the

Table 4–6

Earlier Problems and Severity of Court-Charged Offenses in 1962 for Court-Clinic Cases

	More Severe	Less Severe	Total
	N	N	N
Type I	4	9	13
Type II	9	14	23
No earlier problems	9	10	19
Total	22	33	

Table 4–7

Symptoms at Time of Contact with Child-Guidance and Court Clinics

	Proportion of Children Exhibiting Symptoms Sometimes or Often	
Symptoms	Child Guidance (N = 297)	Court (N = 55)
Making you lose patience	90.2%	76.4%
Being sad or unhappy	66.7	56.4
Disobeying at home	65.0	70.9
Telling lies	52.5	80.0
Staying by himself	46.8	38.2
Crying a lot	45.1	21.8
Failing on examinations	44.1	50.9
Getting into fights	40.7	49.1
Misbehaving at school	40.7	60.0
Destroying things	31.7	18.2
Having bad dreams	31.0	14.6
Taking things	23.6	41.8
Swearing	22.9	38.2
Presenting feeding problems	22.9	10.9
Bed-wetting	19.5	12.7
Keeping bad company	19.5	67.3
Staying out late	11.8	40.0
Truanting	9.8	49.1
Masturbating or playing with self	8.7	5.5
Soiling	8.4	0.0
Setting fires	7.4	1.8
Having problems with opposite sex	4.7	18.2
Threatening suicide	4.7	3.6

time of clinic contact, as compared to only 10 percent of the child-guidance cases, and 42 percent of court-clinic cases were reported as "taking things" while less than one-quarter of the child-guidance cases did so. On the other hand, "having bad dreams" and "crying a lot" were considerably more characteristic of the child-guidance population than they were of the court-clinic population. These facts are in line with what we would expect given the age differences between clinic populations.

Perhaps the more startling and significant finding is the similarity between the two study populations in the distribution of symptoms. For example, although the court-clinic population exceeded the guidance-clinic population in the incidence of "failing examinations" and "getting into fights," the differences were very slight. In addition, a majority of children in each group were reported as "disobeying at home" and as "being sad and unhappy." When the symptoms are ranked, there is a remarkable similarity between the two groups. The Spearman rank-order correlation is 0.70. This correlation further supports our suggestion, based on the apparent shifts between earlier and presenting problems, that by the time of their contact with a guidance or court clinic in 1962, the two samples had much in common.[4] In spite of the similarities, we will continue to analyze the court- and guidance-clinic populations separately because of the differences that characterize the two groups.

Structural and Personal Correlations of Presenting Problems

In the analysis of relationships we are relying on the presenting problems classification rather than on the symptoms checklist, for several reasons. First, this classification into only two types (types I and II) has some basis in the literature.[5] Second, use of the shorter classification over the more-complex checklist is less time-consuming for readers. And, third, the typology is based on clinic data collected at the time of the clinic contact in 1962, whereas the checklist data were collected at the time of the first interview in 1963 and thus rely on the respondents' recall.[6]

The variables that we will consider in addition to the presenting problems are age and sex of the child, and mother's marital status, ethnicity, religion, and social class.

Guidance Clinics

Structural Correlates: Although boys are more likely than girls to prompt parents to contact a clinic, they are only slightly more likely to present the more antisocial problems reflected in the type I category and the relationship is not statistically significant (table 4-8).

We did find that the child's age at the time of the clinic contact was significantly related to the type of presenting problem (see table 4-9). The fact that the child's age was related to the type of presenting problem but not to the type of earlier problem suggests once again the possibility that many of our study-group children showed an acceleration in antisocial behavior over time. Perhaps this increase was especially notable as the children entered adolescence, the time at which our clinics appeared most unable to offer full service.

Of the remaining structural variables included in our analysis of presenting problems, only one stands out: mother's marital status. Before preceeding to the analysis of this family structure variable, however, we would like to present the relatively weak relationships for the other three variables considered: Warner's Index of Status Characteristics (ISC), race, and religion.

Table 4-8
Child's Sex and Presenting Problem in Guidance Clinics

	Male		Female	
	N	%	N	%
Type I	67	34.2	20	27.8
Type II	129	65.8	52	72.2
Total	196		72	
	(73.1)		(26.9)	

$X^2 = 0.71$, 1 df, n.s.

Table 4-9
Child's Age and Type of Presenting Symptoms in Guidance Clinics

	Under 11 Years		11 Years and Over	
Type of Presenting Symptom	N	%	N	%
Type I	31	25.4	56	38.4
Type II	91	74.6	90	61.6
Total	122	100.0	146	100.0

$X^2 = 5.08$; 1 df; $p < .05$

In view of the numerous instances in which social class has been found related to behavioral indexes, it is notable that Warner's ISC was not related to type of presenting problem (see table 4-10). We were less surprised by the relatively weak differences among Catholics, Protestants, and Jews with respect to type of presenting problems, although the direction of these differences is consistent with other research results. The strongest of these three relationships exists for that between race and presenting problems. The apparent stability of this relationship is questionable, however, in view of the small number of blacks (twenty-one) and Asians (two) in our study.

The most substantial relationship found so far among these structural characteristics involves the marital status of the mother. Just as in the case of the other structural variable of class and race, the family has come in for a good deal of attention as a potential source of stress.[7] Croog critically reviewed the relevant literature on the purported role of the broken family in the onset of a variety of problems including crime, delinquency, and mental illness and commented on the weaknesses of such studies. In particular he noted the tendency of these studies to fail to consider possibly important contingent variables such as the availability of parental substitutes or important mediating variables such as social class. Teele, in a discussion of the much-researched relationship between broken homes (homes characterized by death, divorce, desertion, separation, or never-married mothers) and delinquency, has commented on the increasing tendency of researchers to qualify their generalizations. Acknowledging the need to consider a whole range of factors (such as the behavior of police and other enforcement agents, the functioning of unbroken families, and mediating factors such as class), Teele concluded that the structure of the family might still be important in understanding delinquency:

> One can agree with Nye that the broken home is only a *structural feature* and does not, by itself, generate delinquent behavior. But the dynamic features of this structural variable, the associated conditions, the problem-solving resources available, are likely to be present in such a way in most American communities as to make it unwise to ignore or downgrade the statistical association between delinquency and broken homes, however complex that relationship may be.[8]

It is in the light of this view, along with our suggestion that symptoms be considered with the situational context in mind, that we present the relationship between presenting problems and family (or marital) status (table 4-11).

Table 4-11 shows that not only delinquency but a range of norm-violative problems was related to the broken family situation in our study group in 1962. Although we do not want to leap to conclusions about the causal

Table 4-10
**Social Class, Race and Religion and Proportion of Type I Presenting
Problems in Guidance Clinics**

	Proportion Type I	100% =
Social class (ISC)		
Upper (1-5)	26.4	110
Lower (6-9)	35.6	149
$X^2 = 2.07$; 1 df; ns		
Race		
White	30.8	234
Nonwhite	47.8	23
$X^2 = 3.43$; 1 df; ns		
Religion		
Jewish	27.6	58
Protestant	31.7	82
Catholic	37.4	107
$X^2 = 1.75$; 2 df; ns		

Note: No information on presenting problem or social variable in instances where N is less than 297.

Table 4-11
**Marital Status of Mother and Type of Presenting Problem in Guidance-
Clinic Cases**

	Intact Family		Broken Family[a]	
	N	%	N	%
Type I	56	26.0	31	62.0
Type II	159	74.0	19	38.0
Totals	215	100.0	50	100.0
$X^2 = 23.78$; 1 df; $p < .001$				

Note: $N = 265$. No information in thirty-two cases.
[a]Includes the separated, divorced, widowed, and never married.

direction (that is, the broken home might occur after the appearance of a
child's problem), it is certainly possible that family disruption could
increase the risk of emotional or behavioral problems for children.

Since a sizable number of social scientists have found that family status
and social class (or socioeconomic status) are related to delinquency, we
assessed the relationship between family status and type of problem while
controlling for social class.[9] Table 4-12 shows that, at least for the present

Table 4–12

Family Status and Type of Presenting Problem Controlling Social-Class Level at Guidance Clinics

| Presenting Problem | Middle-Class Family Status[a] | | | |
| | Intact Family | | Broken Family | |
	N	%	N	%
Type I	20	21.1	9	69.2
Type II	75	78.9	4	30.8
Total	95	100.0	13	100.0

X² = 13.51; 1 df; $p < .001$

| | Lower-Class Family Status[b] | | | |
	Intact Family		Broken Family	
Type I	33	29.2	20	57.1
Type II	80	70.8	15	42.9
Total	113	100.0	35	100.0

X² = 9.08; 1 df; $p < .01$

Note: $N = 256$. No information on symptoms in 28 cases, on ISC in 10 cases, and on marital status in 3 cases.

[a]ISC scores of 50 or less.

[b]ISC scores of more than 50.

study group, family status is clearly more dominant than social class in predicting the type of problem at the time of clinic contact in 1962. In fact, the relationship between family status and type of presenting problem is slightly more powerful for middle-class than for lower-class families and suggests that more serious behavior (type I) results when the stress of family disruption occurs in middle-class as opposed to lower-class families. The stability of this finding remains to be established more firmly, however, in view of the small number of broken middle-class families.

Personal Correlates: The last factor to consider in connection with the child's presenting problem concerns the respondent's personality. We utilized five so-called personality scales, developed by Leo Srole; these scales, of four or five items each, were designed to measure authoritarianism, anomia, frustration, rigidity, and withdrawal.[10] We had administered these scales during the course of our 1963 interview with respondents because we had assumed that the respondent's personality characteristics might be related to both the child's problem behavior and later development. In presenting the results of this analysis we chose to utilize only the extreme categories of the personality scales (table 4-13).

Only one of the five scales—frustration—comes close to being significantly related to the type of presenting problem. The higher the respondent's level of frustration, the more likely was the child to have type I symptoms ($p < .05$). Of the remaining scales, the one that comes closest to being significantly related is the authoritarianism scale. Since we are not impressed with the magnitudes of these relationships, we do not attach great importance to them. We suspect that the analysis is pitched at too global a level to yield valuable results. Indeed more-refined analyses using two Guttman scales (relation to authority and neurotic behavior), derived from the symptoms checklist, resulted in statistically significant relationships between the relations-to-authority scale and the personality scales in several instances.[11]

Court Clinics

As with the guidance clinics, seven of every ten cases coming to the attention of court clinics in 1962 were boys. In contrast to the cases for guidance clinics, however, there was a substantial difference in court-clinic cases in the relationship between our measure of severity of problems and sex of the child. Girls were charged almost always with being unmanageable (in 94

Table 4-13
Personality Characteristics and Proportion Having Type I and Type II Symptoms for Child-Guidance Cases

	Proportion Having Type I Symptom	Proportion Having Type II Symptom	100% =
Low anomia score (0–1)	34.6	65.4	153
High anomia score (4–5)	32.0	68.0	25
Low authoritarian score (0–1)	30.6	69.4	134
High authoritarian score (4–5)	44.9	55.1	49
Low frustration score (0–1)	30.8	69.2	208
High frustration score (3–4)	51.9	48.1	27
Low rigidity score (0–1)	29.4	70.6	153
High rigidity score (5–6)	35.3	64.7	17
Low withdrawal score (0–1)	31.5	68.5	165
High withdrawal score (3–4)	31.0	69.0	29

percent of the cases) while boys were more often charged with the more-severe offenses against persons, property, or morals (table 4–14).

Although age did not relate to the earlier problems (before 1962) for court-clinic cases, age was substantially related to the offenses with which the children were charged in 1962 (table 4–15).

For both the court- and the guidance-clinic cases, we have reason to believe that the children's problems were getting worse over time. Now, with the finding that the severity of the problems is directly related to the child's age, we began to suspect that the onset of the middle adolescent years was an important milestone for the children and families in our study.

Among our remaining structural variables (race, religion, social class, and marital status of mothers), none was related to the severity of the offense the child was charged with. Since we found marital status to be a powerful corollary of type of presenting problem for guidance-clinic cases, we were somewhat surprised that this variable was not related to the type of charged offense for court-clinic cases. We suspect that because the court-

Table 4–14
Child's Sex and Severity of Offense in Court-Clinic Cases

	Male		Female	
	N	%	N	%
More severe (Property, persons, morals)	21	55.3	1	5.9
Less severe (unmanageability)	17	44.7	16	94.1
Totals	38	100.0	17	100.0
$X^2 = 11.9$; 1 df; $p < .001$				

Table 4–15
Child's Age and Severity of Offenses in Court-Clinic Cases

	9–12 Years		13–17 Years	
	N	%	N	%
More severe	1	10	21	46.6
Less severe	9	90	24	53.4
Totals	10	100.0	45	100.0
$r = -.27$				
$p < .05$				

clinic children were older, we are less justified than for guidance-clinic cases in attempting to develop a typology of problem presenting. Indeed the court cases are more homogeneous in that all of them have been charged with law violations, whereas for guidance-clinic cases all law violations were placed in the type I category. Also, in part because they have a younger average age, there were many neurotic problems among the child-guidance cases while few, if any, of the court-clinic cases could be classified as neurotic. Thus, the categories of more and less severe, which we employed for court-clinic cases, are not really comparable to the type I, type II categories employed for guidance-clinic cases. This is demonstrated by our decision for court-clinic cases to place truants and runaways in the less-severe category, while for guidance-clinic cases they were placed in the more-severe type I category. We were making an effort to find differences among court-clinic cases by grouping their offenses in ways that seemed to make sense. We did not wish to assume, a priori, that the court-clinic children were all alike simply because they were charged with law-violative behavior. While there are, no doubt, differences among them, the present analysis of structural correlates has not revealed differences by the level of severity employed here for our court-clinic cases other than for the child's sex and child's age. Nor did we find any of the respondents' personality scales related to severity of the offense.

Based on the findings so far, we have to assume that the court-clinic cases resembled our type I guidance-clinic cases at the time of the clinic contact in 1962. This conception, however, should not be taken as a contradiction for our earlier statement that as time passed the guidance-clinic cases appeared to be worsening more quickly than did the court-clinic children. Thus, for the most part, we believe we must continue to analyze the two types of clinics separately.

Conclusions

Relying on interview reports by the family and on clinic records and covering several points in time, we have presented data suggesting that waiting time between early recognition of a problem and the family's contact with a clinic merits attention and should be more closely examined by those who investigate treatment outcomes. A host of processes both inside and outside the family unit have been going on, perhaps for a long time, and must be considered by helping agents as well as researchers.

If viewed as cohorts, both the guidance-clinic cases and the court-clinic cases showed an increase in the severity of problems between the time of earlier manifestations and the time of clinic contact in 1962.[12] However, employing the assumption that antisocial and law-violative behavior was more severe than neurotic (type II) behavior for clinic cases and that problems of unmanageability were less severe than offenses against persons, property, and morals for court-clinic cases, we found that guidance-clinic cases appeared to be accelerating more quickly in the undesirable direction than court-clinic cases. This finding seemed to be confirmed by an analysis of symptoms from the checklist employed in our 1963 interview and inquiring about the child's behavior in 1962.

An examination of the structural correlates of the child's presenting problems revealed that the child's age and the mother's marital status were substantially related to type of problem for guidance-clinic cases. More specifically, older children and children from broken homes were overrepresented in the type I category among guidance-clinic cases. Moreover, the relationship involving family or marital status held when social class was controlled for. Among court-clinic cases we found only age and sex correlates of type of offense among the structural variables.

Personality characteristics as indexed by the Srole scales were not related to type of problem-offense for either clinic group.

Notes

1. For example, see Harry Stack Sullivan, *The Interpersonal Theory of Psychiatry* (New York: Norton, 1953).

2. See Thomas Szasz *Ideology and Insanity* (New York: Anchor, 1970).

3. See P. Watzlawik, J. Beavin, and D. Jackson, *Pragmatics of Human Communication* (New York: Norton, 1967).

4. An examination of the checklist symptoms reveals the presence of some of our own assumptions about the nature of children's symptoms. Many of these "symptoms" are not simply reflections of the child's behavior; they are, in fact, perhaps best seen as "aspects of meaningful interpersonal communication," one of the assumptions behind our study. Although our data do not permit a direct test or examination of such an assumption, we think that it permits us to reflect on and to speculate about the meaning of the child's behavior and to comment on the contexts of that behavior. These symptoms should be considered with their context in mind. For example, what does it really mean when a child is "sad or unhappy" or "cries a lot"? Obviously, the child's age, his parent's age, whether the family is intact, the number of siblings, and the child's birth order are just a few of the family structural factors that may frame such "symptoms" and affect the parent perception of such behavior. Indeed each of the symptoms on our checklist could be considered with such situational features in mind.

5. See, for example, Lee Robins, *Deviant Children Grown Up* (Baltimore, Md.: William and Wilkins Co., 1966).

6. Although the presenting problems were recorded in 1962, a couple of the structural variables, such as social class and marital status of the child's mother, were obtained in 1963 and would not reflect possible changes in status subsequent to the 1962 contact. We believe it is reasonable, however, to assume that marital status and social class changed in few cases during the intervening period. Other structural variables employed, such as age and sex of the child and respondent's race and religion are less subject to unknown changes.

7. For example, see Sydney H. Croog, "The Family as a Source of Stress," and James E. Teele, "Social Pathology and Stress," both in Sol Levine and Norman A. Scotch, eds., *Social Stress* (Chicago: Aldine, 1970). On class and race, see Barbara S. Dohrenwend and Bruce P. Dohrenwend, "Class and Race as Status-Related Sources of Stress," also in Levine and Scotch.

8. Teele, "Social Pathology," p. 234.

9. For example, see Leslie T. Wilkins, "Juvenile Delinquency: A Critical Review of Research and Theory," *Educational Research* (February 1963):104-119, and Charles V. Willie, "The Relative Contribution of Family Status and Economic Status to Juvenile Delinquency," *Social Problems* (Winter 1967):326-335.

10. The scale items are "yes-no" questions. The anomia and authoritarian scales were first published by Leo Srole in "Social Integration and Certain Corollaries: An Exploratory Study," *American Sociological Review* 21 (1956):709-716. The items for the remaining scales were developed by Srole and associates in a large-scale study of mental health; see Leo Srole, T. Langner, S. Michael, M. Opler, and T. Rennie, *Mental Health in the Metropolis: The Midtown Manhattan Study* (New York: McGraw-Hill, 1962), vol. 1. Our characterization of these scales as "personality characteristics" is at variance with the manner in which Srole conceptualized them. He saw anomia, for example, as an emergent of the interaction between sociocultural and personality factors.

11. Mike Vickers, in another study of these data, also related the respondents' personality characteristics to symptoms found on the checklist. In his analysis, Vickers utilized the transactional analysis model, generalizing the various life positions ("I'm OK, you're not OK"; "I'm not OK, you're OK") for parents and children, respectively, from the personality scales and symptoms checklist. He confirmed that the underlying structure of each data set paralleled the conceptually defined life positions. More important, he found a congruence of parent-child life positions to be the overall trend, a result suggesting that a systems model, utilizing interaction analysis, is more appropriate than a disease model that examines symptoms discretely. See Michael I. Vickers, "Transactional Analysis as a Sociological Model: A Contribution to the Interpersonal View of Children's Symptomatic Behavior" (Ph.D. diss., Boston University, 1977).

12. We might appear to be making direct statements about processes, at times, based on an examination of symptoms at selected points in time. In fact we qualify all such appearances by stating that the examination of behavioral data at different points in time, while a decided advance over cross-sectional, one-shot studies, only permits the researcher to speculate about process. Later we will present data from respondents' recall of processes and events that will encourage psychiatric researchers to progress beyond the borders of spontaneous remission in evaluating untreated cases.

5 Early Coping Behavior

This chapter chronicles some of the earlier help-seeking activities of the parents, on behalf of their children, leading up to the application in 1962; experiences at the clinic in 1962; and family members' experiences and coping behavior during the interval between application at the clinic and our first interview with respondents in 1963.[1]

In 1963 we assumed that the experiences and reactions of the applicant would be related to social class, the type of clinic, and the type of presenting problem. Thus our presentation is based, in part, on several hypotheses tested in the course of our study:

1. Families of the middle and upper classes seek help earlier than do families of the lower class.
2. Middle- and upper-class families have more satisfying experiences with the clinic than do working-class families.
3. Subsequent to contact with the source clinic, middle- and upper-class families seek professional assistance more often than do families of the working class.

Method

The research design, the selection of the study group, the instruments used, the methods of data collection, and the techniques of data processing and analysis were all, in general, consistent with standard research practice. With respect to the composition and size of the study group, as well as the number of variables considered, our investigation, as far as we know, is unique.

In assessing the factors possibly related to early parental coping behavior we employed the variables used in chapter 4: race, religion, marital status, child's age, child's sex, and measures of the respondent's personality. In addition, we utilized indexes of the respondent's perception of the

Portions of this chapter are reprinted from James E. Teele and Sol Levine, "Experiences of Unsuccessful Applicants to Child Psychiatric Agencies," chapter 6 S. Wheeler, ed., *Controlling Delinquents*, (New York: John Wiley, 1968). Reprinted with permission.

causes of the child's problems and the respondent's feelings about their
clinic experience.

Earlier Sources of Aid

In deriving data on the extent to which these families reportedly sought help
prior to contact with the source agency as well as the specific persons and
agencies whom they reached, guidance-clinic respondents were asked,
"Before the _____ Clinic was contacted, were any of the following
persons or agencies contacted about _____'s problems?" Court-
clinic respondents were asked, "Before _____ came to the attention
of the court, were any of the following persons or agencies contacted?"
Respondents could indicate any of these sources of help: clergymen, psychiatrists, social workers, probation or police officers, schoolteachers,
guidance centers, family-service agencies, and other sources. Those who
named any of these persons or agencies were asked why and when they had
done so.

Careful inspection of the data lends little support to the belief, general
among laymen and professionals, that the underprivileged are indifferent to
the problems of their children. Although this assumption cannot be fully
tested in our investigation because of the composition of the study group,
the findings fail to support it. Although a greater proportion of the families
of the court-clinic cases than of guidance-clinic cases reported no prior contact with any other source of help, the differences are not substantial (see
table 5-1). Moreover, two-thirds of the families of the court-clinic cases did
seek help prior to their contact with the clinic, a finding that hardly
indicates apathy.[2]

We found that a greater percentage of blacks than whites had sought
earlier help; however, the number of cases is small. The only permissible

Table 5-1
**Proportion Seeking or Not Seeking Earlier Help in Guidance and Court
Clinics**

	Guidance Clinic		Court Clinic	
	N	%	N	%
Sought prior help	224	75.1	36	65.5
Did not seek prior help	73	24.9	19	34.5
Totals	297	100.0	55	100.0

inference is that the data do not support the belief, held by some, that blacks are less inclined to seek help for the emotional problems of their children.

Further, our examination of the cross-tabulations of respondents' marital status (intactness of the family) and of the mother's religious identity showed that neither factor was related to the family's early search for assistance. We also considered whether the child's sex or age was related to the prior search for help. Neither was related to seeking such help. Thus our first hypothesis—that middle- and upper-class families with problem children seek help earlier than do families of lower status—was not supported.[3] The result was the same whether we employed Warner's Index of Status Characteristics ($r = -.01$), breadwinner's income ($r = .03$), mother's educational achievement ($r = .05$), or father's occupation. Table 5-2 presents the relationship between social class (indexed by father's occupation) and seeking prior help.

Among the court-clinic families, those of lower status were more likely to have sought prior help than those of the middle class, although the differences are not significant. Thus, on the basis of our findings, there is little to support the belief apparently held by a number of researchers and agencies that lower-class families are more resistant to outside help.

It is possible, of course, that the parents who come to child-guidance clinics may constitute a special help-seeking subsample, on the basis of which we cannot make generalizations about the larger population. However, we can hardly argue that the court-clinic cases come to the attention of the court clinics voluntarily or that they are a peculiar help-seeking group. The fact that a high proportion of court-clinic cases did seek prior help sug-

Table 5-2
Social Class and Seeking Prior Help

Social Class	Sought Prior Help		Did Not Seek Prior Help		
	N	%	N	%	100% =
Guidance clinic ($N = 279$)[a]					
Middle and upper class	117	77.0	35	23.0	152
Lower class	99	78.0	28	22.0	127
Court clinic ($N = 52$)[b]					
Middle and upper class	9	53.0	8	47.0	17
Lower class	24	68.6	11	31.4	35
$X^2 = 1.22$; 1 df; ns					

[a]No data in eighteen cases.

[b]No data in three cases.

gests that many of these families would have taken advantage of preventive programs had they known how and had these programs been available.

It has been observed that families with problems, in their search for help, make considerable use of nonpsychiatric personnel.[4] This is in keeping with our findings and holds for the court-clinic families more than it does for the child-guidance families (see table 5-3). More specifically, when we combined "clergy," "teacher," "probation or police officer," and "any combination of nonpsychiatric agents," we found that 53 percent of court-clinic families and 41 percent of guidance-clinic families reported having sought prior help from these sources. However, only 6 percent of the court-clinic families as opposed to 14 percent of the child-guidance families sought help exclusively from "psychiatrists or social workers" or "child-guidance clinics or family-service agencies." Clearly a great many of the families from court and guidance clinics sought help from some qualified or competent source, psychiatric or otherwise. Such findings belie the notion popular among laymen and professionals that the families seen in court clinics are apathetic in the face of their problem.

It is doubtful if administrators of programs for the prevention and control of delinquency and other childhood problems have explored fully the possibilities of using nonpsychiatric personnel. Since they, more than their psychiatric colleagues, have a great deal of contact with parents of emotionally disturbed children, they may be an effective means of establishing continuing relationships with these families. Even more, if their skills are enlarged and refined through professional consultation, they may serve important case-finding, teaching, and even therapeutic functions.[5]

Placing the Blame

Much like social scientists, parents are often constrained to attempt to explain, at least to themselves, why their child is not developing "like other children" or why they are having problems with a child. Social control theorists offer many examples of a rationale that holds that it is easier to solve a problem if one knows its "cause." Thus we did not think it too unrealistic to assume that parents have "theories" about why their child has a problem and that their theory is related to the urgency of their help-seeking behavior. Early in the interview, and not long after asking the respondents whether they had had earlier problems with their children and had contacted other persons or agencies prior to the contact with the clinic of our study, we inquired about the "cause" of the child's problem. Although our question did not distinguish between the type of earlier problem and the type of problem that led directly to contact with the court or guidance clinic in 1962 and so was not problem specific, we assumed that there probably was a

Table 5–3
Persons or Agencies Contacted Prior to Clinic Contact

	Court-Clinic Cases		Guidance-Clinic Cases	
Type of Agency or Persons Contacted	N	%	N	%
Clergy only	3	8.3	6	2.7
Teacher only	7	19.4	55	24.6
Probation or police officer only	1	2.8	7	3.1
Psychiatrist or social worker only	1	2.8	21	9.4
Child-guidance clinic or family service only	1	2.8	10	4.5
Combination of nonpsychiatric agents	8	22.2	23	10.3
Combination of psychiatric and nonpsychiatric agents	14	38.9	71	31.7
Other	1	2.8	31	13.7
Total	36	100.0	224	100.0

Note: $N = 260$. In 92 cases no earlier contact was reported.

great deal of overlap between these events. The question was, "In your opinion, what caused _____'s problem?" Thus this was an open-ended question.

Responses were coded (in 1963) within a context of "blame" assignment; this was done in order to avoid any later confusion, which we thought might arise from use of imputed "cause." The items, which were derived from responses, were "blaming self," "blaming relatives," "blaming the child," "blaming child's peers," "blaming the environment," and "blaming fate." Each respondent was assigned to either the "yes" or "no" category for each item. Correlation coefficients were computed between each of these blame items and whether earlier help had been sought. The second variable was categorized and coded into no help sought, nonpsychiatric help sought, and psychiatric help sought. The results are presented in table 5–4. With the exception of "fate," all of the relationships for guidance and court cases are in the same direction. Thus, for this analysis, we decided to combine guidance and court cases.

These relationships indicate that parents are more likely to seek early help when they see themselves, other relatives, or society as having some responsibility for the child's problems than when they believe the child or his peers are responsible for the child's problems. Indeed when the child's peers are seen as being blameworthy, the parent was likely not to have

Table 5-4
Relationships between Blame Items[a] and Seeking Earlier Help[b] ($N = 352$)

Blame Categories	Pearsonian Coefficient	Level of Significance
Blaming self	−.10	$p < .05$
Blaming Relatives	−.20	$p < .001$
Blaming the child	.06	ns
Blaming the child's peers	.14	$p < .005$
Blaming the environment	−.09	$p < .05$
Blaming fate	.00	ns

[a]For blame items "yes" was coded as "1" and "No" as "2".
[b]Earlier help was coded as follows: "No help sought" as "1", "non psychiatric" as "2" and "psychiatric" as "3".

sought earlier help for the child. This finding raised our curiosity, and we considered explanations for this apparent reversal of parental concern. We thought that perhaps the age of the child was a factor—that older children would be more likely than younger children to be seen as under peer influence and that parents of such children would be more prone either to feel helpless or to be so annoyed that they would do nothing. Our hunch was correct: although age was unrelated to seeking early help, we found that age was indeed related to blaming peers ($r = -.22, p < .001$). That is, the older the child, the more likely the parents would be to blame the child's peers for his problems. However, it would seem that where peers were not to be blamed, help was sought for older as well as younger children. Age and sex were found unrelated to any of the remaining blame items. Somewhat paradoxically, then, we found that the older child's parents are more likely to put off help-seeking when they believe the child is under peer-group influence. (It is almost as if the parents are converts to peer-group theories of adolescent behavior propounded by sociologists.) This finding takes on added importance in conjunction with our earlier report that the clinics were significantly less likely to give full service to older children when parents applied in 1962 although older children had more severe problems.

Respondent Personality Characteristics as Related to Early Help-Seeking

Because we were intrigued by our finding that parental blame placing was related to the search for help prior to the 1962 call to a child-guidance clinic, we looked for possible relationships between the respondent's personality and the search for earlier help. In so doing, we utilized the five personality scales developed by Srole and employed in chapter 4. In addition, we employed a shortened form of a self-administered vocabulary test, which efficiently predicted scores on general intelligence tests.[6]

We found no relationships between any of the five Srole scales and a search for help prior to the 1962 clinic application. Magnitudes of correlation ranged from $-.01$ for rigidity to $-.06$ for authoritarianism. However a statistically significant relationship was found to exist between the vocabulary test and seeking early help, $r = .11$ ($p < .05$). More specifically, it was found that the higher the respondent's score on the Quick Word Test, the more likely the respondent was to have sought help for the child prior to the 1962 clinic application. This is a fairly impressive finding given the fact that at least some of the children may not have had identifiable problems much sooner than the time of application. To the extent that the child's problem was first observed just prior to the 1962 call for help, no earlier search for help would have been needed. This reasoning, of course, applies to all of our analyses pertaining to the search for early help.

One more finding may be useful as background for our analysis of experiences with the clinic. We have presented data showing that a substantial proportion of our parents in both types of clinic not only reported earlier problems but also were in contact with the clinics in our study soon afterward. We speculated that those who waited the shortest interval between help-seeking activities may in fact have tarried longer in seeking help when the problem first appeared. In short, the question is whether the seriousness of the child's problem was related to the length of the interval between help-seeking events. Data bearing on this issue are presented in table 5-5.

For both court- and guidance-clinic cases, respondents having the shorter waiting interval were more likely to report what we considered to be more-serious problems. Although we cannot be sure of the order of events, it seems that parents who perceived a more-serious problem in their children developed a greater sense of urgency. This difference is more sharply defined for guidance-clinic cases than for court-clinic cases. With respect to court-clinic cases, these cases were referred by the court so there is not the ongoing voluntary appeal that characterizes guidance-clinic cases. Yet many of the court-clinic families had voluntarily sought help before the court referral, and this help-seeking appeared to be directly related to the seriousness of the problem.

To summarize our findings so far, both social factors and personality characteristics appear to be unrelated to the early search for help undertaken by our respondents. However, the respondent's theory about the cause (blame placing) of the problem does appear to be related to whether the respondents initiated an early search for help. Finally, in those cases

Table 5-5

Type of Presenting Symptoms or Offense and Waiting Time between Seeking Help for an Earlier Problems and Contact with Clinic

	Waited 1 Year or Less		Waited More than 1 Year	
	N	%	N	%
Type of presenting problem, guidance clinic[a]				
Type I	32	45.1	26	22.6
Type II	39	54.9	89	77.4
Total	71	100.0	115	100.0

$X^2 = 10.40$; 1 df; $p < .01$

Type of offense, court clinic[b]				
More serious (offenses against persons, property or morals)	9	42.9	3	25.0
Less serious (unmanageability)	12	57.1	9	75.0
Total	21	100.0	12	100.0

$X^2 = 1.05$; 1 df; ns.

[a]$N = 186$. Excludes 73 cases with no earlier problem, 30 cases with no information on presenting problem, and 8 cases with no information on waiting time.
[b]$N = 33$. No earlier problem in 19 cases and no information on waiting time in 3 cases for court-clinic cases.

where the earlier search was rather closely followed by contact with a clinic in 1962, we also found a greater clustering of more-severe problems. We now move to an analysis of some of the experiences which our respondents had when they contacted the clinics in 1962.

Experiences at the Clinic

The clinic is a familiar environment to many agents of social control, and after long occupational socialization they accept and may even internalize its practices, procedures, and rituals. But to a number of clients, the culture and environment might seem puzzling, even frightening. It was important to know, therefore, how comfortable our families felt in discussing problems at the clinic, as well as how they reacted to the advice given them there. Accordingly, interviewers asked, "How comfortable did you feel in talking about _____'s problem to clinic personnel?" and "How did you feel about the advice given by the people at the _____ clinic?"

We were surprised that as many as 60 percent of the respondents who answered the first question reported feeling very comfortable. Of those answering, 18 percent reported feeling somewhat comfortable, 9 percent said they felt only slightly comfortable, and 13 percent admitted that they did not feel comfortable at all. Eleven percent of those questioned refused to answer. We examined these proportions separately in the two types of clinic and found that members of the court-clinic families indicated they felt much less comfortable than did members of guidance-clinic families. For the guidance-clinic families, the proportions were 63 percent, 19 percent, 8 percent, and 10 percent; for court-clinic families, they were 41 percent, 14 percent, 14 percent, and 31 percent. In spite of these differences, it is of interest, and somewhat surprising, that so many informants from each type of clinic stated that they felt very comfortable. On the other hand, considering the special nature and objectives of the clinics, the number claiming to be not completely comfortable and the number who failed to answer might be a point of legitimate concern.

Since the occupation of the father is a key variable in this study, we analyzed the relationship between it and comfortableness at the clinic. As shown in table 5-6, the relationship between father's occupation and comfortableness moves in different directions in the two types of clinic, although in neither case is it statistically significant. That is, the white-collar and professional workers who applied to child-guidance clinics felt more comfortable than did the blue-collar workers; although the difference in court clinics is not as great, the reverse was true.[7] When Warner's ISC was employed as our measure of social class, the result was almost the same as when father's occupation was used. What readily suggests itself is that middle- and upper-class persons who contact child-guidance clinics find themselves in a relatively familiar world, while those of lower status may perceive the clinic as strange and distant. We suggest that the expectation of service and the anticipation of rejection probably characterize the middle- and lower-class people, respectively. At any rate, guidance-clinic personnel and other agents who are asked for help might bear in mind that there may be good reasons why an appreciable number of persons of lower status feel uncomfortable in talking about their problems.

Although it is not surprising to learn that, in general, few people of the upper and lower classes felt very relaxed at the court clinics, their experience is in striking contrast to that of individuals in the child-guidance clinic (see table 5-6). Among court-clinic cases, middle- and upper-class persons reportedly are less comfortable than are those of lower status. This may be explained, in part, by the fact that being in a court probably is conducive to greater feelings of shame in the middle class than in the lower class. In addition, as an authoritarian setting, the court clinic may be more alien to the middle class than to the working class. However, these findings have to be interpreted with some caution; here we are relying upon the respondents' recollections of how comfortable they felt at the time. Possibly the feelings the respondent reported are in part a result of subsequent experience, including contact with the intake worker and other clinic personnel.

In further explication of these findings, we examined the relationship between comfortableness and class of presenting symptom. The data are on

Table 5-6
Social Class and Comfortableness in Discussing Problem

Social Class	Felt Very Comfortable		Somewhat Comfortable		Slightly		Not at All		100% =
	N	%	N	%	N	%	N	%	
Guidance-clinic cases									
Middle and upper class	100	70.9	21	14.9	8	5.7	12	8.5	141
Lower class	62	54.4	28	24.6	11	9.6	13	11.4	114
$X^2 = 7.65$; 3 df; ns									
Court-clinic cases									
Middle and upper class	4	30.8	3	25.1	1	7.7	5	38.4	13
Lower class	11	39.3	3	10.7	5	17.9	9	32.1	28
$X^2 = 0.28$; 1 df; ns[a]									

Note: $N = 296$. Insufficient data on 42 guidance-clinic and 14 court-clinic cases.

[a]In the computation of the chi-square test of significance for court cases, comfortableness was dichotomized between "very" and "somewhat" because of the small theoretical frequencies in several cells.

guidance-clinic cases only since we did not have a comparable classification of symptoms for court-clinic cases (see table 5-7). There was a statistically significant relationship between these variables, with a tendency for those whose children had the most threatening problems (type I) to feel less comfortable than those confronting less serious problems (type II). We then observed the relationship between these variables while controlling father's occupation and found no relationship between type of symptom and comfortableness among persons of higher status. This finding supports our notion that the professional and white-collar families do not feel out of place when they frequent guidance clinics—to such a degree, in fact, that even the most severe problems apparently do not daunt them.

There is a clear relationship between type of symptoms and comfortableness among lower-status persons, however. Only 44 percent of the lower-class respondents with the more-serious symptoms reported that they felt very comfortable as compared with 64 percent of those who had to deal with less-serious pathologies (see table 5-8). Although the number of cases is small, the direction of the findings is even more apparent when we consider the percentage at the other extreme—those who reported not feeling at all comfortable at the guidance clinic. Twenty-four percent of the lower-class individuals with type I symptoms stated that they did not feel at all comfortable as compared with 4 percent of those with type II symptoms.

These findings suggest a need on the part of professional personnel to adapt their practice and approach to the social status of the client. It cannot be assumed that clients varying in social status are equally comfortable in the child-guidance clinics or that the same symptoms have the same meaning and salience for all persons.

We wondered if the attitude of blame and/or the personality indexes were related to respondents' reported feeling of comfortableness during the 1962 application. Of the six measures of blame, we found only blaming peers ($r = -.16, p < .001$) and blaming the environment ($r = .11, p < .03$) to be related to comfortableness; those who blamed peers for the child's problems were the least comfortable and those who blamed the environment were the most comfortable. Earlier we reported that parents who blamed peers were less likely to seek earlier help; now it also seems that such parents did not feel comfortable when they did apply for assistance.[8]

Clinic Recommendations and Applicant Reactions

We next considered the response that clinic personnel reportedly made to those who called about their children's problems and subsequently were not accepted for service. Drawing on our knowledge of the clinics' intake sys-

Table 5-7
Type of Presenting Symptom and Comfortableness in Guidance-Clinic Cases

	Felt Very Comfortable		Somewhat Comfortable		Slightly Comfortable		Not at All		100% =
	N	%	N	%	N	%	N	%	
Type I	48	60.0	13	16.2	6	7.6	13	16.2	80
Type II	112	69.1	31	19.1	10	6.2	9	5.6	162

$X^2 = 7.82$; 3 df; $p < .05$

Note: $N = 242$. Insufficient data in 55 cases.

Table 5-8
Type of Presenting Symptoms and Comfortableness, Controlling Social Class in Guidance-Clinic Cases

	Felt Very Comfortable		Somewhat Comfortable		Slightly Comfortable		Not at All Comfortable		100% =
	N	%	N	%	N	%	N	%	
Middle and upper class									
Type I	30	73.1	5	12.2	2	4.9	4	9.8	41
Type II	63	72.4	13	14.9	5	5.8	6	6.9	87

$X^2 = 0.48$; 3 df; ns

Lower class									
Type II	15	44.1	7	20.6	4	11.8	8	23.5	34
Type II	45	64.3	18	25.7	4	5.7	3	4.3	70

$X^2 = 10.95$; 3 df; $p < .05$

Note: $N = 232$. Insufficient data in 65 cases.

Table 5-9
Clinics' Responses at the Time of Contact

	N	% of Total[a]
Recommendatons at child-guidance clinics		
The clinic could not take on any new cases as it was overloaded	152	53.0
A private psychiatrist should be contacted	37	12.9
The child should be sent away for his own good	10	3.4
Wait for a few months and call back if necessary	86	30.2
Clinic will call back in a few weeks or months	97	33.7
Problem was not a big one and would probably "pass"	24	8.4
It would be a good idea if another clinic that had had experience with this kind of problem were called	71	24.3
The child was too old for this clinic	19	6.5
Recommendations at Court Clinics		
The clinic could not take on any new cases as it was overloaded	—	—
A private psychiatrist should be contacted	1	2.0
It might be better for the family if the child were sent to a detention center	11	22.9
It would be better for the child if he were sent to a detention center	17	35.4
If his family promised to cooperate, the clinic would try to help	20	42.6
The family should try to get the child into a different school	7	14.3
It would be a good idea if he got a job	6	12.2
Another clinic should be called	2	4.1

[a]The total number of responses is greater than the total number of cases, since respondents could report one or more of the listed responses. Percentages therefore add up to more than 100.

tems and information obtained during the exploratory interviews, we made a list of precoded questions to which respondents answered "yes" or "no."

More than half of our guidance-clinic informants reported that they were told by clinic personnel that the clinic was overloaded at the time of the call (see table 5-9). A fairly large proportion of clients were referred elsewhere: 24 percent to other clinics and 13 percent to private psychiatrists. A sizable number of these respondents were told that they should wait for a while and call back or wait for the clinic to call them. The clinic personnel rarely suggested that their problems were not serious or that they would disappear.

Court clinic-respondents were presented with a slightly different list of statements (table 5-9). Typical statements made by court-clinic personnel during the initial clinic interview may be summarized in this way: the clinic would help cooperative clients; the child or the family might be better off if the child were sent to a detention center; and the family should help the child to change either by changing his school or finding him a job.

Both guidance- and court-clinic personnel often have to make recommendations or statements that their prospective clients may not like. Indeed in response to the question, "How did you feel about their advice?" 53 percent of guidance-clinic informants and 35 percent of court-clinic informants indicated that they found the advice unsatisfactory.

Our next hypothesis was that middle- and upper-class persons would report more-satisfying reactions to their experience with the clinic than would those of lower status. Contrary to our expectations, among the guidance-clinic cases, those of upper and middle status were more likely than lower-class persons to view their clinic experience as unsatisfactory: 62 percent of the former as compared with 48 percent of the latter.[9] The findings are still in the same direction when comfortableness is controlled.

We argued that differences in presenting symptoms also could affect the relationship observed between social status and reaction to advice, but when type of symptom is controlled, the relationship between status and reaction to advice obtains only for the more-serious or threatening type I cases (table 5-10). Among those of middle and upper status, 68 percent of the type I cases felt clinic advice was unsatisfactory as compared to 43 percent of those in the lower stratum.

In examining the court-clinic cases, which are roughly equivalent to the type I guidance cases, the relationship between social status and reaction to advice does not hold and, in fact, is slightly reversed. Although the cases are too few to warrant a definite statement, there is a slight tendency for those of lower status to be more dissatisfied than those of higher status. In the court-clinic population, only 20 percent of the middle- and upper-class families expressed dissatisfaction with the advice received as compared with 44 percent of the families from the lower class (table 5-11).

These findings bring to mind the now-classic concept of relative deprivation.[10] This concept is variously defined, but the essential element is that deprivation or dissatisfaction is not merely a function of the individual's objective situation but is influenced by his expectations and the particular world to which he refers in assessing his experience. It appears that the middle and upper classes find the child-guidance clinic a relatively familiar environment and presumably entertain higher expectations of satisfactory service; accordingly they are more disappointed with lack of service than are persons of lower status, at least with regard to the type I cases. There is also some indication that in the formal setting of the court clinic, all, regardless of status, are less confident that they will receive service and less disappointed in learning that they will not receive it. In this milieu—a more familiar one to those of lower status—the lower class expresses greatest dissatisfaction. Our findings and the concept of relative deprivation should

Table 5-10
Social Class and Proportion Who Found Clinic Advice Unsatisfactory,
Controlling Type of Symptom in Guidance-Clinic Cases

Social Class	No Advice Given or Advice Satisfactory		Unsatisfactory		
	N	%	N	%	100% =
Type I					
Middle and upper class	14	31.8	30	68.2	44
Lower class	20	57.1	15	42.9	35
$X^2 = 5.10$; 1 df; $p < .05$					
Type II					
Middle and upper class	41	43.2	54	56.8	95
Lower class	33	45.2	40	54.8	73
$X^2 = 0.07$; 1 df; ns					

Note: $N = 247$. No data in 50 cases.

Table 5-11
Social Class and Reaction to Clinic Worker's Advice for Court-Clinic
Cases

Social Class	No Advice Given		Advice Satisfactory		Advice Unsatisfactory		
	N	%	N	%	N	%	100% =
Middle and upper class	7	46.7	5	33.3	3	20.0	15
Lower class	3	8.8	16	47.1	15	44.1	34
$X^2 = 2.59$; 1 df; ns							

Note: $N = 49$. No data in 6 cases.

serve to remind agents dealing with delinquency that they should not expect clients with similar problems necessarily to react uniformly to advice. Their reactions will depend on many things, including their status, their experiences, and the particular settings in which they are cast.

Help-Seeking Experiences after 1962 Contact with Source Agency

If utilized properly, the referral process, an established procedure of the psychiatric and social-service world, permits effective interagency cooperation with beneficial consequences to the client. But a poor referral may only add to the client's frustration and confirm whatever doubts he may have about his need for help. It is important to ask about the experiences of the families in our study who were referred elsewhere by the source agency.

Of 297 child-guidance applicants, 104 were referred to some other psychiatric professional or agency. All 104 were asked if they had followed up the referral and, if so, where they were referred and what occurred subsequently. Those who did not follow up the referral were asked the reason. Approximately 60 percent of those referred said that they were referred to another child-guidance clinic, 20 percent were referred to a family or social-service agency, 12 percent were referred to a physician, and the remainder were referred to other sources.[11] Of the 104 respondents, 71 indicated that they had followed the suggestion, 31 said they had not done so, and 2 failed to answer (table 5-12).

Almost half of the seventy-one following up the suggestion of a referral did not obtain what could be termed satisfactory service, and only six of the seventy-one reported that they had succeeded in actually getting treatment. However, as many as 39 percent of those following the suggestion reported that they had been seen by the clinic and thus a number of them would probably get treatment for their child eventually. Only 15 percent of those referred reported that the source agency had arranged the referral for them. We know from our intake study that the chances of obtaining service are less if the call is made by a lay person than if it is made by a professional. Therefore it can be assumed that a large number of those referred elsewhere by agencies still did not obtain satisfactory service.

The explanations advanced by the thirty-one informants who failed to follow up a referral from the source agency (table 5-12) make clear that their decision could not be attributed to the child's spontaneous improvement (although this was reported to have occurred in 10 percent of the cases). A large proportion of the informants confessed their indecision or discouragement or their resolve to go it alone. The fact that at the time of the interview, only six of those referred reported having a child under treatment merits concern even if more did receive treatment eventually. Certainly there must be an appreciable number of families who have recognized that their child needs help but who have begun to despair of ever finding it. Our findings on the experiences of those referred clearly demonstrate the need to reexamine the practice of referral and the assumptions underlying it.

Referral is a vital feature of the interagency network. Since no single

Table 5–12
Following Up a Referral to Another Clinic or Person

	N	%
Type of experience		
Was referred elsewhere	10	14.1
Was told to call back	3	4.2
Was told clinic would call back	8	11.3
"Could not take me"	12	16.9
Was seen (at the other clinic)	28	39.4
Child is in treatment	6	8.5
Other	4	5.6
Total	71	100.0
Reasons for not following through		
Decided to handle the problem alone	6	19.4
Decided to put it off	3	9.7
Did not know what to do	2	6.5
Felt discouraged	3	9.7
Did not like agency I was sent to	7	22.5
Child improved	3	9.7
Other	7	22.5
Total	31	100.0

organization offers all of the services required by all types of emotionally disturbed children, to fullfill the general purpose of having care provided to a given child, an agency may have to direct him to a more-appropriate organization. In doing so, the referring agency is linking itself with the services of the receiving agency and, to the extent the referral is successful, may enjoy the goodwill of the satisfied family, the other organizations, and the general community.

There are times when the referral process ends in less-beneficial consequences for the client, the agency world, or the community as a whole. Why, then, do agencies maintain their referral policy when a high proportion of clients can be expected not to follow their recommendations or, worse, will not receive servce if they do so? In part, the answer can be found in the apparent latent functions that the present referral system serves for the referring agency. Agencies that have more work than they can handle or that for one reason or another cannot render the services expected of them may merely be concerned with removing the load or "getting rid of the client." Moreover, by sending a client to an agency that does not render the desired service, the initiating body may exert pressure on the second one to expand its domain and extend its services. For example, a child-guidance agency may wish to specialize in providing service to children with learning problems or to those who are mentally retarded and does not feel adequate to handle delinquents or children with sexual problems. Still it may be under constant pressure from the community to provide services for such children. If the agency in question can encourage another one to assume these functions, it may put an end to public harassment while continuing to specialize in the cases for which it feels it has appropriate interest and expertise. Therefore, an agency may refer a child to another organization that is not in a position to accept him. While we can understand the persistence of the present referral process in terms of organizational needs and behavior, it is hard to justify it in consideration of the patient's welfare and convenience.

Informants in 1963 were asked to indicate if, subsequent to their experience with the source agency, they had been in touch with a clergyman, a psychiatrist, a child-guidance center, a social worker, a probation officer, a court clinic, a family service agency, or a schoolteacher. We then classified guidance centers, psychiatrists, and social workers as "psychiatric or social service" and teachers, probation officers, and clergymen as "nonpsychiatric," the court clinic being retained as a separate category. Of all informants, 43 percent reported that they had seen or contacted either a psychiatrist, social-service worker, or psychologist, 2 percent had seen or contacted court-clinic personnel only, 23 percent had seen or contacted nonpsychiatric persons only, and 32 percent reported not having seen anyone at all. It is important to contrast these figures with the fact that during the previous year all of these respondents had contacted child psychiatric clinics in the attempt to solve the problems presented by their children. Thus, for whatever reason, nearly three-fifths of our respondents apparently have been out of touch with psychiatric professionals.

Our third hypothesis was that subsequent to contact with the source agency, middle- and upper-class families are more prone than lower-class families to seek professional psychiatric assistance. This is supported, but only in the case of the guidance clinics (table 5–13). Thus, 51 percent of child-guidance families of higher status had seen or contacted a psychiatrist, psychologist, or social-service professional subsequent to their contact with the source agency, as compared with 38 percent of those of lower status. On the other hand, 31 percent of persons of lower status had seen or contacted only nonpsychiatric personnel such as ministers, teachers, and probation officers, as compared with approximately half that percentage in the middle- and upper-class families. Here again we witness how important nonpsychiatric personnel may be in the total child-care spectrum, especially with regard to the emotional problems of lower-class children.

An opposite though not significant trend is apparent among the court-clinic families. Here, lower-class families made more use of psychiatric personnel and upper-class families made more use of nonpsychiatric personnel. The number is small, and it is difficult to interpret the findings. In two respects, however, the postclinic data for child-guidance cases and court-clinic cases are quite consistent. First, about one-third of the cases in each

Table 5–13
Social Class and Persons or Agencies Seen or Contacted after Contact with Source Agency

Persons or Agent Seen or Contacted [a]	Middle and Upper Class		Lower Class	
	N	%	N	%
Guidance clinics				
Has seen psychiatrist, psychologist, or social-service personnel	80	51.3	50	39.1
Has seen nonpsychiatric personnel only	27	17.3	40	31.2
Has seen no one since clinic contact	49	31.4	38	29.7
	156		128	
$X^2 = 4.22$; 1 df; $p < .05$				
Court clinics				
Has seen psychiatrist, psychologist, or social-service personnel	4	23.5	18	51.4
Has seen nonpsychiatric personnel only	6	35.3	6	17.2
Has seen no one since clinic contact	7	41.2	11	31.4
	17		35	
$X^2 = 3.65$; 1 df; ns				

Note: $N = 336$. No data in 16 cases.

[a]Help-seeking agents, for the purpose of the chi-square test, are dichotomized between psychiatric and other.

population saw or contacted no one after contact with the source clinic. Second, approximately one-quarter of the cases in each population were in contact with nonpsychiatric personnel.[12]

In examining the relationship between type of presenting complaint to the guidance clinic and number of postclinic contacts with psychiatric agents, we found that 56 percent of the type I cases and 45 percent of the type II cases had seen or contacted a psychiatric agent since contact with the source agency. This finding suggests that the families with the more-serious problems (at least more serious from a legal view) continue to seek help more frequently than those with less-serious problems. To be sure, from a societal point of view, it would be desirable if more type I problems were further attended to by the families concerned. However, one of the main findings of our study is that most of the families at some time did attempt to do something but were generally unsuccessful in their search. Thus from this perspective, perhaps the primary social problem is to determine how to find qualified help for those who both need and want it.

When major type of symptom is controlled, persons from the middle and upper classes are more likely to have seen or contacted a psychiatric agent than those from the lower class. Moreover, the proportion of those seeking help within each group decreases as one moves from type I to type II of the behavior problems. Thus, although there is a good deal of independence between the two variables of occupational class and type of symptom, there is also interaction between them with respect to postclinic contacts with psychiatric professionals. The fact that professional and white-collar workers appear more able than blue-collar workers to make the second effort to find psychiatric assistance takes on added importance when we recall that within the general population, those of lower status seemed less likely than those of higher status to initiate applications to child guidance clinics for service.

Demographic Factors and Help-Seeking

Other demographic variables were then considered in the analysis of coping effort. We examined the relationship of mother's age, child's age, mother's marital status, mother's religious identity, and race to help-seeking. The findings are summarized in table 5–14. In the computation of tests of significance (chi-square or Kendall's tau) the help-seeking variable was dichotomized between psychiatric personnel (including psychologists and social workers) and other.

The results of the tests of significance revealed that none was significant. In only one case was the .05 level almost attained and that involved marital status for court clinic cases ($X^2 = 3.19, p < .10$). The other important revelation is that there are no Jewish children among court-clinic cases in this study.

Blame Placing, Personality Characteristics, and Help-Seeking after 1962 Contacts with Clinic

Finally we undertook the analysis of possible relationships between blame placing and personality characteristics on one hand and help-seeking between the 1962 contact and our 1963 interview on the other hand. We found no relationship between any of the blame categories and later help-seeking; this contrasts with our reported finding that type of blame was significantly related to early help-seeking in four of six blame categories. In contrast, we found that two of the five Srole personality scales, authori-

Table 5-14
Selected Demographic Variables and Psychiatric Help-Seeking

Child's Age and Proportion Seeking Psychiatric Help

	Under 6	6-10	11-14	15 and over
Guidance	50%	44.6%	49%	41.5%
100% =	(24)	(112)	(96)	(65)
Court	—	50%	23.6%	32.4%
	—	(4)	(17)	(34)

Mother's Age and Proportion Seeking Psychiatric Help

	20-29	30-39	40-49	50 and over
Guidance	45.5%	46.3%	46.2%	40.0%
100% =	(33)	(147)	(91)	(15)
Court	—	38.1%	28.6%	—
	(2)	(21)	(28)	(3)

Mother's Marital Status and Proportion Seeking Psychiatric Help

	Married	Separated, Widowed, Divorced
Guidance	47.2%	40.6%
100% =	(235)	(59)
Court	50%	26.1%
	(32)	(23)

Mother's Religion and Proportion Seeking Psychiatric Help

	Protestant	Catholic	Jewish	Other
Guidance	41.3%	44.3%	53.2%	60.0%
100% =	(92)	(122)	(62)	(10)
Court	30.4%	24.1%	—	—
	(23)	(29)	(0)	(3)

Race and Proportion Seeking Psychiatric Help

	White	Black
Guidance	46.9%	50.0%
100% =	(263)	(22)
Court	35.5%	47.4%
	(31)	(19)

Note: Numbers on which proportions are based are in parentheses.

tarianism ($r = .10, p < .05$) and rigidity ($r = .13, p < .01$), were related to later help-seeking. That is, authoritarian and rigid persons were significantly less likely to have sought help during the year subsequent to the 1962 application. This finding contrasts with our earlier finding that none of the Srole scales was related to preapplication help-seeking. Nor did we find the word test related to subsequent help-seeking ($r = -.03$); this also contrasts with the case for early help-seeking.

Summary and Conclusions

In this chapter the focus has been on the history of coping activities employed by parents whose children presented them with problems in the early 1960s. The data were gathered in 1963 in interviews with respondents approximately a year after they had all had contact with psychiatric clinics for children. In all cases, the clinic contact had not apparently resulted in the anticipated assistance. Specifically we presented data on coping activities both prior to and subsequent to the 1962 clinic contact; in addition we presented data on respondents' experiences with clinic personnel during the application process.

In examining the extent to which help was sought prior to the 1962 clinic contact, we found that a substantial majority of both guidance- and court-clinic respondents had sought earlier help. An assessment of social factors possibly related to early help-seeking was undertaken. The factors examined included age, sex of child, race, marital status, and religion of the mother, and social-class level (variously indexed). None of these factors was significantly related to the earlier search for help. This is a most important finding in itself and suggests that the assumptions made about the extent to which certain families are caring about their children may be unjustified.

We then examined attitudinal and personal factors in connection with earlier help-seeking. Parents were thought to have some ideas or "theories" about why their child might be having problems, and we referred to this as "placing the blame." We found that early help-seeking was more likely to occur when parents blamed themselves, other relatives, or environmental factors than when they blamed the child or his peers for the problem. In fact, we found that when the child's peers were blamed, parents were most likely not to have sought help early. In connection, we observed that while child's age was unrelated to seeking early help, it was related to blaming peers; that is, the older the child, the more likely parents were to blame peers.

None of the Srole personality factors was found related to the search for prior help. However, there was a statistically significant relationship for the Quick Word Test, an efficient predictor of general intelligence scores. The higher the respondent scored on the word test, the more likely the respondent was to have sought earlier help.

In examining respondents' experiences with the clinics, we focused on their feelings of comfortableness with clinic personnel and on their reactions to any advice given them. We found that guidance-clinic families felt more comfortable than those at court clinics. However, interesting differences existed when social class was examined within each type of clinic. Although middle-class respondents were more at ease in guidance clinics than were their lower-class counterparts, this was not true in the court clinics. The difference was not statistically significant, but there was a tendency for lower-class families to feel more comfortable than middle-class families in the court-clinic setting.

Perhaps consistent with these class-related feelings of comfortableness were our findings concerning clients' reactions to clinic advice. In the guidance clinics, the middle-class respondents were more likely to feel that the advice was unsatisfactory, while in court clinics, lower-class respondents tended to be more dissatisfied with the clinic response to their problems. It seems consistent to us to observe that when clients feel comfortable, they will feel freer to criticize or complain about the clinic advice, especially when the clinic does not proffer the expected assistance.

The final analysis in this chapter focused on respondents' help-seeking activities after the 1962 contact with the source clinic. First we noted that of the respondents referred elsewhere, approximately one-third did not carry out the referral. We observed that the referral system stands in need of substantial improvement.

When we examined the extent to which our respondents had reported subsequent contacts after the 1962 experience, we found that over half of them had not established contact with a psychiatric professional and that one-third had seen no one about their child's problems. Among guidance-clinic families, the middle-class respondents had been more likely than those in the lower class to seek professional help; an opposing tendency appeared in court clinics. When severity of presenting symptoms was examined, it was found that those with the more serious type I problems were more apt to continue the search for help.

Although some of these findings are tenuous, we believe the following general statement is clearly supported by our data: contrary to some beliefs, the more deprived do not appear to be weaker in their problem-solving efforts on behalf of their children. We found abundant evidence that strong problem-solving efforts were made regardless of social class, marital status, race or religion, both before and subsequent to the 1962 clinic contact.

Notes

1. Nearly all of the data in this chapter comes from the 1963 interview.

2. The higher mean age of the court-clinic cases is the only evidence

found suggesting that these families may have been less attentive to the needs of their children.

3. In analysis of these data, we included professional, proprietor, managerial, and clerical workers in the category "middle and upper classes," and manual, service, and farm workers in the "lower class."

4. See, for example, Earl Lomon Koos, *Families in Trouble* (New York: King's Crown Press, 1946), pp. 86–87, and Allen Bergin, "The Evaluation of Therapeutic Outcomes," in Bergin and Sol Garfield, eds., *Handbook of Psychotherapy and Behavior Change* (New York: John Wiley, 1971).

5. See Gerald Caplan, *Principles of Preventive Psychiatry* (New York: Basic Books, 1964).

6. The first forty items of the second column of E.F. Borgatta and R.J. Corsini, *The Quick Word Test (Form B)* (New York: World Book Co., 1960).

7. When "comfortableness" is dichotomized between "very" and "somewhat," the relationship is statistically significant at the .05 level for guidance-clinic cases.

8. It would seem that the categories of transactional analysis, employed by Vickers, represent another assessment or index of blame-placing. See Michael Vickers, "Transactional Analysis as a Sociological Model: A Contribution to the Interpersonal View of Children's Symptomatic Behavior" (Ph.D. diss., Boston University, 1977).

9. In the computation of the chi-square test of significance, the categories of "no advice given" and "advice satisfactory" were combined.

10. Samuel Stouffer, Edward Suchman, L. De Vinney, Shirley Star, and Robin Williams, Jr., *The American Soldier: Adjustment during Army Life* (Princeton, N.J.: Princeton University Press, 1949), vol. 1. See also Robert K. Merton, *Social Theory and Social Structure,* rev. ed. (New York: Free Press, 1957), pp. 241–271.

11. Table 5–9 shows that thirty-seven informants said the clinic had suggested that they "contact a private psychiatrist"; however, only twelve of them said they were specifically referred by the clinic to a psychiatrist.

12. In the computation of this relationship, the variable "person seen since contact" was divided between the second and third categories.

6 Short-Term Outcome

As our study progressed, we realized that the issue of the problem-solving behavior of families who could not, apparently, find clinic assistance in their efforts to deal with their child-rearing problems was profoundly relevant to many contemporary evaluative issues. First, we were rather startled to find that there were few differences between the families accepted by psychiatric clinics and those who were not, particularly with respect to the children's presenting problem. Thus it seemed that the caution to researchers about undertaking evaluative studies on groups selected in unknown or mysterious ways is well made. The temptation, especially in studies evaluating the effects of child psychotherapy, is then to assert or to accept the assertion that the children share some ailment differentiating them from other children. Second, as we perused the research literature on psychotherapy for children, keeping in mind our findings regarding selection, our interest began to focus on the rather disturbing research conclusion that clinic treatment for those selected did not seem to have much effect. At least this conclusion seemed to be reached by a number of social science researchers, most emphatically by H.J. Eysenck (for adult psychoneurotics) and by E.E. Levitt (for emotionally disturbed children). Indeed both Eysenck and Levitt decided that not only did the control groups, in the studies reviewed, do as well as treatment groups but that these effects were spontaneously reached. But the time for relying on the notion of spontaneous remission has passed, and researchers in this area need to examine the facts. Such an examination should include not only a focus on selection but must also analyze both the history of the problem and the history of clients' coping behavior. The findings presented so far strongly suggest that researchers undertaking evaluative studies should make fewer assumptions about the experiences, or the lack of experiences, of their control or comparison group subjects.

Our data on short-term outcome, collected in 1963, focus in part on the adjustment of the child around the time of our 1963 interview with parents. We also focus on parents' reports of changes in the children's behavior occurring between the time of the family's contact with the source clinic in 1962 and the time of the interview in 1963, a period spanning, on the average, almost a year.

Our conceptual model is essentially a stress-coping one. Indeed, all along we have emphasized the need for research on the problem-solving behavior of families under stress. Thus we have presented three general hypotheses (chapter 1) derived from our stress model that are relevant to our analysis of long-term outcome. The framework and the hypotheses articulate the interrelationships among cognitive processes, mediating resources, coping responses, and outcome. Resources particularly are affected by conditions and events that exist and occur within the family. Thus family size and social-class level are viewed as conditions that affect resource availability, as are death and divorce.

It is easy to accept the stress model since all of our families felt that they had had problems with a child, had sought help at a clinic, and had not been accepted for service. Our problem was not an issue of the etiology of stress but an issue of how these parents coped with their or their children's problems after their failure to win acceptance into the clinic's service program.[1] Although our hypotheses pertained to long-term outcome, our model (figure 6–1) should also have some utility with respect to short term outcome.

Change Measures

Since this study addresses the issue of short-term as well as long-term outcome, it was important for us to acknowledge the difficulties that must be faced in such a task. In an important and relevant paper, Strupp and his colleagues reviewed a number of problems and issues surrounding research on

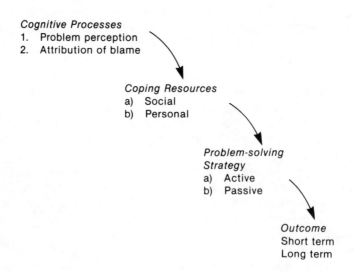

Figure 6–1. Stress-Coping Model

outcome.[2] Although they were primarily interested in evidence concerning the negative effects of psychotherapy, they also discussed the meaning of mental health from different perspectives and developed a tripartite model of therapeutic outcomes. They observed that the relevant research on negative effects was not convincing because of weaknesses in conception (what was the training of the therapist? what type of therapy was employed? what outcome measures were employed? what were the strengths and weaknesses of these measures?) and design (were both short-term and long-term outcomes assessed? was there a control group? what procedures were used in sample selection? what was the extent of sample mortality?) Strupp et al. argued that there is good reason to conduct research on possible negative effects and that to deny the likelihood of negative effects is to trivialize psychotherapy.

For us, the most relevant feature of the paper by Strupp and his associates was their discussion of the diverse meanings of mental health and of subsequent outcome measures. Although most of the studies they reviewed appear to be focused on adult subjects and so do not deal with the issue of maturation effects for children, their discussion of the complexities involved in the assessment of outcome are relevant here. They focused on three interested parties who produce divergent definitions of outcome: society (including significant persons in the patient's life), the individual patient, and the mental health professional. They note that society is concerned primarily with "behavioral adaptation and conformity to its social code," that individuals (patients) "define mental health in terms of subjective feelings of well-being," and that the mental health professional "defines mental health largely with reference to a theoretical model of a 'healthy' personality structure." They then discuss the types of measures subsumed under these definitions.

This brief discussion of the paper by Strupp and his associates helps to place our own outcome measures in perspective. First, we did not attempt to obtain the children's subjective view of their sense of well-being. Such data might be interesting and useful, but their value would seem questionable for the younger children in our study, and we never considered the utility of such a measure in 1963. Second, because of the nature of our study group, we do not have the therapist's or professional's outcome assessment. Some of our subject children received professional assistance during the year between the clinic contact and our 1963 interview, but this assistance was most diversified and its nature, from the professional perspective, could not be fully specified in a large-scale study of the type we undertook. More specifically, we undertook to assess the fate of a large number of children who were not accepted by clinic staffs; thus we believed that the parents were the logical respondents in our study. (We did obtain information in 1963 on the type of help received, but we got this information from the parents.)

The third perspective discussed by Strupp and his associates dealt with societal concerns within which they included the views of significant others. This perspective is the one most closely approximated in our study. We view the parents (and our interviews were usually with mothers) as the most significant persons in a child's life, and so all of our short-term outcome measures were mediated through the views of the concerned parent.

Behavioral Measures of Short-Term Change

The principal measures of change we employed are two behavioral-change measures derived from the application of Guttman scaling techniques to our twenty-three-item checklists (see table 4-6).

During our 1963 contact, we solicited responses to the checklist at two points in the interview. First, fairly early, we invited respondents to indicate how frequently—never, rarely, sometimes, or often—their children exhibited any of the symptoms around the time of the respondent's 1962 clinic contact. Then much later in the interview, we again asked for responses to the checklist, but this time we requested that respondents consider the child's behavior around the time during which our interview was taking place. The Spearman rank-order correlation between the guidance- and court-clinic subjects at the time of the 1962 contact was .70 and around the time of our interview in 1963 was .82.

In developing our measures of behavioral change, we employed both logical and empirical procedures. Our analysis of the symptoms, taking into account both the conceptual fit and the empirical distributions, suggested that there were two dimensions along which Guttman scales (scales measuring degree to which a characteristic is exhibited) might be developed. The first of these apparent dimensions seemed to be the child's ability to observe rules of authority (which we refer to here as the authority dimension, not to be confused with our measure of the respondent's authoritarianism) and included the following actions and the proportion of children committing these acts "sometimes" or "often" prior to the 1962 clinic contact:

"Disobeying at home": Guidance clinics, 65 percent, court clinics, 71 percent.

"Getting into fights": Guidance clinics, 41 percent, court clinics, 49 percent.

"Taking things": Guidance clinics, 24 percent, court clinics, 41 percent.

The items we selected for the dimension assumed to tap neurotic

behavior (the neurotic scale) included the following actions and the proportion of children committing them "sometimes" or "often" prior to the
1962 clinic contact:

"Being sad or unhappy": Guidance clinics, 67 percent, court clinics,
56 percent.

"Crying a lot": Guidance clinics, 45 percent, court clinics, 22 percent.

"Having bad dreams": Guidance clinics, 31 percent, court clinics,
15 percent.

The court-clinic cases more frequently violated rules of authority and
guidance-clinic cases displayed more neurotic behavior.

The ranking of the items in each dimension was consistent between the
two types of clinic although the spread for court-clinic cases between the
second and third items for each dimension was less desirable than the spread
for guidance-clinic cases with respect to the requirements for Guttman scaling. However, because the two dimensions made sense to us and because the
ranking of the items was consistent between the two types of clinic (and also
because inspection did not reveal any better sets of items), we decided to see
if Guttman scales could be developed. We then utilized zero-cell analysis,
and our results were consistent with the requirements of Guttman's
cumulative scales.[3] Each set of items resulted in a four-point scale with
cumulative scores ranging from "0" to "3." The Pearsonian correlation
coefficient for the relationship between the authority and neurotic dimensions at the time of the clinic contact in 1962 was .40. While the relationship
is strong, it is obvious that the two dimensions are somewhat independent.
Scales were also constructed for the child's symptoms around the time of
the interview in 1963. The dichotomized distribution on these scales, for
both points in time, are presented for both guidance and court clinics in
table 6-1. Throughout our analysis of the authority dimension, the twenty-
four preschoolers in our guidance-clinic study group were excluded because
we felt it unrealistic to take seriously the notion that preschoolers would
engage in certain antisocial behavior, such as stealing and fighting, in the
same sense with which older children might engage in such behavior.

Table 6-1 shows that court-clinic cases were more frequently found to
have higher scores than guidance-clinic cases on the authority scale at both
points in time; however, on the neurotic scale, the guidance-clinic cases
more frequently had scores of "2" or "3" in 1962, and the court-clinic
cases showed a greater frequency of high scores in 1963. Indeed the court-
clinic scores on the neurotic scale in 1963 are the only instance in which the
scores suggest more deterioration than improvement.[4] The skewed distribution for court cases on the neurotic scale in 1962, however, is a caveat.

Table 6-1
Authority Scale and Neurotic Scale Scores, 1962 and 1963

Guttman Score	1962				1963			
	Guidance		Court		Guidance		Court	
	N	%	N	%	N	%	N	%
Authority scale								
0-1	156	57.1	27	49.1	188	68.9	30	54.5
2-3	117	42.9	28	50.9	85	31.1	25	45.5
Total	273[a]		55		273[a]		55	
Neurotic scale								
0-1	149	50.2	43	78.2	207	69.7	30	54.5
2-3	148	49.8	12	21.8	90	30.3	25	45.5
Total	297		55		297		55	

[a]Twenty-four preschool children were not included in this scale.

We then cross-tabulated these scales by running the 1962 scale against the 1963 scale on each dimension. The resultant categories reflect whether the child's behavior changed and the direction of change, if any. The categories are:

1. Improved from a "poor" score ("2" or "3") in 1962 to a good score ("0" or "1") in 1963.
2. Little or no evidence of this behavior at either time; no change.
3. Scored high ("poor") on the scale at both times; no change.
4. Deteriorated from a "good" score ("0" or "1") in 1962 to a "poor" ("2" or "3") score in 1963.

The proportion of cases in each of the above categories is presented for the two types of clinic in tables 6-2 and 6-3.

Analysis of table 6-2 shows that there was greater improvement than deterioration for each type of clinic case, with the guidance clinics having considerably less deterioration (and slightly less improvement) than court-clinic cases. However, when we confine our attention to those who scored "2" or "3" on the 1962 authority scale (table 6-1), we note that almost three-fifths of these cases continued to have problems in both guidance and court clinics (table 6-2). This evidence of the unchanging nature of these problems over the year covered shows that remission was not demonstrably widespread. Moreover, in view of the evidence of widespread help-seeking

Table 6–2
Authority Change Categories

	Guidance Clinic		Court Clinic	
	N	%	N	%
Improved over the year	49	17.9	12	21.8
No difficulty at either time	139	50.9	18	32.7
Problems at both times	68	24.9	16	29.1
Deteriorated over the year	17	6.3	9	16.4
Totals	273[a]		55	

[a]Excludes twenty-four prescholers.

Table 6–3
Neurotic Change Categories

	Guidance Clinic		Court Clinic	
	N	%	N	%
Improved over the year	73	24.6	3	5.5
No difficulty at either time	134	45.1	27	49.0
Problems at both times	75	25.3	9	16.4
Deteriorated over the year	15	5.0	16	29.1
Total	297[a]		55[a]	

[a]Includes detention cases.

presented in chapter 5, we suggest that the notion of spontaneity of remission will provide an implausible explanation for the changes that do occur.

Table 6–3 reveals the same pattern of greater improvement than deterioration for guidance-clinic cases but shows a striking and unexpected form reversal for court-clinic cases. For guidance-clinic cases, there are five times as many improved cases as there are deteriorated cases, but for court cases, there are five times as many deteriorated cases as there are improved cases. It is quite likely that regression effects are operating here for court cases since so few of these children gave evidence of neurotic behavior in 1962. However, this effect presents yet another facet among the complexities ignored when spontaneous remission is employed to explain change. What seems most clear about the data in tables 6-2 and 6-3, however, is that there was a fair amount of improvement, a rather small amount of deterioration (with one exception), and much unchanged behavior.

These data clearly justify one of the emphases we have highlighted in our research: that spontaneous remission is an assumption that demands investigation, a study for which our study group is ideally suited. The data also show the importance of the issues raised by Strupp and his associates concerning negative as well as positive change. Thus, their criticism of outcome research that utilized only a global index of change and assumes that change indexes miss out on the fact that some patients may improve in one between our court- and guidance-clinic cases on the dimensions presented in tables 6-2 and 6-3. Indeed various other writers have suggested that global change index miss out on the fact that some patients may improve in one aspect of their behavior but deteriorate in another, while others from the same cohort may exhibit the opposite pattern; were a single change index employed for the cohort that combined such differing dimensions, the consequence would likely be a masking of the differences.

Yet another problem, commented upon by Strupp and his associates, may be observed in the data in tables 6-2 and 6-3: the tendency to combine categories. Some researchers have combined the deteriorated with the "no change" category and labeled these as "unimproved." Not only does such an operation mask deterioration; it also masks the nature of no change. Sometimes the "no change" label itself assumes group subjects started with the same problem and/or with similar levels of seriousness. In fact, if the problem is not unitary and/or if the subjects differ on extent to which they initially manifest specific symptoms or behavior, then the outcome category of "no change," especially if employed in a global measure, will have little meaning.

A good example of this problem may be inferred from an examination of table 6-2 or table 6-3. Imagine that "improved" constitutes one category and that the three remaining categories are combined into a category labeled "unimproved." The category of "unimproved" would then mask the fact that some of our subjects did not manifest such behavior at either examination point in the period covered, that some of the subjects exhibited the index behavior at both points, and that other subjects did not manifest the measured behavior at the first point but did so at the second point. Such a procedure of combining the categories would be misleading, and this is why we have presented four change categories on each measure. Our procedure, typically, will be to maintain the separation of our change categories in the interest of clarity and chi-square will be the preferred test of significance, although Kendall's tau will also be employed since it is a measure of association and indicates direction of the relationship. Even so, we realize that our procedures do not yet describe the complex nature of change. For example, did the child improve in his ability to obey the rules of authority but continue to exhibit the symptoms of neurosis, or did the child deteriorate on both dimensions? In an effort to show these and other complexities of outcome, later we present the results of the analysis of a combined measure of change.

Although the children's outcomes presented in tables 6-2 and 6-3 are based on behavioral checklists completed by parents (as opposed to therapists, for example), these parents were also the persons who reported the presenting problems, and so we believe it is reasonable that we employed their perceptions in the assessment of outcome. To summarize, then, our data suggest that on the two dimensions discussed so far, the majority of our children showed little change in behavior. Still, approximately one-fifth of the guidance- and court-clinic cases showed improvement on the dimension indexing observance of the rules of authority; on the dimension of change in neurotic behavior, about a quarter of the guidance-clinic cases but only a twentieth of the court-clinic cases exhibited improvement. With respect to negative change, the proportions are considerably smaller than those recorded for improvement in all but one case: court-clinic cases on the dimension indexing neurotic behavior, where about 30 percent of the children were seen as deteriorating.

Factors Related to the Measures of Change

Among the variables to be initially examined in connection with outcome are the behavioral, social, attitudinal, and personal characteristics introduced earlier. In addition, the following independent variables are introduced here for the first time: mother's age in 1963, mother's rating of the degree of happiness in her marriage, an index of the extent of marital agreement as seen by the respondent, extent of parental agreement on child-rearing practices, and three measures of social participation (frequency of attendance at religious services, frequency of visits with relatives, and a combined index of social isolation). Our index of marital agreement is based on eleven "yes-no" items derived from the work of Burgess and Wallin.[5] Respondents were given a score based on the number of affirmative responses. (See appendix B for scale reliability.) The index of parental agreement on child-rearing practices was constructed from eight four-point items tapping this dimension. Our measure of social isolation was constructed from three variables: visiting with friends, participation in voluntary association, and participation in social hobbies. (See appendix B.) All of the independent variables employed in our analysis of short-term outcome are presented in table 6-4.

Coping Behavior

One of the most interesting questions before us is the extent to which parental coping was associated with change in the child's behavior over the period between 1962 and 1963. Relationships (in proportions) between problem-solving factors and the direction of change on the authority and neurotic dimensions are presented in table 6–5.

Examination of the guidance-clinic cases shows that the type of early help sought was not related to a change in the observance of rules of authority but was substantially related to change in neurotic behavior. Parents who sought early help from psychiatric professionals more often reported improvement in the neurotic dimension for their children than did those who sought no assistance or who sought the assistance of nonpsychiatric professionals. A similar result for guidance-clinic cases was found for the relationship between subsequent help-seeking (after the 1962 clinic contact) and behavior change. That is, although no relationship was found between subsequent help-seeking and change in the observance of rules of

Table 6–4
Independent Variables Employed in Assessment of Short-Term Outcome

Variables	Code Categories
Problem-solving variables	
Years waited between seeking early help and contact with the clinic	1 = 1 year or more, 2 = more than 1 year
Type of early help sought	0 = none sought, 1 = nonpsychiatric, 2 = psychiatric
Type of person or agency contacted or seen subsequent to 1962 clinic contact	1 = none, 2 = nonpsychiatric professional, 3 = psychiatric
Presenting problems at clinic in 1962 (clinic record)	Type I problem (most severe; predominantly law violation)
	Type II (predominantly neurotic, so considered less severe)
Demographic and social variables	
Mother's age	1 = 40 years, 2 = 40–50 years, 3 = 50 years
Mother's race	1 = black, 2 = white
Mother's religion	1 = Jewish, 2 = Protestant, 3 = Catholic, 4 = other
Mother's marital status	1 = married, 2 = separated, 3 = divorced or widowed
Chief breadwinner's income	1 = under $3,901, 2 = between $3,901 and $9,199, 3 = more than $9,200
Mother's education	1 = elementary school only, 2 = high school only, 3 = some college or better
Warner's ISC	1 = upper class (score of 1, 2, or 3); 2 = middle class (score of 4, 5, or 6); 3 = lower class (score of 7, 8, or 9)
Child's sex	1 = male, 2 = female
Child's age	1 = preschooler (1–5 years), 2 = latency (6–10 years), 3 = early adolescence (11–12 years), 4 = middle adolescence (13–15 years), 5 = late adolescence (16–18 years)

Table 6–4 continued

Variables	Code Categories
Respondent's perceptions and attitudinal or personal characteristics	
Blames self for child's problems	1 = yes, 2 = no
Blames relatives for child's problems	1 = yes, 2 = no
Blames peers for child's problems	1 = yes, 2 = no
Blames child for child's problems	1 = yes, 2 = no
Focus of blame (combined index).	1 = older generation, 2 = younger generation, 3 = fate or don't know
Quick Word Test (index of IQ)	1 = 1st quartile (low), 2 = 2d quartile, 3 = 3d quartile, 4 = 4th quartile
Srole scales: authoritarianism[a]	1 = low (0–1), 2 = medium (2–3), 3 = high (4–5, most authoritarian)
Anomia[a]	1 = low (0–1), 2 = medium (2–3), 3 = high (4–5, most anomic)
Frustration[a]	1 = low (0–1), 2 = medium (2), 3 = high (3–4)
Rigidity[a]	1 = low (0–1), 2 = medium (2–4), 3 = high (5–6)
Withdrawal[a]	1 = low (0–1), 2 = medium (2), 3 = high (3–4)
Hopefulness for child's future	1 = very hopeful, 2 = mildly hopeful, 3 = not hopeful
Marital happiness variables	
Repondent's estimate of degree of marital happiness	1 = very happy, 2 = happy, 3 = unhappy
Combined index of respondent's assessment of extent of marital agreement with spouse (includes 11 items, such as finances and religion)[a]	1 = little agreement (agreed on 2 or fewer items), 2 = some agreement (agreed on 3 to 5 items), 3 = much agreement (agreed on 6 or more items)
Parental agreement on child-rearing practices (based on eight items, such as household chores and allowances)[b]	1 = nearly always agree, 2 = predominant agreement, 3 = frequent disagreements
Behavioral Indexes (social participation variables)	
Frequency of visits with relatives in month prior to interview	1 = rarely (one or more), 2 = some (2 to 4 in month), 3 = frequently (more than one visit per week)
Frequency of attendance at religious services in month prior to interview	1 = none or once, 2 = fairly regularly (2–3), 3 = regularly (4 times), 4 = more than once a week
Social isolation scale (cumulative scale, based on visits with friends, participation in voluntary associations, and participation in social hobbies)	0 = isolate (no visits with friends and no participation in clubs or hobbies), 1 = visits friends but does not participate in clubs or hobbies, 2 = either participates in voluntary associations or social hobbies or both and typically have friends

[a]See appendix B for reliability of these scales.

[b]We averaged the eight agree-disagree items for each respondent and assigned this as the index score. If more than three items were missing, the case was excluded. We then trichotomized the distribution in order to obtain somewhat equivalent categories.

Table 6-5
Indexes of Problem-Solving and Short-Term Change in Observance of Rules of Authority and Neurotic Behavior

	Authority Change[a]					Neurotic Change[b]				
	Improved	Unchanged[c] (+)	Unchanged (−)	Deteriorated	100% =	Improved	Unchanged (+)	Unchanged (−)	Deteriorated	100% =
Guidance clinics										
Type of help sought prior to 1962 clinic contact										
None	23.7	49.2	22.0	5.1	59	22.1	54.4	20.6	2.9	68
Nonpsychiatric	14.5	53.0	23.9	8.6	117	18.9	51.2	23.6	6.3	127
Psychiatric	18.6	49.5	27.8	4.1	97	33.3	31.4	30.4	4.9	102
	$X^2 = 4.45$, 6 df, ns; Kendall's tau (C) = .03, ns					$X^2 = 14.41$, 6 df, $p < .05$; Kendall's tau (C) = −.00, ns				
Type of person or agency contacted or seen since 1962 clinic contact										
None	16.9	59.0	24.1	—	83	18.7	47.3	29.6	4.4	91
Nonpsychiatric	16.9	49.2	26.2	7.7	65	17.4	58.0	20.3	4.3	69
Psychiatric	19.2	46.4	24.8	9.6	125	32.1	37.2	24.8	5.8	137
	$X^2 = 9.55$, 6 df, ns; Kendall's tau (C) = .06, ns					$X^2 = 12.11$, 6 df, $p < .10$, Kendall's tau (C) = .08, $p < .10$				
Time waited between seeking early help and 1962 clinic called[d]										
One year or less	18.4	46.1	30.2	5.2	76	28.2	43.6	23.1	5.1	78
More than one year	14.6	52.8	25.2	7.4	123	24.6	43.3	26.1	6.0	134
	$X^2 = 1.60$, 3 df, ns; Kendall's tau (C) = .00, ns					$X^2 = 0.49$, 3 df, ns; Kendall's tau (C) = .05, ns				

Court clinics	+[A]				N	+[B]				N
Type of help sought prior to 1962 clinic contact										
None	31.6	42.1	15.8	10.5	19	10.5	63.2	15.8	10.5	19
Nonpsychiatric	25.0	25.0	30.0	20.0	20	5.0	45.0	40.0	10.0	20
Psychiatric	6.3	31.3	43.8	18.6	16	—	37.4	31.3	31.3	16
	$X^2 = 6.54$, 6 df, ns; Kendall's tau C $= .25$, $p < .05$					$X^2 = 8.10$, 6 df, ns; Kendall's tau C $= .24$, $p < .05$				
Type of person or agency contacted or seen since 1962 clinic contact										
None	30.0	40.0	20.0	10.0	20	5.0	65.0	20.0	10.0	20
Nonpsychiatric	38.5	—	46.1	15.4	13	7.6	30.8	38.5	23.1	13
Psychiatric	4.5	45.5	27.3	22.7	22	4.5	45.5	31.8	18.2	22
	$X^2 = 13.88$, 6 df, $p < .05$; Kendall's tau C $= .22$, $p < .05$					$X^2 = 4.05$, 6 df, ns; Kendall's tau C $= .13$, ns				
Time waited between seeking early help 1962 clinic contact[d]										
One year or less	9.6	38.1	33.3	19.0	21	4.8	47.6	38.1	9.5	21
More than one year	16.7	8.3	50.0	25.0	12	—	16.6	41.7	41.7	12
	$X^2 = 3.47$, ns; Kendall's tau (C) $= .15$, ns					$X^2 = 6.33$, $p < .10$; Kendall's tau (C) $= .23$, ns				

[a] For the guidance clinics, $N = 273$; for the court clinics, $N = 55$.

[b] For the guidance clinics, $N = 297$; for the court clinics, $N = 55$.

[c] The "unchanged" category in which behavior was not manifested at either time is labeled as (+), and the unchanged category in which the behavior was present at both times is labeled (−).

[d] N includes only those cases which sought early help and responded to this question.

authority, it was again found that seeking help from psychiatric professionals was associated with more improvement on the neurotic dimension (although this difference was statistically significant only at the .10 level on the chi-square test). The third variable presented in table 6–5—time waited between early help-seeking and calling the source clinic—was related to neither of our two change dimensions.

A slightly different pattern emerges with regard to court-clinic cases. Basing our analysis on Kendall's tau we found that type of help sought, either prior to or subsequent to the 1962 contact with the source clinic was significantly related to change in the authority dimension. Parents who did not seek any help or who sought help from nonpsychiatric agents were more likely to report improvement than were parents who sought help from psychiatric professionals. On the neurotic dimension, perhaps the most striking phenomenon is the substantial deterioration taking place among court-clinic children who received or sought any help either prior to or subsequent to the 1962 clinic contact. While only seeking prior help is statistically significant, these results on the neurotic dimension are quite different from those for guidance-clinic families.

These data suggest that psychiatric professionals, especially in their traditional guidance-clinic settings, have more success with children having neurotic behavior problems—that is, if we can assume that help-seeking results in at least some time spent with those whose help is sought. This is not a surprising finding; it confirms some of our earlier findings based on psychiatric professionals' self-reports. However, Levitt's conclusions would vary from this since he did not find that psychotherapy resulted in additional improvement (over spontaneous remission) for neurotic children.[6]

It is more difficult for us to make sense out of the substantial relationship between type of help sought after the 1962 contact and changes in the child's observance of conduct rules among court cases. However, we suggest that the nature of the child's problems, the older average age of the court children, and the fact that contact with the court-clinic psychiatrist did not have the voluntary character of guidance clinics combined to minimize the effectiveness of subsequent contacts with psychiatric professionals. A different and less plausible interpretation is that their training does not adequately prepare psychiatric professionals to work with youths who violate the law.

Another conclusion also emerges: there is little reason to assume that much of the improvement reported was spontaneous. When we examined all "improved" guidance-clinic cases, we found that less than 30 percent of these had reported not seeking any assistance between 1962 and 1963 on either of the two dimensions: 28.6 percent and 23.3 percent, respectively, on the authority and neurotic scales. Moreover, since the Pearsonian correlation coefficient between these two scales is only .30, we can infer that even fewer cases could be attributed to spontaneous remission on both dimensions. Although the proportion of court-clinic cases that improved without aid presents a brighter picture, the impression is misleading, for several reasons. First, the number of "improved" cases is small—twelve and three for the authority and neurotic dimensions, respectively. Second, the court-case parents had not voluntarily contacted the court psychiatric personnel in 1962; thus it is possible that prior and subsequent contacts with psychiatric personnel were also involuntary. If such contacts were court mandated, then it seems inappropriate to assume that such contacts are bona-fide attempts at coping. Although our short-term outcome data do not permit us to address properly the nature of such contacts, our long-term follow-up data will allow us a more sensitive examination of coping behavior for both guidance and court clinics. The long-term data will be particularly important in examining the presence and effects of voluntary coping behavior for court-clinic cases. In the meantime, it appears that speculations or statements here about spontaneous remission are appropriately confined to guidance-clinic cases.

Because we believe that our guidance-clinic cases constitute a study group that is highly comparable to the usual untreated control group, we argue that these findings demonstrate the weakness of the claim that 65 percent or 70 percent of untreated controls experience spontaneous remission. Although it is certainly true that some children outgrow their problems (in this sense, their remission may be considered spontaneous) and some children change for the worse, it is also true that parents spend a great deal of time and effort working to alleviate perceived problems. Even our short-term data suggest that coping appears preferable to spontaneity in the explanation of change.

It is important to acknowledge that the nature of the data presented so far on coping behavior has weaknesses that caution us against strong conclusions about the effectiveness or ineffectiveness of psychiatric assistance. First, we are looking at short-term outcome; the long-term outcome data may produce different results, especially since they are far richer data in detail. Second, it is possible that most of the parents who sought psychiatric help subsequent to the 1962 clinic contact suffered their 1962 fate of not finding the help they sought. In other words, "seeking help" does not automatically mean that help was found. Finally, parents do not call professionals unless they perceive a serious problem. Thus it is quite possible that coping or help-seeking behavior should not be thought of as an independent variable employed in explaining the scale or dimension score in table 6-5 but that the child's position on the scale should be construed as the independent variable employed in the explanation of help-seeking.

The Primary Presenting Problem

At this point in our analysis, we wondered if the primary presenting problem, recorded by the guidance clinic in 1962, was related to change status on
either the authority or neurotic dimension. Because there is obviously some
overlap between the presenting-problems typology of type I and type II and
our two change dimensions, we were skeptical of this analysis. However, we
wondered if the presenting-problem classification, amorphous as its
categories are, would be useful in the prediction of change dimensions. The
results are not very useful in the explanation of change, for on both dimensions the type I presenting problem was more likely to show improvement.
There was indeed some overlap between the typology and the dimension of
observance of rules of authority at the time of the 1962 application, (r =
.24) but virtually no overlap between the typology and the dimension of
neurotic behavior in 1962 (r = .01). For the court-clinic cases, there was an
absence of any relationship between our classification of type of offense
("more" or "less" serious) and our two dimensions of change. Thus, we
concluded that our typologies of presenting problems and offenses were too
amorphous and contained too many dimensions of behavior to be useful in
the prediction of change.

Demographic and Social Variables

We examined the following social variables with respect to our two dimensions of behavior change: mother's age, mother's marital status, race,
Warner's ISC, mother's religion, child's age, and the sex of the child. The
data are presented in table 6–6. (In this analysis, the continuous background
variables of mother's age, Warner's ISC and child's age were collapsed.)

Mother's age: There was no relationship between mother's age and change
on either dimension for guidance-clinic cases. For court-clinic cases,
although no difference was found employing the chi-square test, there was a
difference employing Kendall's measure of association. This was due to a
tendency for older mother's children to improve on the authority dimension
and for the children of younger mothers to deteriorate on both dimensions.
This deterioration effect was most evident for mothers under forty. A caution for the court-case relationship on the neurotic dimension, however, is
that there was considerable skewness toward an absence of neurotic symptoms in 1962.

Table 6-6

Selected Background Factors and Short-Term Change in Observance of Rules of Authority and Neurotic Behavior

Guidance clinics	Authority Change [a]					Neurotic Change [b]				
	Improved	Unchanged (+)	Unchanged (−)	Deteriorated	100% =	Improved	Unchanged (+)	Unchanged (−)	Deteriorated	100% =
Mother's age in 1963										
Under 40 years	20.1	43.4	29.6	6.9	159	25.6	39.4	27.8	7.2	180
40–49 years	13.5	61.8	19.1	5.6	89	24.2	54.9	19.8	1.1	91
50 years and over	20.0	60.0	16.0	4.0	25	19.2	50.0	26.9	3.9	26
$X^2 = 9.46$, 6 df, ns; Kendall's tau (C) = −.06, ns						$X^2 = 9.88$, 6 df, ns; Kendall's tau C = −.05, ns				
Mother's marital status in 1963										
Married	17.1	53.0	23.0	6.9	217	24.7	46.8	25.5	3.0	235
Divorced or widowed	27.6	48.3	20.7	3.4	29	25.7	45.2	22.6	6.5	31
Separated	16.0	32.0	48.0	4.0	25	25.0	28.6	28.6	17.8	28
$X^2 = 10.16$, 6 df, ns; Kendall's tau (C) = .01, ns. No information in 2 cases						$X^2 = 13.91$, 6 df, $p < .02$; Kendall's tau C = .04, ns. No information in 3 cases				
Mother's race										
Black	9.5	42.9	38.1	9.5	21	30.5	47.8	13.0	8.7	23
White	18.4	51.0	24.5	6.1	245	24.4	44.0	27.1	4.5	266
$X^2 = 2.86$, 3 df, ns; Kendall's tau (C) = −.06, $p < .05$. No information in 7 cases						$X^2 = 2.75$, 3 df, ns; Kendall's tau C = .03, ns. No information in 8 cases				
Warner's ISC										
Upper class	19.4	36.9	11.1	5.6	36	22.5	45.0	30.0	2.5	40
Middle class	12.3	56.2	28.1	3.4	89	25.3	40.0	30.5	4.2	95
Lower class	19.6	44.9	26.8	8.7	138	25.0	47.4	21.0	6.6	152
$X^2 = 10.10$, 6 df, ns; Kendall's tau (C) = −.06, ns. No information in 10 cases						$X^2 = 4.54$, 6 df, ns; Kendall's tau (C) = −.03, ns. No information in 10 cases				

Table 6-6 continued

	Authority Change [a]					Neurotic Change [b]				
	Improved	Unchanged (+)	Unchanged (−)	Deteriorated	100% =	Improved	Unchanged (+)	Unchanged (−)	Deteriorated	100% =
Mother's religion										
Jewish	22.2	64.8	11.1	1.9	54	22.6	41.9	30.7	4.8	62
Protestant	12.5	54.5	27.3	5.9	88	25.0	47.9	22.8	4.3	92
Catholic	18.7	42.9	30.4	8.0	112	24.6	43.5	27.0	4.9	122
Other	20.0	30.0	30.0	20.0	10	30.0	60.0	10.0	—	10

$X^2 = 17.44$, 9 df, $p < .05$; Kendall's tau (C) = .12, $p < .05$
No information in 9 cases

$X^2 = 3.51$, 9 df, ns
No information in 11 cases

	Authority Change [a]					Neurotic Change [b]				
	Improved	Unchanged (+)	Unchanged (−)	Deteriorated	100% =	Improved	Unchanged (+)	Unchanged (−)	Deteriorated	100% =
Child's age										
Preschool (under 5)	—	—	—	—	—	20.8	16.7	37.5	25.0	24
Latency (6–10)	19.6	42.9	29.5	8.0	112	22.3	43.8	27.6	6.3	112
Early adolescence (11–12)	22.4	46.9	22.4	8.3	49	26.5	42.9	28.6	2.0	40
Midadolescence (13–15)	13.8	54.2	27.8	4.2	72	27.8	51.4	19.4	1.4	72
Late adolescence (16–18)	15.0	72.5	10.0	2.5	40	25.0	57.5	17.5	—	40

$X^2 = 14.10$, 9 df, ns; Kendall's tau (C) = −.06, ns

$X^2 = 35.00$, 12 df, $p < .001$; Kendall's tau (C) = −.15, $p < .001$

	Authority Change [a]					Neurotic Change [b]				
	Improved	Unchanged (+)	Unchanged (−)	Deteriorated	100% =	Improved	Unchanged (+)	Unchanged (−)	Deteriorated	100% =
Child's sex										
Male	18.4	48.3	26.8	6.5	201	21.5	50.7	21.9	5.9	219
Female	16.7	58.3	19.4	5.6	72	33.3	29.5	34.6	2.6	78

$X^2 = 2.39$, 3 df, ns; Kendall's tau (C) = −.04, ns

$X^2 = 13.99$, 3 df, $p < .01$; Kendall's tau (C) = −.02, ns

	Authority Change [a]					Neurotic Change [b]				
	Improved	Unchanged (+)	Unchanged (−)	Deteriorated	100% =	Improved	Unchanged (+)	Unchanged (−)	Deteriorated	100% =
Court Clinics Mother's age in 1963										
Under 40 years	13.0	34.9	21.7	30.4	23	—	43.5	8.7	47.8	23
40–49	28.6	28.6	35.7	7.1	28	10.6	53.6	17.9	17.9	28
50 years and over	25.0	50.0	25.0	—	4	—	50.0	50.0	—	4

$X^2 = 7.72$, 6 df, ns; Kendall's tau (C) = −.21, $p < .05$

$X^2 = 11.94$, 6 df, ns; Kendall's tau (C) = −.22, $p < .05$

	Authority Change [a]					Neurotic Change [b]				
	Improved	Unchanged (+)	Unchanged (−)	Deteriorated	100% =	Improved	Unchanged (+)	Unchanged (−)	Deteriorated	100% =
Mother's marital status in 1963										
Married	15.6	34.3	31.3	18.8	32	6.3	43.7	21.9	28.1	32
Divorced or widowed	38.5	46.1	15.4	—	13	7.7	76.9	7.7	—	13

					N					N
Separated	20.0	10.0	40.0	30.0	10	—	30.0	10.0	60.0	10

$X^2 = 9.22$, 6 df, ns; Kendall's tau (C) $= -.06$, ns $X^2 = 10.46$, 6 df, ns; Kendall's tau (C) $= .04$, ns

Mother's race					N					N
Black	22.7	22.7	36.4	18.2	22	4.5	40.9	13.7	40.9	22
White	19.4	41.9	22.6	16.1	31	6.5	54.8	16.1	22.6	31

$X^2 = 2.36$, 3 df, ns; Kendall's tau (C) $= -.09$, ns $X^2 = 2.08$, 3 df, ns; Kendall's tau (C) $= -.19$, ns
No information on race in 2 cases   No information on race in 2 cases

Warner's ISC					N					N
Upper class	50.0	50.0	—	—	2	—	50.0	—	50.0	2
Middle class	40.0	20.0	20.0	20.0	5	—	60.0	20.0	20.0	5
Lower class	19.2	34.0	29.8	17.0	47	6.4	48.9	17.0	27.7	47

$X^2 = 3.15$, 6 df, ns; Kendall's tau (C) $= .09$, ns $X^2 = 1.39$, 6 df, ns; Kendall's tau (C) $= .01$, ns
No information in 1 case

Mother's religion					N					N
Jewish	—	—	—	—	—	—	—	—	—	—
Protestant	21.8	34.8	30.4	13.0	23	8.8	39.1	13.0	39.1	23
Catholic	24.1	27.6	27.6	20.7	29	3.5	55.2	17.2	24.1	29
Other	—	—	—	—	—	—	—	—	—	—

$X^2 = 0.72$, 3 df, ns; Kendall's tau (C) $= .05$, ns $X^2 = 2.38$, 3 df, ns; Kendall's tau (C) $= -.11$, ns
No information on religion in 3 cases   No information on religion in 3 cases

Child's age					N					N
Preschool (under 5)	—	—	—	—	—	—	—	—	—	—
Latency (6–10)	50.0	50.0	—	—	4	—	100.0	—	—	4
Early adolescence (11–12)	33.3	33.3	16.7	16.7	6	—	66.6	16.7	16.7	6
Midadolescence (13–15)	18.2	18.2	31.8	31.8	22	4.6	22.7	22.7	50.0	22
Late adolescence (16–18)	17.4	43.5	34.8	4.3	23	8.7	60.9	13.0	17.4	23

$X^2 = 12.45$, 9 df, ns; Kendall's tau (C) $= .01$, ns $X^2 = 3.14$, 3 df, ns; Kendall's tau (C) $= -.08$, ns

Child's sex					N					N
Male	26.3	28.9	31.6	13.2	38	5.3	52.6	10.5	31.6	38
Female	11.8	41.2	23.5	23.5	11	5.9	41.2	29.4	23.5	17

$X^2 = 2.71$, 3 df, ns; Kendall's tau (C) $= .12$, ns $X^2 = 3.14$, 3 df, ns; Kendall's tau (C) $= .03$, ns

[a] $N = 273$ for guidance-clinic cases, and $N = 55$ for court-clinic cases.
[b] $N = 297$ for guidance-clinic cases, and $N = 55$ for court-clinic cases.

Marital Status: There is no relationship between marital status and change on the authority dimension for guidance-clinic cases; however, there is a significant difference between marital status and neurotic change, due almost exclusively to deterioration of the children of separated women. One is tempted to speculate that there is more turmoil among women occupying the uncertain status of marital separation and that this stress results in the appearance of neurotic behavior in the children. For court-clinic cases there is a very similar trend on the neurotic dimension for the children of separated women; however, the difference is not statistically significant, probably due to the small number of cases of separated women.

Race and Religion: Race is not related to either dimension of change for guidance- or court-clinic cases when the chi-square test is employed. However, a significant difference on the authority dimension appears for Kendall's tau in guidance-clinic cases where white children show more improvement. The magnitude is decidedly weak, however, so race would not be expected to have much predictive utility.

Religion of the mother shows a significant difference for guidance-clinic cases, but only on the authority change dimension. Here, however, both of the tests show a statistically significant difference, with Jewish children showing both the most improvement and the least deterioration. Somewhat contrasting, Jewish children showed less improvement than Christians on the neurotic dimension. This finding is consistent with expectations that since Jews emphasize family harmony and scholarly achievement, they would find nonobservance of the rules of authority distasteful and unrewarding. In the court clinics, where no Jewish children are reported, there is no difference between Protestants and Catholics.

Social Class: Somewhat surprising, there is no relationship between Warner's ISC and change on either dimension for both types of clinic cases. The skewness of Warner's ISC among court-clinic cases, however, forced us to examine the relationship between other indexes of class (breadwinner's income and mother's schooling) and change. Here, where skewness was not a problem, an absence of any relationship between class and change persisted. We shall continue to examine social class, however, since we believe it to be a powerful mediator of social stress; it is possible that it will prove to have more power when examined in conjunction with other potential sources of change.

Child's Age: While the child's age at the time of application was unrelated to change on the authority dimension for guidance-clinic cases, there was a powerful relationship on the neurotic change index, with younger children showing less improvement and more deterioration than older children ($p <$

.001). If we consider the two change categories of "unchanged negative" and "deterioration" on each dimension, it is clear that by late adolescence, there is very little evidence of undesirable behavior among guidance-clinic cases. One must wonder if this result is due to developmental processes, to the coping processes in evidence, or, as we suspect, to the interaction of these factors. One also wonders not only if such behavior will wane in late adolescence for the younger children but whether it will reemerge later.

Some evidence from the analysis of our court-clinic cases may provide a clue to one answer. It is that age-related change is not much in evidence for court-clinic cases. If developmental processes are operating for guidance-clinic cases so as to induce a fairly consistent reduction of symptoms over age, such processes must be working quite differently for court-clinic cases. Thus we strongly suspect that coping skills and coping processes, social factors, and developmental processes are all operating in the production of outcome and that they are operating in distinctly different ways for guidance- and court-clinic cases.

Child's Sex: There is no relationship between child's sex and outcome on the authority dimension for either guidance- or court-clinic cases; however, there is a significant difference (chi-square test) on the neurotic dimension for the guidance-clinic cases, with females showing more improvement on this dimension. The difference, though, is due more to the diverging proportions of "unchanged" (+) and (−) cases than to differing proportions of "improved" or "deteriorated" cases among males and females.

Regarding background factors as they are related to change, it seems that mother's age, mother's marital status, mother's religion, and child's age have the best potential as predictive variables. Interestingly enough, mother's age is the only background factor of promise as far as court-clinic cases are concerned. Of the remaining three factors, mother's religion is the only predictor of change on the authority dimension, while both marital status and child's age bear potential as predictors of change on the neurotic dimension.

Personality Factors

Here we present the relationships between the Srole personality scales and the dimensions of change. We show only the proportions improved for the trichotomized categories on each of the five Srole scales (table 6-7).

For guidance-clinic applicants, three of the five scales show a significant difference on the authority dimension when the chi-square test is employed: authoritarianism, frustration, and withdrawal. Respondents

Table 6-7
Personality Factors (Srole Scales) and Proportion Improvement on Change Dimensions

	Guidance[a]				Court[b]			
	Authority (% Improved)	100% =	Neurotic (% Improved)	100% =	Authority (% Improved)	100% =	Neurotic (% Improved)	100% =
Authoritarianism								
Low	21.9	128	26.4	144	22.2	9	—	9
Med	13.6	88	26.3	95	23.5	17	5.9	17
High	15.8	57	17.2	58	20.7	29	6.9	29
	$X^2 = 13.2$, 6 df, $p < .05$ K. tau (C) = .13, $p < .01$		$X^2 = 4.0$, 6 df, ns K. tau (C) = .04, ns		$X^2 = 3.64$, ns K. tau (C) = -.10, ns		$X^2 = 4.25$, 6 df, ns K. tau (C) = -.12, ns	
Anomia								
Low	18.1	160	23.2	168	21.1	19	—	19
Med	17.4	86	27.5	102	31.8	22	4.5	22
High	18.5	27	22.2	27	7.1	14	14.3	14
	$X^2 = 4.06$, 6 df, ns K. tau (C) = .04, ns		$X^2 = 10.9$, 6 df, ns K. tau (C) = .01, ns		$X^2 = 4.38$, 6 df, ns K. tau (C) = .06, ns		$X^2 = 7.4$, 6 df, ns K. tau (C) = -.06, ns	
Frustration								
Low	19.6	209	25.6	227	22.6	31	—	31
Med	8.8	34	21.6	37	25.0	8	12.5	8
High	16.7	30	21.2	33	18.8	16	12.5	16
	$X^2 = 15.9$, 6 df, $p < .05$ K. tau (C) = .12, $p < .01$		$X^2 = 7.4$, 6 df, ns K. tau (C) = .07, $p < .05$		$X^2 = 8.35$, 6 df, ns K. tau (C) = -.05, ns		$X^2 = 7.73$, 6 df, ns K. tau (C) = -.08, ns	

Rigidity								
Low	16.4	146	25.0	164	22.2	9	—	9
Med	18.7	107	25.9	112	22.6	31	6.5	31
High	25.0	20	14.3	21	20.0	15	6.7	15
	$X^2 = 9.12$, 6 df, ns		$X^2 = 5.4$, 6 df, ns		$X^2 = 2.67$, 6 df, ns		$X^2 = 1.37$, 6 df, ns	
	K. tau (C) $= .06$, ns		K. tau (C) $= .04$, ns		K. tau (C) $= .05$, ns		K. tau (C) $= -.03$, ns	
Withdrawal								
Low	13.9	165	26.4	178	13.6	22	4.5	22
Med	28.4	74	23.8	80	26.3	19	5.3	19
High	14.7	34	17.9	39	28.6	14	7.1	14
	$X^2 = 16.73$, 6 df, $p < .05$		$X^2 = 10.03$, 6 df, ns		$X^2 = 3.58$, 6 df, ns		$X^2 = 1.04$, 6 df, ns	
	K. tau (C) $= -.04$, ns		K. tau (C) $= .10$, $p < .05$		K. tau (C) $= -.09$, ns		K. tau (C) $= .05$, ns	

[a] $N = 273$ on the authority dimension and 297 on the neurotic dimension.

[b] $N = 55$ on both the authority and neurotic dimensions.

who score low on authoritarianism report the most improvement on this dimension. The relationship involving withdrawal is curvilinear; those in the middle range report the most improvement. When the measure of association—Kendall's tau—is employed, the relationship regarding withdrawal is not statistically significant since this measure does not pick up nonlinear relationships. Our measure of association, however, shows significant relationships involving frustration and authoritarianism.

On the neurotic dimension for guidance-clinic cases, there are no differences when the chi-square test is employed; however, frustration and withdrawal are both significantly related to the neurotic dimension, with the low scores reporting the most-desirable behavior.

In the court-clinic cases, there was not a single statistically significant relationship between the personality scales and the two dimensions of change on either of the two tests of significance. And indeed, the directions, or signs, tended to be the opposite of those for guidance-clinic cases. Thus, whereas nine of ten signs were positive for the guidance clinics, in the case of court clinics, seven of the ten were negative. The most striking of these reversals involves the relationship between respondent's authoritarianism and the child's change in observance of rules of authority. For guidance clinics, the less authoritarian the parent, the more observant the child became of authority rules, but for court-clinic cases, the less authoritarian the parent, the less observant the child became of authority rules (although this association was not statistically significant).

Attribution of Blame

In dealing with problem solving, parents were likelier to start looking for help when they blamed themselves or other relatives for the child's problems. Now we wish to ascertain whether the focus of blame is related to either or both of our short-term outcome measures (table 6-8).

Employing both of our usual tests of significance (and, for the moment, ignoring the combined index of blame), we see that both blaming oneself or one's relatives for the child's problems are related significantly to authority change on the chi-square test, and blaming relatives is also significant on Kendall's tau for guidance-clinic cases. Blaming relatives, then, is the more stable of the two variables and is of a stronger magnitude on the Kendall test. More to the point, respondents who blamed relatives for their children's problems were more likely to report undesirable behavior in their children as indexed by the change measure. The "unchanged" categories are at least as responsible for the relationship as are the "improved" or "deteriorated" categories. Thus if relatives are blamed, there is less movement away from undesirable behavior ("unchanged") and toward improvement than is the case when relatives are not blamed. A similar argument holds, but less firmly, in the case of blaming oneself.

When the guidance-clinic cases are assessed on the relationships between blame attribution and change as indexed on the neurotic dimension, there is not a single significant relationship. At this point in our analysis, we constructed a combined index of blame. We reasoned that since blaming self and blaming relatives were empirically related in similar ways to change on the authority dimension, perhaps they could be combined. Examining the relationships for blaming peers and blaming the subject child, we saw that there was at least some similarity; each had a positive sign on the Kendall test. When either the child or his peers were blamed, there was more movement away from undesirable behavior than was the case when they were not blamed. Thus, empirically, there was a substantial difference between self and relatives on one hand and peers and child on the other, at least with respect to direction of movement on the authority dimension. We then combined self and relatives into the "older generation" and the child and peers into the "younger generation." We now had the first two categories of the combined locus-of-blame index. We had also recorded instances where respondents attributed the child's problems to "fate" or had said they "didn't know." These two responses are combined to form the last category of our combined-blame index.

An examination of the relationship between the combined-blame index and the change categories of the authority dimension show a statistically significant difference on the chi-square test. The difference is in the expected direction given the manner in which the index was contrived. When the "older generation" was blamed for the child's problems, there was considerably less movement away from rule-violative behavior toward improvement than was the case when the "younger generation" was blamed. Those who blamed fate or who said they did not know why the child acted as he did were between the two generations in extent of desirable change on the authority dimension.

This situation is somewhat reversed regarding the relationship between the index of blame and the neurotic dimension for guidance-clinic applicants. Here when the older generation was blamed, there was slightly more movement away from neurotic behavior than was the case for either of the other two categories although the difference is not statistically significant on the chi-square test ($p < .10$).

In the court-clinic cases, there was not a single statistically significant chi-square difference between any of the blame measures and the two change dimensions. Blaming relatives is significantly related to the authority change dimension, on the measure of association, and in the same manner as for guidance-clinic applicants. The combined index is also related to change in observance of rules of authority, and again the pattern is quite

Table 6-8
Attribution of Blame and Change in Observance of Rules of Authority and Neurotic Behavior

	Authority[a]					Neurotic[b]				
	Improved	Unchanged (+)	Unchanged (−)	Deterio-rated	100% =	Improved	Unchanged (+)	Unchanged (−)	Deterio-rated	100% =
Guidance Clinics										
Blames self										
Yes	20.5	37.2	34.6	7.7	78	24.6	36.4	31.8	7.1	85
No	16.9	56.6	21.0	5.6	195	24.6	48.6	22.6	4.2	212
	$X^2 = 8.95$, 3 df, $p < .05$; K. tau (C) $= -.08$, ns					$X^2 = 4.92$, 3 df, ns; K. tau (C) $= -.07$, ns				
Blames relatives										
Yes	14.8	37.0	43.3	4.9	81	30.7	34.1	27.5	7.7	91
No	19.3	56.7	17.2	6.8	192	21.8	50.0	24.3	3.9	206
	$X^2 = 20.78$, 3 df, ns; K. tau (C) $= -.17$, $p < .002$					$X^2 = 7.66$, 3 df, ns; K. tau (C) $= .00$, ns				
Blames peers										
Yes	15.0	70.0	5.0	10.0	20	25.0	65.0	10.0	—	20
No	18.2	49.4	26.5	5.9	253	24.5	43.7	26.4	5.4	277
	$X^2 = 5.57$, 3 df, ns; K. tau (C) $= .03$, ns					$X^2 = 4.94$, 3 df, ns; K. tau (C) $= .04$, ns				
Blames Child										
Yes	27.0	45.9	24.4	2.7	37	19.6	51.2	26.8	2.4	41
No	16.5	51.7	25.0	6.8	236	25.4	44.1	25.0	5.5	256
	$X^2 = 3.03$, 3 df, ns; K. tau (C) $= .06$, ns					$X^2 = 1.58$, 3 df, ns; K. tau (C) $= -.01$, ns				
Comined index (locus of blame)										
Older generation	16.2	43.2	34.3	6.3	111	30.8	34.2	27.5	7.5	120
Younger generation	27.0	52.3	15.9	4.8	63	20.9	52.2	23.9	3.0	67

Fate or don't know or no response	14.1	58.6	20.2	7.1	99	20.0	52.8	23.6	3.6	110
	X^2 = 13.45, 6 df, $p < .05$; K. tau (C) = $-.06$, ns					X^2 = 11.40, 6 df, ns; K. tau (C) = $.01$, ns				
Court Clinics										
Blames self										
Yes	12.5	25.0	37.5	25.0	8	12.5	37.5	12.5	37.5	8
No	23.4	34.0	27.7	14.9	47	4.3	51.1	17.0	27.6	47
	X^2 = 1.2, 3 df, ns; K. tau (C) = $-.11$, ns					X^2 = 1.4, 3 df, ns; K. tau (C) = $-.02$, ns				
Blames relatives										
Yes	11.8	17.6	41.2	29.4	17	—	35.3	23.5	41.2	17
No	26.3	39.5	23.7	10.5	38	7.9	55.2	13.2	23.7	38
	X^2 = 6.65, 3 df, ns; K. tau (C) = $-.33, p < .01$					X^2 = 4.30, 3 df, ns; K. tau (C) = $-.26, p < .05$				
Blames peers										
Yes	18.8	37.5	12.5	31.2	16	6.2	50.0	6.3	37.5	16
No	23.1	30.7	35.9	10.3	39	5.1	48.8	20.5	25.6	39
	X^2 = 5.45, 3 df, ns; K. tau (C) = $-.09$, ns					X^2 = 1.98, 3 df, ns; K. tau (C) = $-.03$, ns				
Blames child										
Yes	35.8	21.4	35.8	7.0	14	7.2	64.3	7.1	21.4	14
No	17.1	36.6	26.8	19.5	41	4.9	43.9	19.5	31.7	41
	X^2 = 3.65, 3 df, ns; K. tau (C) = $.14$, ns					X^2 = 2.34, 3 df, ns; K. tau (C) = $.16$, ns				
Combined index										
Older generation	11.8	23.5	41.2	23.5	17	5.9	29.4	17.6	47.1	17
Younger generation	29.0	32.3	22.6	16.1	31	6.5	58.0	12.9	22.6	31
Fate or don't know	14.3	57.1	28.6	—	7	—	57.1	28.6	14.3	7
	X^2 = 6.41, 6 df, ns; K. tau (C) = $-.20, p < .05$					X^2 = 6.13, 6 df, ns; K. tau (C) = $-.18$, ns				

[a] N = 273 for guidance-clinic cases, and N = 55 for court-clinic cases.
[b] N = 297 for guidance-clinic cases, and N = 55 for court-clinic cases.

similar to that found for guidance-clinic cases; there is little movement toward improvement when the older generation is blamed but considerable improvement when the younger generation is considered at fault.

With respect to the neurotic dimension, we have already remarked on the considerable deterioration taking place among court-clinic cases. Still there is no improvement when relatives are blamed, and this contributes to the finding of a significant relationship here. More important, however, is the fact that considerably more deterioration is evidenced in those cases where relatives are blamed as opposed to those who are not blamed. Similar differences in deterioration effects are found between blaming the older and younger generations although the difference does not result in a statistically significant effect.

Previously we found that parental coping behavior was related to blame placing; moreover, we found that child's age was importantly related to at least one locus of blame, the child's peers. Such findings, when considered with those just presented, indicate that blame placing is an important and a complex factor in short-term behavior change.

Marital Harmony

Here we present three indexes of marital harmony, each representing an ordinal scale: (1) respondent's prestructured estimate of the extent of happiness in the parents' marriage, (2) extent of marital agreement based on eleven "yes-no" items, and (3) extent of parental agreement on child-rearing practices based on eight four-point items designed to tap child-rearing agreement. (See table 6-9.)

In examining the relationships between the marital harmony variables and the authority dimension for guidance-clinic cases, we found that only the respondent's estimate of extent of marital happiness attains statistical significance. This is due to the greater amount of movement from undesirable to improved behavior among the children of the "very happily" married in contrast to the experience of those less happy in their marriages. On the neurotic dimension, none of the three indexes of harmony shows a substantial relationship.

The court-clinic cases present a different picture. Here there is no relationship between respondent's estimate of marital happiness and the authority dimension, but there is one between the extent of marital agreement and change as shown on the authority dimension. Respondents who report much marital agreement experience considerable improvement in their children, while those reporting less agreement experience no improvement in their children's behavior. We emphasize, however, that the numbers are small of those reporting little or some agreement. Another interesting difference between court- and guidance-clinic cases is presented when we observe the relationship between agreement on child-rearing practices and change on the authority dimension. For guidance-clinic cases, there was hardly any association at all, while for court-clinic cases there was an inverse relationship. That is, the more the parents agreed on child-rearing practices, the less likely the child was to show any improvement. Here it seems important for parents of children referred to court clinics to debate and to question each other's child-rearing philosophy as it applies to children who have violated the law. In this case, it would seem that one parent would have to take the lead in forcing a change in their child-rearing practices, and a change that can have important and beneficial effects for the children.

The last important difference between the court- and guidance-clinic cases here is with respect to the neurotic dimension. Although there were no differences for guidance-clinic cases on this dimension, there is a difference for court-clinic cases between the extent of marital agreement and change in the child's neurotic behavior: respondents who reported much marital agreement had fewer cases of deterioration when contrasted with parents reporting less marital agreement. Again, however, the small number of court case parents reporting little or some agreement requires cautious interpretation.

The Social Network

The last set of factors concerns three measures of social participation: visits with relatives, frequency of church attendance, and a combined measure of social isolation. The relationships between these variables and our dimensions of change are presented in table 6–10.

None of the measures of social participation is related to either dimension of change for guidance-clinic cases, but four of the six cross-tabulations show a statistically significant association for court-clinic cases, with all four being in the anticipated direction. Apart from our surprise at the lack of significant relationships for guidance-clinic cases, the major unexpected finding was presented in the court-clinic data for visiting relatives. Surprisingly, respondents who reported rare visits with relatives also reported the most improvement and least deterioration on the authority dimension ($p < .10$). This finding, however, at least for court-clinic cases, is quite consistent with the data presented in table 6–8 where we saw that far less improvement was reported in the cases where relatives had been blamed for the child's presenting problem. On the other measures of social participation, the court-clinic respondents who attended church regularly and who reported the most extensive (voluntary) social network also reported

Table 6-9
Marital Harmony and Change in Observance of Rules of Authority and Neurotic Behavior

	Authority[a]					Neurotic[b]				
	Improved	Unchanged (+)	Unchanged (−)	Deteriorated	100% =	Improved	Unchanged (+)	Unchanged (−)	Deteriorated	100% =
Guidance clinics										
Respondent estimate of marital happiness										
Very happy	17.7	57.8	18.4	6.1	147	26.4	48.4	21.4	3.8	159
Happy	15.2	42.4	34.8	7.6	66	17.8	39.7	35.6	6.9	73
Unhappy	19.1	38.3	36.2	6.4	47	27.5	41.2	23.5	7.8	51

Authority: $X^2 = 11.5$, 6 df, ns; K. tau (C) = .10, $p < .05$; no information in 13 cases

Neurotic: $X^2 = .8.51$, 6 df, ns; K. tau (C) = .08, ns; no information in 14 cases

	Improved	Unchanged (+)	Unchanged (−)	Deteriorated	100% =	Improved	Unchanged (+)	Unchanged (−)	Deteriorated	100% =
Extent of marital agreement										
Little	23.8	47.6	28.6	—	21	18.2	54.5	27.3	—	—
Some	22.6	45.2	25.8	6.4	31	31.4	34.3	20.0	14.3	35
Much	16.8	52.0	24.4	6.8	221	24.2	45.8	25.8	4.2	240

Authority: $X^2 = 2.8$, 6 df, ns; K. tau (C) = .03, ns

Neurotic: $X^2 = 10.3$, 6 df, ns; K. tau (C) = −.00, ns; no information in 22 cases

	Improved	Unchanged (+)	Unchanged (−)	Deteriorated	100% =	Improved	Unchanged (+)	Unchanged (−)	Deteriorated	100% =
Extent of agreement in child-rearing practices										
Nearly always	17.1	63.2	15.8	3.9	76	25.0	50.0	20.0	5.0	80
Substantial agreement	15.4	48.1	26.9	9.6	104	25.0	41.4	28.4	5.2	116
Frequent disagreement	19.4	43.1	31.9	5.6	72	23.3	46.8	24.7	5.2	77

Authority: $X^2 = 10.9$, 6 df, ns; K. tau (C) = .08, ns; no information in 21 cases.

Neurotic: $X^2 = 2.24$, 6 df, ns; K. tau (C) = .03, ns; no information in 24 cases.

Court clinics

Respondent estimate of marital happiness					
Very happy	8.8	47.8	13.0	30.4	23
Happy	5.9	64.7	23.5	5.9	17
Unhappy	—	25.0	8.3	66.7	12

$X^2 = 13.0$, 6 df, $p < .05$; K. tau (C) = .19, ns; no information in 3 cases

Extent of marital agreement					
Little	—	66.7	33.3	—	3
Some	—	—	—	100.0	6
Much	6.5	54.4	17.4	21.7	46

$X^2 = 17.6$, 6 df, $p < .01$; K. tau (C) = −.18, $p < .05$

Extent of agreement on child-rearing practices					
Nearly always	4.5	36.4	18.2	40.9	22
Substantial agreement	7.9	61.5	23.1	7.7	13
Frequent disagreement	5.9	52.9	5.9	35.3	17

$X^2 = 6.05$, 6 df, ns; K. tau (C) = −.13, ns; no information in 3 cases

Respondent estimate of marital happiness					
Very happy	21.8	30.4	30.4	17.4	23
Happy	29.4	47.1	17.6	5.9	17
Unhappy	16.7	8.3	41.7	33.3	12

$X^2 = 8.45$, 6 df, ns; K. tau (C) = .09, ns; no information in 3 cases

Extent of marital agreement					
Little	—	66.7	33.3	—	3
Some	—	—	50.0	50.0	6
Much	26.1	34.8	26.1	13.0	46

$X^2 = 11.43$, 6 df, ns; K. tau (C) = −.18, $p < .05$

Extent of agreement on child-rearing practices					
Nearly always	9.1	27.2	36.4	27.3	22
Substantial agreement	23.1	46.1	23.1	7.7	13
Frequent disagreement	35.3	29.4	23.5	11.8	17

$X^2 = 7.12$, 6 df, ns; K. tau (C) = −.29, $p < .05$

[a]$N = 273$ in guidance-clinic cases, and $N = 55$ in court-clinic cases.
[b]$N = 297$ in guidance-clinic cases, and $N = 55$ in court-clinic cases.

Table 6-10
Social Networks and Changes in Observance of Rules of Authority and Neurotic Behavior

	Authority[a]					Neurotic[b]				
	Improved	Unchanged (+)	Unchanged (−)	Deteriorated	100% =	Improved	Unchanged (+)	Unchanged (−)	Deteriorated	100% =
Guidance clinics										
Visits relatives										
Rarely	18.7	48.4	26.6	6.3	64	28.3	41.8	26.9	3.0	67
Sometimes	11.9	55.3	28.9	3.9	76	24.1	45.8	22.9	7.2	83
Frequently	20.1	50.0	21.8	8.1	124	22.4	46.4	26.1	5.1	138

$X^2 = 4.62$, 6 df, ns; K. tau (C) = −.03, ns; no information in 9 cases $X^2 = 2.45$, 6 df, ns; K. tau (C) = .03, ns; no information in 9 cases

	Authority[a]					Neurotic[b]				
	Improved	Unchanged (+)	Unchanged (−)	Deteriorated	100% =	Improved	Unchanged (+)	Unchanged (−)	Deteriorated	100% =
Frequency of church attendance last month										
None or once (0–1)	16.6	49.2	29.2	5.0	120	25.7	39.0	28.7	6.6	136
Fairly regularly (2–3)	19.1	53.2	21.3	6.4	47	25.6	52.9	17.6	3.9	51
Regularly (4)	16.7	50.0	25.0	8.3	48	22.4	53.2	22.4	2.0	49
Devout (5 or more)	15.6	53.3	22.2	8.9	45	23.4	42.6	27.6	6.4	47

$X^2 = 2.56$, 9 df, ns; K. tau (C) = −.00, ns; no information in 13 cases $X^2 = 6.55$, 9 df, ns; K. tau = −.02, ns; no information in 14 cases

	Authority[a]					Neurotic[b]				
	Improved	Unchanged (+)	Unchanged (−)	Deteriorated	100% =	Improved	Unchanged (+)	Unchanged (−)	Deteriorated	100% =
Social isolation scale										
Isolate	15.4	53.8	23.1	7.7	26	13.3	56.7	30.0	—	30
Visits friends only	18.3	45.0	30.0	6.7	120	27.3	40.9	25.0	6.8	132
Either clubs or hobbies and friends	16.9	56.5	21.0	5.6	124	24.3	46.2	25.0	4.5	132

$X^2 = 3.96$, 6 df, ns; K. tau (C) = .05, ns; no information in 3 cases $X^2 = 6.03$, 6 df, ns; K. tau = −.2, ns; no information in 3 cases

	Guidance clinic				N	Court clinic				N
Court clinics										
Visits relatives										
Rarely	28.6	42.9	19.0	9.5	21	—	61.9	14.3	23.8	21
Sometimes	25.0	16.7	25.0	33.3	12	—	33.3	16.7	50.0	12
Regularly	15.8	26.3	42.1	15.8	19	15.8	42.1	15.8	26.3	19

$X^2 = 7.09$, 6 df, ns; K. tau (C) = .19, $p < .10$; no information in 3 cases

$X^2 = 8.66$, 6 df, ns; K. tau (C) = −.02, ns; no information in 3 cases

Frequency of church attendance										
None or once	12.5	29.2	20.8	37.5	24	—	33.3	16.7	50.0	24
Fairly regularly	14.2	42.9	42.9	—	7	—	71.4	—	28.6	7
Regularly	38.4	30.8	30.8	—	13	15.4	53.8	23.1	7.7	13
Devout	20.0	20.0	60.0	—	5	—	60.0	20.0	20.0	5

$X^2 = 15.36$, 9 df, $p < .10$; K. tau = −.25, $p < .05$; no information in 6 cases

$X^2 = 14.2$, 9 df, ns; K. tau (C) = −.28, $p < .01$; no information in 6 cases

Social isolation scale										
Isolate	20.0	—	40.0	40.0	5	—	20.0	20.0	60.0	5
Visit friends only	17.1	37.2	28.6	17.1	35	2.8	48.6	14.3	34.3	35
Either clubs or hobbies and friends	33.3	33.3	25.0	8.4	12	16.7	58.3	16.7	8.3	12

$X^2 = 5.28$, 6 df, ns; K. tau (C) = −.19, $p < .05$; no information in 3 cases

$X^2 = 7.96$, 6 df, ns; K. tau (C) = −.27, $p < .01$; no information in 3 cases

[a] $N = 273$ in guidance-clinic cases and $N = 55$ in court-clinic cases.
[b] $N = 297$ in guidance-clinic cases and $N = 55$ in court-clinic cases.

the most improvement and the least deterioration on each of the two change measures.

Several important conclusions may be presented about these data on social networks. The first is that the conflicting findings for familial and social interactions not only underscore the quality component in these networks but emphasize the complementary roles that family and social interactions probably play.[7] This is more apparent for the court-clinic cases, where, perhaps, the informal sources of assistance are of critical importance in problem solving. Our second statement about the social network pertains to the guidance-clinic families where there was an absence of relationships. Perhaps these families have other resources available to them that are more crucial in affecting their children's behavior: money and educational achievements, which permit them some independence from family and social networks. Perhaps guidance-clinic families either attempt to find the professional help they think is required or rely on their own perceived ability to cope, unaided by others. In any case, these findings, with respect to social and family networks suggest that a number of factors, different ones for guidance- and court-clinic cases, are involved in a complex relationship with the changes in the children's behavior.

Combined Measure of Change

Now that we have presented data on outcome in a simple form, we will introduce a combined measure constructed from our two change dimensions. Such a measure brings us back to the notion recently emphasized by Strupp and his associates that not only should we include deterioration effects in the consideration of outcome but we should beware that an individual may show positive change in one aspect of functioning and retrogress in another area.[8] Our combined measure will amplify this feature of change.

Before we present our combined measure, we would like to discuss a related problem. By the time of our 1963 interview, twenty-five of the children in our study group had been placed in detention. Of these, twenty-two were court-clinic cases. Initially interviewers had been instructed not to administer the symptoms checklist assessing behavior just prior to the time of the interview if the child was in detention since it was felt that respondents would be reluctant to discuss the child's behavior if he were in detention. We were afraid, in particular, that such parents would be annoyed that their child was in detention and so might not wish to admit the possibility that the child "deserved" detention. Our pilot interviews showed that we were wrong and that the parents of detained children were not reluctant to discuss the child's behavior around the time of detention. Our interviewers were instructed, in those cases where the child had been placed in detention during the year's interval (between contact with the clinic and the time of the interview), to administer the symptoms checklist and to request the respondent to indicate the child's behavior just prior to detention. Thus we were able to ascertain the nature of the child's behavior over time (as indexed on our change dimensions) and to ascertain the relationship of this behavior to detention status. The question then was the extent of the correlation between the two and whether a separate analysis of detention was required.

The answer is that being in detention appears to be strongly predicted by the child's behavior on each dimension. Among court-clinic cases where twenty-two of the twenty-five detention cases are found, every one of the twenty-two was in one of the two cells that indicated the presence of undesirable behavior ("unchanged" or "deteriorated") on both change dimensions. On the Kendall test, the association was .91 and .90, respectively, on the authority and neurotic dimensions for court-clinic cases. These associations also mean that in most (90 percent) court-clinic cases where behavior was undesirable on both of the two change measures, the child was in detention.[9] Among guidance-clinic cases, all three of the cases in detention exhibited undesirable behavior on both change measures; however, the association was not as strong as in the case for court clinics as the large majority of guidance-clinic cases whose behavior was undesirable on both dimensions were not in detention. This overlap between behavior and detention suggested that we did not have to present a separate analysis for detention cases since they were nearly always included in the change categories reflecting undesirable behavior.

We wonder, of course, if the court-clinic children were tagged as "bad" after they were placed in detention. We cannot answer this question. If, indeed, they were tagged as guilty of undesirable behavior after they were detained, they were tagged by their parents and not by court or court-clinic authorities. It is possible that some parents gave up on their children and that the court was aware of such negative attitudes and decided that the child might be better off if he were sent into detention. Such parents might then have rationalized this decision by indicating that the child's behavior was such as to justify detention. In Goffman-like terms then, the detention decision might actually have been instigated by the child's close relatives.[10] This is speculation, of course, because we do not know enough about the dynamics of detention for these children. Indeed we think that many parents would be concerned that their child was in detention and regretted that such action had been taken. Moreover, all of the court-clinic cases that had been charged with law violations, were known to the authorities, and could have been placed in detention because of new or additional legal infractions. A range of speculations could be applied to our finding. We will simply accept the notion that being placed in detention was not independent of the child's behavior; thus we have decided not to present separate analysis of detention cases. The irony, perhaps, is that for court-clinic cases we can identify 90 percent of the detention cases from the change scores. We now wish to examine the cross-tabulation of the authority change and neurotic change dimensions (table 6-11).

Table 6-11 shows how we obtained our combined index of change. In the table each of the two subtables (guidance and court) is divided into four quadrants. For guidance clinics, the three detention cases are located in the lower-right quadrant, but for court-clinic cases, all of the twenty-two cases in this quadrant were in detention by the time of our interview. The two dimensions are strongly related, with more independence evidenced for guidance-clinic cases than court-clinic cases. These four quadrants—for each type of clinic—represent the four categories in the combined index of change. The number in parentheses in each quadrant represents the score assigned to the categories in the combined index. Analysis of table 6-11 shows that guidance clinics have more cases in the symptom-free quadrant (quadrant 1) than do court clinics (57 percent to 50 percent), while court clinics have more cases in quadrant 4, where the most undesirable behavior is located (40 percent to 15 percent). Beyond this, there is little to choose between quadrants 2 and 3. Quadrant 2 contains those children whose behavior appears acceptable on the authority index but is undesirable on the neurotic index; the opposite is true for quadrant 3. Some readers may disagree with this ordering, but we believe that antisocial behavior would seem more likely to concern and involve a wider circle of people than would neurotic behavior. Relationships (Kendall's tau) between our independent variables and this combined index of change are presented in table 6-12.

The analysis of the tau coefficients presented in table 6-12 shows clearly that our variables are differentially related to the combined change index for guidance- and court-clinic cases. For example, among the twenty-six independent variables, eleven have a statistically significant relationship for guidance clinics and six for court clinics. The important revelation, however, is that in only two cases (both in the area of blame attribution) do these significant relationships apply to both types of clinics. Another interesting difference is shown by the fact that coefficient signs ($+ -$) are in opposite directions for the two types of clinics in eleven of the twenty-six cases. For example, relationships between authoritarianism and change are $+12$ ($p < .01$) and -12 (ns) for guidance and court cases, respectively. Apparently nonauthoritarian persons have more success with children in guidance-clinic cases while high-authoritarian respondents had the most success with children among court-clinic cases. Other intriguing examples of sign divergence appear for frustration, child's age, number of years waited before the clinic contact, the marital agreement index, and visiting with relatives.

Table 6-11
Cross-Tabulation of Authority Change and Neurotic Change Dimensions

Authority Change	Improved		Neurotic Change Unchanged (+)		Unchanged (−)		Deterio- rated		100% =
	N	%	N	%	N	%	N	%	
Guidance clinics									
Improvement	(1) 19	38.8	24	49.0	(2) 6	12.2	—	—	49
Unchanged (+)	33	23.8	79	56.8	26	18.7	1	0.7	139
Unchanged (−)	(3) 15	22.1	18	26.5	(4) 28	41.2	7	10.2	68
Deteriorated	1	5.9	9	52.9	6	35.3	1	5.9	17
	68		130		66		9		273
Court Clinics									
Improved	(1) 1	8.3	10	83.4	(2) 1	8.3	—	—	12
Unchanged (+)	1	5.6	15	83.2	1	5.6	1	5.6	18
Unchanged (−)	(3) 1	6.2	2	12.5	(4) 6	37.5	7	43.8	16
Deteriorated	—	—	—	—	1	11.1	8	88.9	9
	3		27		9		16		55

Note: N = 273 for guidance-clinics and N = 55 for court clinics.

Table 6-12
Relationships (Kendall's Tau) between Independent Variables and
Combined Index of Change

Independent Variables	Guidance Clinics (N = 273)	Court Clinics (N = 55)	Code
Problem solving			
Earlier help sought (prior to 1962)	.07	.26	0 = none, 1 = nonpsychiatric, 2 = psychiatric
Subsequent help sought (between 1962-1963)	.05	.15	0 = none, 1 = nonpsychiatric, 2 = psychiatric
Number of years waited before entering clinic (in 1962)	− .00	.30*	1 = 1 year or less, 2 = more than 1 year
Background factors			
Mother's age in 1963	− 12**	− .12	1 = under 40 years, 2 = 40–49, 3 = and up
Mother's marital status in 1963	.05	.01	1 = married, 2 = Divorced, widowed or never married, 3 = separated
Mother's race	− .04	− .16	1 = black, 2 = white
Warren's Index of Status Characteristics, 1963	.04	.04	1 = upper class, 2 = middle class, 3 = lower class
Mother's religion[a]	.10*	− .02	1 = Jewish, 2 = Protestant, 3 = Catholic
Child's age in 1963	− .14**	− .02	1 = preschool, 2 = latency (6–10), 3 = early adolescence (11–12), 4 = middle adolescence (13–15), 5 = late adolescence (16 = 18)
Child's sex	.14**	.05	1 = male, 2 = female
Personality factors (respondents)			
Authoritarianism	.12**	− .12	1 = low, 2 = medium, 3 = high
Anomia	.04	.02	1 = low, 2 = medium, 3 = high
Frustration	.13***	− .06	1 = low, 2 = medium, 3 = high
Rigidity	.09*	− .01	1 = low, 2 = medium, 3 = high
Withdrawal	.02	.02	1 = low, 2 = medium, 3 = high
Attribution of blame (respondent)			
Blames self	− .16**	− .07	1 = yes, 2 = no
Blames relatives	− .18***	− .31**	1 = yes, 2 = no

Table 6–12 continued

Independent Variables	Guidance Clinics (N = 273)	Court Clinics (N = 55)	Code
Blames child's peers	.07	.02	1 = yes, 2 = no
Blames child	.01	.10	1 = yes, 2 = no
Combined index of blame	− .10*	− .20*	1 = older generation, 2 = younger generation, 3 = fate, don't know, or no response
Marital harmony			
Respondent's estimate of mental happiness	.15**	.12	1 = very happy, 2 = happy, 3 = unhappy
Respondent's score on 11-item marital agreement index	.01	− .16*	1 = little agreement, 2 = some agreement, 3 = much agreement
Parental agreement on child rearing	.15**	− .30*	1 = nearly always agree, 2 = substantial agreement, 3 = frequent disagreement
Social network			
Visits with relatives (last month)	− .03	.15	1 = none or rarely, 2 = sometimes, 3 = often (more than once a week)
Church attendance (last month)	− .03	− .17	1 = None or rarely, 2 = fairly regularly, 3 = frequently, 4 = devout (more than weekly)
Social isolation scale	− .04	− .20*	0 = no friends, clubs, or hobbies, 1 = friends only, 2 = participants in clubs or hobbies and sees friends

  * = $p < .05$
 ** = $p < .01$
*** = $p < .001$
[a]No Jews in court clinics.

There is one interesting similarity here: for both types of clinic, the strongest relationship involves blaming relatives for the problem. In each case when relatives are blamed, the child's behavior was more often reported to be undesirable than when relatives were not blamed.

Coefficients of association do not tell very much when relationships are not linear. We are unable to present cross-tabular tables for these relationships in table 6–12, so we have selected one of the independent variables for cross-tabular presentation: mother's marital status. This variable is of theoretical importance in our study and had a somewhat curvilinear association with the combined index of change (see table 6–13).

Table 6–13
Mother's Marital Status versus Combined Index of Change

	Marital Status		
Combined Index[a]	Married	Divorced, Widowed, or Never Married	Separated
Guidance clinics[b]			
Quadrant 1	57.3	62.2	40.0
Quadrant 2	12.4	13.8	8.0
Quadrant 3	16.1	10.3	20.0
Quadrant 4	13.9	13.7	32.0
100% =	217	29	25 271
Court Clinics			
Quadrant 1	43.8	76.9	30.0
Quadrant 2	6.2	7.7	—
Quadrant 3	6.2	7.7	—
Quadrant 4	43.8	7.7	70.0
100% =	32	13	10 55

[a]Quadrant 1 = acceptable on both authority and neurosis; quadrant 2 = acceptable on authority but not on neurosis; quadrant 3 = acceptable on neurosis but not on authority; quadrant 4 = undesirable on both authority and neurosis.
[b]Two cases with no information on marital status.

In table 6–13 for guidance-clinic cases, some curvilinearity is evident across the top row. The divorced, widowed, or never-married respondents (only one never-married respondent) report the most acceptable behavior, followed by married persons, and last, the separated. The separated parents, conversely, more often report their children's behavior as undesirable on both change dimensions. We suggested earlier that the separated respondents probably live under the most unsettled conditions and that the attendant anxieties may have negative consequences for both their coping ability and for their children.

With respect to court-clinic cases, these trends are exaggerated. There is curvilinearity, with the married respondents taking the middle position between the high frequency of quadrant 1 placements for the divorced, widowed, and never married and the low frequency of such placement for the separated. Somewhat surprisingly, then, married respondents have less success than those who are ex-marrieds, widowed, or never married (only one respondent reported never having been married). These findings sustain the notion held by some social scientists that the quality of a marriage may be more important than whether a home is broken. Thus it seems that certain factors, such as marital happiness and agreement on ways of running the home and rearing the children, may be interacting with the structural features of the home. Ironically it is possible that two redeeming features of a broken marriage may be that there are no longer husband-wife disagreements over daily decisions and happiness with one's spouse ceases to be a concern except in cases like separation where the relationship continues after it is physically terminated.

These complex issues demand a more complex analysis than have been presented so far. Thus we have undertaken regression analysis in order to ascertain the relative importance of our various independent variables in the explication of change. In doing so, we took steps to minimize the confusion that could have resulted from an inclusion of variables like marital status that have a nonlinear relationship to change. The precautions to be taken are necessitated by the assumptions underlying regression analysis, with perhaps the most important of these being that variables are measured on a continuous scale. For this reason, we employ continuous variables whenever posssible. In the case of marital status, a nominal variable, we employ two dummy variables: separated versus all other marriage categories and divorced, widowed, or never married versus all other marriage categories.

The Regression Analysis

In this analysis we attempted to isolate which variables would most clearly help us explain short-term outcome. The zero-order analyses presented so far cannot indicate the most powerful of the variables for purposes of explanation. Thus we turned to regression analysis in order to ascertain the combined as well as the individual power of our independent variables in accounting for variation in our outcome measures. We had two aims with respect to assessment of outcome: to ascertain the power of a given independent variable when other variables are controlled and to ascertain the power of a given combination of variables in the explanation of outcome.

The dependent variables in the regression analysis are somewhat different from those employed in the cross-tabular analysis presented above where we utilized three measures of change: relations to authority, neurotic behavior, and a combined index of change. Now we employ two outcome measures best described as measures of adjustment. These two adjustment measures, first presented in table 6-1, are the two Guttman scales that tap relations to authority and neurotic behavior at two points in time: 1962 and 1963. Our change measures were derived from combining the two scales presented in tables 6-2 and 6-3. The assignment of scores to the change categories would be somewhat arbitrary, especially since "no change" often was as complex as "change." Thus, for example, it is debatable as to whether "deterioration" is more undesirable than the (unchanged) manifestation of undesirable behavior at two points in time. Indeed the advantage of our cross-tabular analysis was that it permitted an examination of categories without being constrained by the arbitrary assignment of numbers. However, if we are to carry the analysis to a higher level and attempt to assess the relative power of our independent variables, it is essential that the dependent (outcome) measures should be unambiguous, continuous variables, attributes that do not describe our change measures. For this reason we chose to employ the child's adjustment (behavior) at the time of the 1963 interview as the basis for our outcome measures and use the 1962 scale scores as independent variables. The Guttman scales seemed to contain the qualities that we wished our measures of outcome to have.

We also decided that the results of our use of the combined index (where we combined the two dimensions of relation to authority and neurotic behavior) argue against the presentation of a combined index in the report of our regression analysis. Specifically a number of the independent variables are related differently to the two dimensions, and the combined analysis washed out many of the relationships that existed in the more refined analysis.

Twelve independent variables appear in the reported regression analysis. A series of regression analyses were, in fact, undertaken as we sought to eliminate the variables that did not heighten our understanding. Our first analysis involved twenty independent variables, including those that either showed a substantial relationship to one of our two change measures in the cross-tabular analyses or were of theoretical importance in our study. The second regression analysis involved fourteen independent variables, and the third one (the results of which are presented here) had twelve variables.

These twelve independent variables, listed in table 6–14, include indexes of the respondent's cognitive processes, coping resources, and coping behavior. A comparison of the variables listed in tables 6–4 and 6–14 will reveal those variables that, based on cross-tabular and the first two regression analyses, appeared only weakly related to outcome and so were omitted from the analysis reported here.

The results of the third set of regression analyses, involving our two adjustment measures (child's behavior at the time of the 1963 interview, approximately one year after the clinic contact) and the twelve independent variables are presented in table 6–15. The individual coefficients reflect the explanatory power of one independent variable when the effects of the other variables are controlled. The combined power of the independent variables is reflected in the table note.

We present both *B*'s and the beta coefficients in the regression table. We are presenting *B* coefficients (unstandardized regression coefficients) since they reflect the natural metric of our variables and we believe this metric is interpretable in our analysis. The unstandardized regression coefficients allow us to make some comparisons between guidance- and court-

Table 6-14
Independent Variables Used in Regression Analyses of 1963 Adjustment

Variables	Code Categories
Warner's Index of Status Characteristics (social class)	1-9, with 9 high
Child's age, Jan. 1, 1963	1-18 years (numbers)
Blames relatives for child's problems	0 = no, 1 = yes
Blames child's peers for child's problems	0 = no, 1 = yes
Authoritarianism (five-item summary scale)	0 = not authoritarian, 5 = high on authoritarianism
Frustration (four-item summary scale)	0 = not frustrated, 4 = high on frustration
Social isolation scale (three-item cumulative scale based on visiting with friends, participation in clubs, and participation in social hobbies)	0 = sees no friends and does not participate in clubs or hobbies, 1 = sees friends but does not participate in clubs or hobbies, 2 = either participates in clubs or social hobbies or both and typically has friends
Type of help sought subsequent to 1962 agency contact and prior to 1963 interview	1 = none, 2 = nonpsychiatric, 3 = psychiatric
Respondent is separated?	0 = no, 1 = yes
Respondent is divorced, widowed, or never married?	0 = no, 1 = yes
Child's sex	0 = male, 1 = female
1962 Guttman score on the symptoms scale, Relations to Authority or Neurotic, depending on dependent variable	1 = Guttman score of 0, 4 = Guttman score of 3

clinic cases. We are presenting the beta coefficients (standardized regression coefficients) because they will permit us to assess the relative strength of our variables within type of clinic. In fact, we emphasize the beta coefficients since we are primarily interested in the relationships within each type of clinic.

First of all, we would like to call the reader's attention to the overall variance (r^2) accounted for by our predictor variables. In each of the four overall results presented in table 6-15, a fair amount of the variance is accounted for. Indeed in each case, the overall F test shows that a statistically significant amount of variance is accounted for by our independent variables, with the results being more impressive for guidance clinics as opposed to the court clinics.

Table 6-15
Standardized and Unstandardized Regression Coefficients of Child's Short-Term Outcome on Twelve Independent Variables

	Authority				Neurotic			
	Guidance		Court		Guidance		Court	
	B	Beta	B	Beta	B	Beta	B	Beta
Social class	-.01	-.02	-.14	-.15	.05	.09	-.05	-.05
Child's age, Jan. 1, 1963	-.02	-.07	.07	.12	-.04*	-.13	.03	.05
Blames relatives	.27*	.13	.63	.22	.13	.06	.55	.18
Blames peers	.01	.00	.18	.06	-.21	-.05	.04	.01
Authoritarianism scale	.08*	.12	-.24	-.27	.03	.05	-.25	-.27
Frustration scale	.11*	.11	-.14	-.14	.13*	.13	-.11	-.10
Social isolation scale	.05	.04	-.89*	-.38	-.02	-.01	-.99*	-.39
Subsequent help sought	.14*	.12	.24	.16	-.03	-.02	.11	.07
Respondent is separated	.00	.00	.67	.19	.08	.02	.81	.22
Respondent is divorced or widowed	-.26	-.08	-.43	-.14	-.11	-.03	-.47	-.14
Child's sex	-.17	-.18	.70	.25	.00	.00	.57	.19
Symptom scale score (1962)	.44***	.47	.39*	.34	.40***	.41	.45*	.29
	Overall F = 12.33; df = 12/250, p < .001; r² = .37, adjusted r² = .34		Overall F = 2.34; df = 12/37; p < .05; r² = .45, adjusted r² = .26		Overall F = 6.95; df = 12/272, p < .001; r² = .23, adjusted r² = .20		Overall F = 2.15; df = 12/37 p < .05; r² = .43, adjusted r² = .23	

Note: On the F test, significance levels are indicated as follows: * = p < .05, ** = p < .01, *** = p < .001.

Authority Dimension

Focusing on the guidance clinics, it is easily apparent that the most powerful predictor among all of the independent variables is the child's symptomatic behavior in 1962. Perhaps this is not surprising, given the fact that a fairly short time span existed between the two points in time for which respondents indicated the child's behavior. On the authority dimension, in addition to the 1962 symptom score, blaming relatives, seeking help, and respondent scores on the measures of frustration and authoritarianism each account for a significant amount of variance when the other variables are controlled. More specifically, the child appears to have a low symptom score (fewer symptoms) in 1963 when the following conditions exist: relatives are not blamed for the problem, respondent is low on frustration and authoritarianism, the child had a low score on the authority dimension in 1962, and psychiatric help was not sought during the year after clinic contact was made. In connection with help-seeking, it seems fair to surmise that parents may be more inclined to call a psychiatric professional when the child exhibits difficulty in obeying the rules of authority than when other behavior is manifested. If this is so, and it is certainly one interpretation of the finding, then psychiatric professionals (psychiatrists, psychologists, and social workers) frequently would see some of the more recalcitrant or difficult cases. A competing hypothesis is that those who received psychiatric assistance responded negatively to the intervention. The fact that the data on help-seeking between 1962–1963 and the 1963 outcome data were both obtained during our 1963 interviews makes it imperative that we delay drawing conclusions about this relationship until we have analyzed the long-term data (1975–1976).

The children of divorced, widowed, or never-married women exhibited substantially fewer symptoms in 1963 than did children whose parents were married or separated. This result, while not statistically significant, is consistent with the direction of this association found at the zero level and reported in table 6–6.

Focusing on the court clinics, we observe that the overall *F* shows that a statistically significant amount of the variance is accounted for by the array of independent variables, though only the .05 level of significance is attained. Turning to the power of the individual variables, only two independent variables account for a significant portion of the variance when all other independent variables are controlled: the respondent's social isolation score and the child's score on the 1962 authority scale, with the former being the stronger. Parents who were the most sociable and whose children were low scorers on the 1962 authority scale were more likely than their counterparts to report low scores on the 1963 scale. Other variables that appear to be influential, though not statistically significant, when the other independent variables are controlled include child's sex, mother's marital status, blame attribution, and help-seeking. As was the case for guidance clinics, not getting psychiatric help appeared to result in better adjustment for the child with respect to observance of rules of authority. However, this relationship may mean that the court-clinic parents sought psychiatric help only when they felt their child's behavior was undesirable and/or deteriorating. We are unwilling to guess as to the interpretation at this point because the short-term data do not reveal a precise ordering of events.

Just as intriguing and equally hazardous is the issue of the relationship between marital status and short-term outcome. Although one can speculate that marriages that end (divorce or widowhood) spur the surviving mother to take effective action when contrasted with those still married or separated, it is wise to acknowledge that this is just speculation. We do not know when the status of divorce or widowhood was attained; the marriage could have ended during the period between our two measures of the child's behavior and thus support the speculation offered above, or the marriage could have ended before the child's behavior became a problem in 1962 and make it unwise to assume that the termination of the marriage bond is related to the child's behavior in 1963.

Neurotic Dimension

For the guidance-clinic cases, the overall F is significant at the .001 level on the 1963 neurotic scale, the same level as was reached on the 1963 authority scale. However, the r^2 of .23 on the 1963 neurotic scale is somewhat lower than the r^2 of .37 on the 1963 authority scale. As might be expected from this difference in overall amount of explained variance, only three of the twelve individual variables account for a significant amount of the neurotic scale variance when all other independent variables are controlled, whereas five were so productive on the authority scale. Once again, the most powerful of the individual variables, for guidance clinics, is the child's symptomatic behavior in 1962. (Beta coefficient is .41.) The other two significant predictors of the child's 1963 score on the neurotic scale are child's age and the respondent's score on the frustration scale. That is, the child's neurotic symptoms scale score tended to be lower for respondents who scored low on the frustration scale and for the older children. Examining the B coefficients, the decrement seemed to amount to .04 symptoms for each additional year of age. Thus, a fifteen-year-old child would have, on average, four-tenths fewer symptoms than a five-year-old.

The role of age may become clearer if the relationship between neurotic change and child's age presented in table 6–6, is reexamined. While the neurotic change variable employed in the cross-tabulation is somewhat different from the Guttman scale employed in the regression analysis, one can probably more clearly see there the importance of the developmental process. Maturation indeed seems to be an important factor in the dimension of neurotic behavior, with the largest decrease in neurotic behavior apparently taking place as soon as the child enters school. Indeed if spontaneous remission were to have any meaning in the explanation of change or outcome, it would seem to be largely limited to the indication of maturation.

Among court-clinic cases, the overall F is significant at the .05 level of significance for the neurotic scale, the same level found on the authority scale. Yet another parallel is that the same two independent variables appear as significant in examining the power of the individual variables with all other variables controlled: respondent's social isolation score and the child's score on the 1962 symptom scale. Once more, the social isolation scale score seems the more powerful of the two, taking the beta coefficient as well as the individual F score into account. We surmise from this that the social network is especially vital to the coping strategy employed by the court-clinic families.

Discussion of Regression Analysis

The ony statistically significant predictor variable common to both guidance- and court-clinic cases is the child's symptomatic behavior in 1962. Thus it is clear that we are dealing with two rather different populations and that it was probably wise to have maintained the separate analyses of them. The two types are probably most noticeably different in the matter of the social network variable: court-clinic cases are strongly affected by the extent to which respondent-parents are engaged in voluntary social activities, while the behavior of guidance-clinic children in 1963 appears little affected by the parent's voluntary social engagement. This difference between the two types of cases is intensified when one examines other variables. Thus the respondents' scores on frustration account for a significant amount of the variance when other factors are controlled among guidance-clinic cases; among court-clinic cases, this factor is not only not significant but the sign is reversed. Among guidance-clinic cases, respondents who are frustrated are likelier than nonfrustrated parents to have children who score high on both 1963 outcomes measures; but among court-clinic cases, there is a tendency for more-frustrated parents to report a smaller number of symptoms than the less frustrated. A similar reversal of signs is shown for authoritarianism.

The other major observation about the regression analysis concerns the differences between the two outcome dimensions. There are only two statistically significant variables that are common to both 1963 outcomes scales for each type of clinic case. One of these, the child's symptomatic behavior in 1962, applies to both types of clinic. For guidance-clinic cases, the other common variable is respondent's score on the frustration scale, and for court-clinic cases, the variable that is significant on both dimensions of short-term outcome is the respondent's social isolation score. The small number of court-clinic cases is probably responsible for the small number of significant common factors found for the court cases; thus blaming relatives and marital status appear fairly strong and will continue to warrant our attention.

For the guidance clinics, variables unique to a dimension are child's age on the neurotic dimension and blaming relatives, authoritarianism, and subsequent help sought on the authority dimension. Although no startling impressions emerge as a result of the unique variables, it nevertheless is of some importance that there appears to be confirmation of the existence of two independent dimensions for the guidance clinics. This is in contrast to the case for the court clinics and is further confirmation of the difference between guidance- and court-clinic cases. Support for this conclusion was also found in the fact that the Pearsonian coefficient for the relationship between the 1963 authority and neurotic scales is .35 for guidance-clinic cases but .89 for court-clinic cases. Thus there is more independence between the two dimensions among guidance-clinic cases in comparison with the court-clinic cases.

The final comment about our regression analysis concerns the issue of its consistency with hypotheses derived from the stress paradigm presented in figure 6–1. These hypotheses were developed for employment in the analysis of long-term outcome. However, it was thought that no harm would come from the preliminary examination of them in connection with short-term outcome. Briefly we thought that (1) the perceptions, feelings, and expectations of parents would be related to outcome, with the more-hopeful and less-frustrated parents reporting more-favorable outcome. Problem-solving behavior would intervene, of course, between cognition and outcome. (2) Thus our second hypothesis states that problem-solving resources are important to problem outcome and that resources, such as higher status and intelligence, would be related to a favorable outcome. (3) The third hypothesis is that extensive coping behavior will result in more favorable outcomes.

There is only mixed support for our first hypothesis; guidance-clinic parents who scored high on the frustration scale reported less-favorable short-term outcome on both scales. However, court-clinic parents who scored high on frustration had a tendency (not statistically significant) to report more-favorable outcome on both scales. Perhaps, when the parents of guidance-clinic children are frustrated, they may suffer an inability to initiate appropriate problem-solving behavior. Other variables bearing on cognition, such as parent's expectation of child's future behavior will be more appropriate to our analysis of long-term outcome and thus were not included in our analyses of short-term outcome. Finally, with respect to parent's perceptions, although data on attribution of blame have been presented in this analysis, we had not offered any clearly derived hypotheses based on the blame attribution.

With respect to our second hypothesis, again there are mixed results. Social-class level was not found to be predictive of short-term outcome on either dimension within either category of clinic. Intelligence, as indexed by the Quick Word Test, was not found related to either of the measures of symptomatic outcome for either type of clinic. Indeed we did not even include the intelligence measure in the regression analyses presented here. It remains to be seen, however, whether the availability of such resources as intelligence, social status, extensive education, or marital happiness (data gathered in 1963) will be predictive of the long-term outcome for the children in our study. Right now, we must emphasize that not much time had elapsed between the 1962 clinic contact and the interview in 1963, and this might explain, in part, the absence of strong relationships here.

The same reasoning can be used in explaining the absence of much support for our third hypothesis that extensive coping would result in more-favorable outcomes. Indeed there is only one instance (involving guidance-clinic cases on the authority dimension) in which help-seeking subsequent to the 1962 clinic contact was statistically related to the child's outcome, and that instance is not in the predicted direction. Various qualifications must be made about this relationship. One is that there is no guarantee that people who sought help ever actually got it in the short run (between 1962 and 1963). Still, at least some of the people who sought help did receive assistance. However, because the length of the contact was not specified, it is difficult to say how much assistance or treatment was actually received by the family during the relatively brief period between the clinic contact in 1962 and our 1963 interview. In the present study, another reason demands a consideration of alternative interpretations of the unexpected relationship between help-seeking and short-term outcome. When they applied for their help in 1962, approximately one-third of our respondents were told to "call back, if necessary," that is if the problem continued or got worse. We think that many of the parents simply followed the clinic's advice and called the same clinic or some other psychiatric agency if they thought the problem persisted. Since our short-term data on help-seeking and 1963 outcome were collected together in 1963, we thought it more likely that parents who perceived their children as "worse" or engaged in continuing undesirable behavior would then seek psychiatric help rather than the case that seeking and/or obtaining professional or psychiatric help would result in the child's getting worse. At this stage in the analysis, since it seems that either interpretation is possible, we are inclined to the view that our long-term data may clarify the direction of this relationship.[11] We should also reserve judgment, of course, on the short-term relationship between help-seeking and the neurotic dimension.

In connection with our third hypothesis, the social network seems to be an important and effective resource for the court-clinic parents but not for guidance-clinic cases. We surmise that the voluntary character of the utilization of social networks serves similar purposes for lower-class, court-clinic families as does the guidance-clinic for middle-class families. Again, we are most interested in assessing the long-term effects of the utilization of the social network for both court and guidance cases.

Summary

This chapter presents the results of our short-term analysis of the children's outcome. We utilized two main types of symptomatic outcome: the use of change scores in a cross-tabular, zero-order analysis, and the use of 1963 adjustment scores in a regression analysis. These scores were distributed on two dimensions, the rules of authority dimension and the neurotic dimension. Our analyses, reported as well as unreported, showed a more substantial degree of consistency between the two types of procedures for the guidance clinics as opposed to the court-clinic cases; this may be due in part to the small number of court-clinic cases in our study.

The regression analysis seemed to support more strongly the existence of two dimensions for guidance-clinic cases than for court-clinic cases. Inspection of the r^2 values showed that a statistically significant amount of the variance was accounted for by the array of independent variables in each of the four instances presented in table 6–15.

Perhaps it is not surprising that the most powerful predictor of the child's 1963 outcome score in the regression analysis was the child's 1962 symptoms score. No doubt it is more accurate to state that this suggests the stability and lack of change in the children's behavior. This is why we have focused so much of our attention on the other independent variables in our regression analysis.

The short-term outcome analysis leaves many questions, which we will return to in considering the long-term experiences and problem-solving activities of the parents and the long-term effects for their children.

Notes

1. The parents' perception of the causes of the child's problems, however, are relevant to their coping behavior.

2. See Hans Strupp, Suzanne Hadley, Beverly Gomes, and Stephen Armstrong, "Negative Effects in Psychotherapy: A Review of Clinical and Theoretical Issues Together with Recommendations for a Program of Research" (unpublished paper, Vanderbilt University, May 1976).

3. That is, the coefficients of reproducibility were satisfactory (see appendix B for summary data on the validity of cumulative scales). For an example of zero-cell analysis, see James E. Teele, "Measures of Social Participation," *Social Problems* 10 (Summer 1962):31–39.

4. It is also notable that on each scale approximately 70 percent of guidance-clinic cases had low scores in 1963. This is very similar to the proportions reported as improved by Eysenck and others for "untreated" controls and apparently attributed to spontaneous remission. Many assumptions, some of which are examined here, surround such attribution.

5. E.W. Burgess and P. Wallin, *Engagement and Marriage* (Chicago: J.B. Lippincott, 1953).

6. E.E. Levitt, "Psychotherapy with Children: A Further Evaluation," *Behavior Research and Therapy* (1963):326–329.

7. This point has been made repeatedly in the sociological literature. For examples of empirical and conceptual analyses, see J. Teele, "Measures of Social Participation," and E. Bott, *Family and Social Network,* 2nd ed (New York: Free Press, 1971). Also see J. Kosa, I. Zola and J.A. Antonovsky, "Health and Poverty Reconsidered," in their *Poverty and Health,* (Cambridge: Harvard University Press, 1969), p. 327.

8. H. Strupp, S. Hadley, B. Gomes, and S. Armstrong, "Negative Effects," (unpublished).

9. None of the three court cases, where the child's behavior was undesirable only on the authority dimension was in detention.

10. See Erving Goffman, *Asylums* (Garden City, N.Y.: Anchor, 1961).

11. Pearlman and Schooler, in a related finding, found that self-reliance was more effective in reducing stress in parenting than was the seeking of other's help. Their study, however, was cross-sectional and the authors noted the need for longitudinal studies in this area. See Leonard Pearlin and Carmi Schooler, "The Structure of Coping," *Journal of Health and Social Behavior* (March 1978):9, 10.

7

Procedures for the Long-Term Study

Many of the issues we faced could not be resolved without longitudinal data. For example, the relationship between the type of help sought and short-term outcome was shadowed by several factors. These included the fact that "help sought" is not the same as "help received." We could not ignore the fact that in 1963 we had asked respondents whether they had seen or contacted various helping sources between 1962 and 1963. Moreover we did not inquire as to how long the child had received assistance, if any, from the various possible helping sources. Such unfocused questioning was avoided in our 1976 follow-up interview. (See appendix D.) Although the short-term study provided an abundance of valuable information, it was clear that a long-term follow-up study could examine a number of highly relevant issues important to clinicians, researchers, and policy makers.

There is a dearth of longitudinal studies focusing on some of the issues addressed in this book. These issues include but are not limited to the following questions: (1) Can evidence be obtained that clarifies what historical processes typically occur among problem children and their families who are members of control (untreated) groups? (2) What long-term problem-solving strategies are employed by parents who experience difficulty in finding professional assistance for children perceived as having problems? (3) How are factors such as type of initial problem, family structure, life events, parent attitudes, and coping strategy related to the child's well-being in adulthood?

Clearly these are questions that can be best studied through longitudinal research. This is not to dispute the fact that time-series studies, analyses of different cohorts, and various types of experimental and quasi-experimental designs have become valuable tools in the social sciences. Perhaps because of the special difficulties encountered, the validity of results have, nevertheless, persistently plagued much of the evaluative research on emotionally disturbed children and adults. These validity problems appear to stem, at least in part, from issues of selection, of maturation, and of history. We believe that past failure to conduct clarifying research on these issues have led to some of the emphasis on the role of spontaneous remission in research on child psychotherapy. Although our study is not a psychotherapy evaluation study, its longitudinal design enables it to address and clarify many matters that are significantly relevant to the evaluation of psychotherapy. Indeed our study group resembles the type of comparison or control group frequently employed in research on child psychotherapy effects. As such, it would seem to be an ideal study group—in long-term analysis—for examining not only the notion of spontaneous remission but also for better understanding the historical processes associated with both the problem-solving behavior of parents and the adjustment of their children in adulthood.

At a well-publicized meeting of the Society for Psychotherapy Research, held at Oxford, England, in 1979, the two-hundred participants apparently reached a consensus that psychotherapy works. However, they commented on the lack of clinically relevant knowledge, the difficulty of obtaining supportive evidence, the problem of judging improvement, and the phenomenon of spontaneous remission. Spontaneous remission was presented as not being spontaneous at all but a result of informal therapy or treatment offered by nonpsychiatric agents.[1] One conference conclusion was that better-designed research was needed in focusing on these issues.

The dearth of longitudinal research in this field is in part a result of the difficulties that must be overcome in implementing plans for such research. Like other long-term research studies, we encountered the full range of problems typically associated with such studies.[2]

Problems in Conducting Longitudinal Research

The central problem faced in such research appears to be the retention of the study group. Although many researchers are so pessimistic about this problem that they avoid longitudinal research, some researchers have surmounted the problem of study group mortality.[3] Study group mortality takes a variety of forms, including the failure to relocate respondents or subjects, the failure to obtain respondent agreement to participate once they are relocated, and the death of some respondents. In our study, a fourth type of sample loss took place as a result of a second major consideration that researchers must place priority on and that is the concern about ethical issues. Our concern for our respondents' mental well-being led us to make decisions not to request interviews with those subjects whom our relocation search revealed to have extensive family problems and whose mental well-being we feared might be worsened by participation in the long-term phase of the study. This was the case for six respondents, representing about 2 percent of our study group.

Relocating and Interviewing Respondents

In 1963 our respondents numbered 352; thus this was the number of respondents we set out to relocate when the second interview stage was begun in 1975. We had made no contact with respondents during the first eleven years of this interval since we had not anticipated the long-term follow-up. In 1974, however, we did attempt to locate ten respondents in order to assess the feasibility of doing a follow-up study. (The result of the pilot relocation effort was encouraging.) With such a long no-contact period we anticipated that a considerable number of our respondents would have changed either their address or their telephone number or both. We also anticipated that some of our respondents would have a name change, due to divorce or/and remarriage. Indeed both residential mobility and extent of name changing were so extensive that it took fifteen months to relocate and reinterview participating respondents. One reason the interview process took so long was that the investigator was greatly concerned with adhering to procedures that protected the rights of participants. Thus the research staff relied on public documents in efforts to find subjects who were difficult to locate.

Typically our first step was to try the old telephone number of the respondent, dating from the time of the 1963 interview. With the assistance of telephone operators who sometimes supplied new numbers for persons who changed their numbers fairly recently, we located about 35 percent of our families. A search through old telephone directories covering the interval between 1963 and 1975 allowed us to match names with telephone directory addresses for the town lived in at the time of our 1963 interview. In this way we located an additional 15 percent of our respondents who had moved within the same town during the twelve-year interval and, of course, also got their new telephone numbers. The search through the old telephone directories was time-consuming, but we were greatly aided when the telephone company allowed us into the telephone directory storehouse, which contained a copy of every telephone directory issued over a period covering many years. (Public libraries, also, often have a full set of telephone directories for their area of the state.)

The most difficult part of our task was now before us for we had to locate that 50 percent of our cohort who had not only moved but had often moved from the town or the state lived in in 1963. Moreover, many of them were women who for one reason or another had changed their last name. We eventually discovered that approximately 60 percent of our original cohort of 352 respondents moved one or more times during the interval and 21 percent moved two or three times; 36 percent had moved to another town or metropolitan area or state during the interval. Over 65 percent had a new telephone number, often under a different name or, in some cases, unlisted or unpublished. Moreover, 17.1 percent of the respondents had changed their name through divorce or/and remarriage. The specific sources employed in our procedures, along with proportion of cases in which they were used, were as follows:

Telephone unchanged from 1963, 35.0 percent

Past telephone directories, 1963–1975, 55.0 percent

City directories or town clerk, 49.0 percent

Vital records (birth, marriage, death), 28.0 percent

Voter registration and assessor records, 21.0 percent

Motor vehicle registration, 19.0 percent

Relatives contacted, 24.1 percent

Neighbors contacted, 21.0 percent

Reverse telephone directory, 2.0 percent

Education department, 3.0 percent

Divorce records, 1.0 percent

Employer, 3.0 percent

We contacted a relative, a neighbor, or a former employer only in those cases where the lack of any public record suggested that the respondent had left the area. In such cases, care was exercised in the protection of the respondent's privacy, and the caller spoke only in general terms of our interest in locating the respondent.

The use of all these procedures resulted in our finally locating all but five of our respondents (98.6 percent). Of those located, 12 (3.4 percent) were found to be deceased. We succeeded in interviewing 81.5 percent of the 340 respondents still alive, for a total of 277 respondents. Our overall success in relocating and reinterviewing members of our original interview study group twelve to thirteen years later should encourage more social scientists to undertake longitudinal studies.[4] Although there were differences between our study groups, our follow-up success rate was similar to that reported by Lee Robins—81.6 percent.[5]

Among the 63 respondents not reinterviewed, 19 (5.4 percent) refused to be interviewed. Thirty-three persons (9.4 percent) failed to respond to either of two letters sent them. We had confirmed the location of these 33 persons through two or more of our locating procedures and thus must count them as refusals. In addition to the 5 persons whom we could not locate, there were 6 instances in which we declined to request an interview because we obtained information suggesting that these families were in great turmoil.[6]

Seventy percent of our interviews took place in 1976 and the remainder during the last three months of 1975.

The interview schedules contained a combination of open-ended and semistructured questions designed to give respondents an opportunity both to relate their experiences in their own words and also to ensure the research team of systematic coverage in selected areas. The interviewing was done primarily by professional social workers after they had undergone an orientation period under the direction of the research director. Members of the research team conducted interviews only when special circumstances arose. In general, the interviews took approximately one and one-half to two hours to complete. Most of the respondents (80.1 percent) were mothers. The fathers were interviewed in 9.4 percent of cases, with foster mothers, grandparents, and aunts accounting for the remainder of respondents. In 1963 the figures for mothers and fathers were 79.8 percent and 10.4 percent, respectively.

Of the 277 respondents interviewed during 1975–1976, 53 percent were face-to-face interviews, and 47 percent took place over the telephone. No differences were found between telephone and face-to-face interviews. For the most part the telephone interviews were full-length interviews, conducted over the telephone for the convenience of our respondents. Typically such respondents were motivated by the desire to ensure the privacy of the interview, especially in those cases where the child still lived with them. In fact, in 9 percent of our cases, while the respondent was willing to be interviewed, they were unwilling to give us a full interview for fear that a full-length interview would lead to complications in the home. They either were afraid that another family member would get suspicious and want to know the content of the interview or were afraid that reopening their past experiences would be upsetting. In these cases, the respondent agreed to talk to us and to answer some of our questions, but only for a relatively brief period. After a couple of experiences like this, we developed a shortened interview form to be used when we encountered such a situation. This shortened, or collapsed, interview was devoted to questions on the respondent's coping and the child's outcome. Our resort to the collapsed interview in these cases is one reason we had a relatively small number of refusals. The main advantage in employing the collapsed interviews is that important adult outcome and long-term parental coping are available for these cases and can be utilized in connection with the 1963 baseline data. The disadvantage is that some important second-stage explanatory material is missing in these cases.

Comparisons between Those Interviewed and Those Not Interviewed

All interviews were edited by the field director and then coded by research team members employing a code manual prepared by the principal investigator.

Intercoder reliability was systematically checked and found to be highly satisfactory. Early during the coding process, we found that the agreement among coders over all coded items was about 93 percent. The disagreements, mainly over a few subjective items, were then reviewed by the research team and subsequently reduced. Overall intercoder agreement, assessed at the end of the process, was found to be over 95 percent.

We then conducted an analysis in order to determine whether our study group appeared to be biased by the loss of respondents for the second interview. To assess this, we decided to examine the relationships between selected background variables from the first interview and whether the second interview was completed.

First, for guidance-clinic cases, we examined the relationships involving a large number of background (time I) factors that included presenting problems in 1962, scores on the authority and neurotic symptoms scales in 1963, child's sex, child's age, respondent's marital status, age of the mother, Warner's ISC, the mother's education, respondent's social participation, and other variables. None of these factors was significantly related to completion of the second interview on the chi-square test. However, when Kendall's test was applied, both child's age (Kendall's tau = .08) and authority symptoms score (Kendall's tau = .10) were significantly related to completion status at the .05 level. Specifically, guidance-clinic respondents with older children and respondents with children having a high score on the authority scale were more likely not to have participated in the second interview. We were not surprised to find that the symptoms scale was related to completion status in view of our decision not to attempt interviews in several cases where the study-group child and family were having very substantial problems.

We then combined the court-clinic cases with the guidance-clinic cases in our analysis of the interview completion status. The strength of the relationships involving child's age and authority symptoms score was greatly increased. What had been borderline differences became magnified. Significant differences were found for each on both the chi-square ($p < .01$) and Kendall tests. On the latter test, coefficients reached a magnitude of .16 for both child's age and authority symptoms ($p < .001$). In addition, when clinic cases were combined, a significant difference was found for Warner's ISC (Kendall's tau = $-.10, p < .05$), the relationship indicating that more lower-class respondents had not participated in the second stage.

These findings meant that the attrition problem was substantially greater for the court-clinic cases than guidance-clinic cases. Indeed while we reinterviewed over 81 percent of all cases at time II, this broke down into 85 percent and 54 percent, respectively, for guidance- and court-clinic cases. We took age as an example of how attrition affects the two types of clinic cases differently.

Thus, among guidance-clinic cases reinterviewed, the mean age of the children on January 1, 1976, was 23.5 years; if all of the guidance clinic

1963 respondents had been reinterviewed, then the children's mean age would have been 23.7 years. For court-clinic cases reinterviewed, the mean age in 1976 was 27.2 years; however, among all the court-clinic cases the mean age for children was 27.6 years. Thus whereas the guidance cases lost two-tenths of a year in average age, the court cases lost four-tenths of a year.

The differences between the guidance- and court-clinic cases, already demonstrated during the first stage of our study, are now in even greater evidence. These differences led us to adapt a different strategy for the presentation of second-stage data.

Second-Stage Analysis

Since the substantial difference between the guidance- and court-clinic cases seemed to be accelerating with age, we began to think that different research and/or conceptual approaches might be necessary in considering them. Indeed because of our failure to reinterview 46 percent of the court-clinic cases, we realized that any analysis of follow-up data for these cases probably would succeed only in raising questions about the effects of attrition on the findings. Thus on methodological grounds and also because we wished to enhance clarity of presentation, we eventually decided to present our data on guidance- and court-clinic cases in separate chapters in the seccond-stage section of the book, reserving one chapter for court-clinic cases. In the meantime, in 1979, we decided to make renewed efforts to gain access to adult criminal history records, at least for the court-clinic cases. Those efforts had been made earlier, but a moratorium on research access to these records existed in Massachusetts and had continued to exist for several years after the beginning of the second stage of our study. Fortunately, access to such records, with appropriate safeguards to enhance privacy rights, was eventually made possible, and we were able to request and obtain criminal histories on the fifty-five court-clinic cases, covering the period of our study.

A preliminary analysis of the criminal history data not only supported our decision to handle the court-clinic cases separately but also convinced us that the conceptual framework developed for the analysis of the long-term data does not seem to be appropriate for court-clinic cases. Thus whereas only a handful of the guidance-clinic children apparently had any serious problems with the law after 1963, we found that about 75 percent of the court-clinic cases had at least one nontraffic conviction during the period between our two interviews. In fact, about 60 percent had at least two convictions during that time. Three-fifths of all court-clinic cases had been charged with quite serious offenses ranging from "moderately" severe charges of breaking and entry or prostitution up to the "most" severe charges such as attempted murder, armed robbery, rape, and murder. It now seems clear that different processes were going on within the court-clinic families and that the stress-coping paradigm developed for guidance-clinic cases did not apply in cases where the coping process either did not take place or operated within very different boundaries, with different underlying assumptions. We will need to consider the assumptions and premises of labeling theory and conflict theory in the analysis of data in court-clinic cases.

Thus we decided to postpone further consideration of the adult outcome for court-clinic cases until we have developed a more-relevant paradigm. The meanings and assumptions we developed about data for guidance-clinic families obviously do not apply to all of these families, but they apparently apply to few of the court-clinic families. We were unprepared for this great lack of variation among court-clinic cases. (See appendix A for a table on these data.) If these families are not in great distress, that would be yet another mark of their difference.

Notes

1. See, for one report, *The New York Times,* July 10, 1979.
2. See James E. Teele, Phyllis Blake, Marty Sawzin, and Gina Abeles, "Sample Maintenance and Ethical Issues in a Longitudinal Research Study" (paper presented at the 1978 Meetings of the American Sociological Association, San Francisco.
3. See, for example, Bruce Eckland, "Retrieving Mobile Cases in Longitudinal Surveys," *Public Opinion Quarterly* 32 (1968):51–64.
4. For a fuller discussion of our relocation efforts, see Teele et al., "Sample Maintenance." Because of the importance of sample maintenance in longitudinal studies and the lack of descriptions, we are preparing a monograph detailing our search procedures and experiences.
5. Lee Robins, *Deviant Children Grown Up* (Baltimore: Williams and Wilkins, 1966), pp. 32–33.
6. At the time of our initial interview in 1963, those six cases displayed a considerable amount of problem behavior. Two of the children involved were in a juvenile detention center, and three of the remaining four had serious problems with authority.

8

Long-Term Coping among Guidance-Clinic Cases

The unique feature of our study is the history of help-seeking and problem-solving behavior of parents facing stressful child-rearing situations. For a number of reasons, not altogether clear, no long-term studies evaluating psychotherapy have focused on this issue. Certainly the Pearlin and Schooler and Langner and Michael studies have contributed valuable findings pertaining to the relationship between stress and coping; however, both reported on cross-sectional data, which limits their relevance. Moreover, neither study purported to evaluate the outcome of child psychotherapy.[1] There have also been a number of studies focusing on developmental issues, but perhaps the best of such studies have been concerned primarily with "normal" children. As a result, there seems to be a great divide between those social scientists concerned with the evaluation of psychotherapy and those interested in child-rearing processes. Some bridging is needed. In the childrens' field especially, there is a great need for information helping to clarify the effects of psychotherapy and of other treatment approaches designed to help children with emotional problems. Ours is not a study that evaluates the effects of psychotherapy per se, but we think it will be helpful to such studies. Moreover, among those interested in the problems facing the family, there appears to be a dearth of information about problems and problem-solving behavior in connection with child-rearing. The important study by Lee Robins, perhaps because the data were collected primarily from the children who had had problems and not the parents, did not contain information on parental problem-solving behavior. It is our contention that coping behavior is an important and neglected area of research and that increasingly social scientists will be drawn to its investigation.

Recently Pearlin and Schooler also focused on the fact that social scientists have paid much more attention to the conditions that are potentially deleterious to well-being (such as certain status categories and opportunity deficits) than to coping behavior, leaving the latter primarily to clinicians.[2] In this book, and particularly in this chapter, we intend to help rectify this discrepancy. We do not deal with the extreme forms of coping, such as impending death, but with the more mundane problem of child-rearing.

Our dependent variable inevitably focuses on the type of assistance sought and received by parents. We note also that coping mechanisms include changing perceptions of problems or redefining them so as to remove threat, disciplinary tactics, and changing one's own behavior. Yet another coping mechanism involves changing the situation out of which threat grows, such as ending a troubling marriage or moving to a new neighborhood. Data were also collected on life events that occurred among our respondents subsequent to our 1963 interview. Coping resources, such as amount of income, intelligence, and personality characteristics, are some typical independent variables in the analysis.

Recall of Events

In this study we define coping as steps the parents have taken in trying to resolve the problems they perceived in their children. Indeed that is consistent with the way our study commenced in 1962: with parents who had contacted a child psychiatric clinic for assistance with a problem. The coping measures described here pertain to the period between 1963 and 1975–1976 and deal with the following questions: (1) Who was contacted and gave assistance? (2) How long was the assistance given? (3) What was the nature of the assistance given? In our 1975–1976 interview, we asked each respondent to try to list all of the places they went and people they saw for help, those who gave assistance, and the length of time they received service in connection with their child's 1962 presenting problem between 1963 and the time of the second interview. We thus have data on contacts on the sources of the help received, the number of different helping agents who actually gave assistance, specific type of assistance given, and the length of time that a particular service or helping program was administered.

There were essentially three major sources of assistance given that we coded from the data: psychiatric service, nonpsychiatric professional service, and informal service (friends, relatives, and others). In this analysis we were careful to separate the number of attempts to find service from the number of times that these efforts resulted in service being given. This is a major difference from our analysis of the help-seeking efforts made by parents between 1962 and 1963; this earlier analysis was less useful in the examination of outcome since help received had not been clearly distinguished from help sought.

In this analysis we emphasize that parents were asked to describe their help-seeking behavior in connection with the child's early problem behavior as presented to the clinics in 1962. Since their responses were dependent on their ability to recall events, we needed to obtain some indication that our respondents had good memories. We were in a fortunate position since I had also directed both stages of the study and knew that data collected in 1962 (clinic records) and 1963 (the first interview) would be relevant to a check on the respondents' recall powers in 1975–1976.

Since we had to tell our would-be respondents, either by telephone or letter, why we wished to interview them in 1975 and 1976, we could not use their recall of our initial interview as a test of their recall power. Still the success of our endeavor is an indication that respondents recalled participating in the earlier study. In any event, the vast majority of the respondents indicated their recall of the initial interview.

Early in the second interview we asked respondents if they recalled their initial call to the clinic of contact in 1962; the majority of respondents (78 percent) said that they did. In most cases where respondents did not recall a specific clinic contact, it appeared that they had searched so widely for help that they had lost track of which helping sources they had contacted in 1962. Moreover, all of our respondents had failed to find the assistance they sought at the clinic contacted in 1962; in many cases, they had had only a single telephone conversation with intake personnel, and so it is understandable that between the brevity and the disappointing results of the call some parents would not recall that contact.

We felt that a better assessment of recall power would involve the respondents' ability to recall the nature of the presenting problem that led them to contact the clinic in 1962. Employing both frequency and cross-tabular analyses, we checked on the consistency of grouped responses between presenting problems in 1962 and respondents' recall in 1975–1976. The analysis was complicated by the fact that in a number of cases, multiple problems were cited at both times; thus citations as well as number of cases were used in the analysis. A high degree of recall ability was evident in the crosstabular analysis, confirming our hunch that parents have a high degree of recall power where problems with their children are involved. Evidence of this is contained in table 8–1, where the proportions of problem citations are presented for the two efforts among guidance-clinic respondents.

We could not compare on all of the specific presenting-problem categories since not all categories were mentioned at both times. For example, obesity was cited a couple of times in 1962 but not mentioned at all in 1975–1976. Similarly, hyperactivity was mentioned in 1975–1976 but had not been cited at all in the clinic record in 1962. In fact, hyperactivity represents a new diagnostic category that did not become much discussed until after 1962. Thus the categories employed by clinicians and parents in 1975–1976 were somewhat different from those employed in 1962. Adding to this problem is the possibility that in at least some cases, the clinic intake worker in 1962 might have used different terms from the parents in categorizing or classifying the parent's description of the problem.

In spite of these cautions, we were gratified by the extent to which respondents recalled their specific reasons for contacting the clinics in 1962. In setting out the data, we stayed away, in general, from broad categories of presenting problems such as "emotional" problems because we did not think they would fairly test the power of recall. Our final array, in fact, sug-

Table 8-1
Recall of Presenting Problems

Problem	Presenting Problem, 1962[a]	Respondent's Recall of 1962 Presenting Problem in 1976[b]
Learning	23.2%	23.7%
Aggressive behavior	14.5	17.6
Night terrors	7.4	9.3
Stealing	7.7	10.8
Running away	2.7	8.1
Shy and inhibited	7.1	14.6
Retarded	3.0	6.2
Lying	3.0	5.4
Eneuresis	2.4	2.8
Soiling	1.7	2.3
Sexual	1.7	4.2

[a]$N = 297$. Data come from clinic record.
[b]$N = 252$. Forty-five guidance-clinic respondents for 1963 were not reinterviewed in 1976.

gests that the respondents were more specific in their later discussion of the 1962 presenting problems than was revealed by clinic records. One interpretation, of course, is that later events colored the respondents' recall of the 1962 problems. Although we did obtain data about problems subsequent to the 1962 presenting problems, we cannot be certain that earlier and later problems did not begin to merge for some of our parents. However, with the exception of a couple of presenting problems, we think there is good reason to conclude that the respondents' memories are reliable. In the case of "running away" and "sexual problems," we suggest that it was likely that later emerging problems became mingled with earlier problems. Overall we feel that our confidence in relying on the parents' recall of their problem-solving efforts between 1963 and 1975-1976 is justified, although in some cases the reported problem-solving efforts may have involved some later-developing problems.

Measures of Coping

We had three major sources of assistance received: psychiatric, nonpsychiatric professional, and informal. We developed continuous measures of each, based on the number of times each particular type of service was received. In addition, we constructed a measure of the amount of time ser-

Table 8-2
Persons and Agencies from Whom Help Was Sought by Guidance-Clinic Respondents

Contact Source	Number of Contacts	% of All contacts
Nonspecific	6	1.0
Psychiatric professional		
Private psychiatrist	55	9.1
Psychiatric clinic (includes psychologists		
and social workers)	134	22.3
Social work agency	25	4.2
Family service	21	3.5
Nonpsychiatric professionals		
Physicians or medical hospital	64	10.6
Clergy	26	4.3
Teachers	72	12.0
Speech therapist or occupational training	11	1.8
Private schools	37	6.1
Informal		
Friends, neighbors	21	3.5
Relatives	56	9.3
Voluntary associations	16	2.7
Police or court	13	2.1
Institutions (rehabilitation)		
Mental hospitals	18	3.0
Reform schools or prisons	11	1.8
Foster homes	12	2.0
Drug center	4	0.7
Totals	602	100.0

vice was given, a measure of the specific type of service obtained, and a combined index based on whether the service was psychiatric, nonpsychiatric, informal, or a combination of different sources of service. Thus we had six measures that focused on the problem-solving or coping behavior of our respondents.

Table 8-2 presents the nature of assistance sought by respondents in their efforts to find help for their child's problems between 1963 and the time of our interview in 1975-1976. Subsequent tables will be devoted to the source, type, and amount of assistance actually given. The table, which applies only to guidance-clinic cases, shows that 602 contacts were made. There were 229 cases responding to this question; including 26 who said they had not sought any help. Fifteen more respondents who actually reported receiving assistance later on during the interview did not specify a search for help and are not included here. Such cases actually may have been called by a clinic on whose waiting list they had been placed. Also some of our respondents did not think that asking a friend or neighbor for advice was help-seeking and are not included here. Thus some of our respondents who did not report seeking help are not included in table 8-2 but do appear later on in our data reporting on assistance received.

Table 8-2 presents a very clear picture: seeking help was epidemic among our respondents. There is an average of 2.6 reported help-seeking contacts for each respondent, subsequent to the time of our 1963 interviews, in connection with their child's presenting problems. Thus all contacts prior to and including the 1962 clinic contact and efforts made between the 1962 contact and our 1963 interview are not included in table 8-2. Were these included, we would have an average of four or more contacts per respondent. We thus have a picture of many concerned guidance-clinic parents who sustained a search for help for their children over a period of years.

The immediate question that comes to mind concerns the extent to which our respondents found the help they sought. In connection with this question, we counted the number of times each respondent reported finding assistance in connection with the child's problem. Although we have taken note of the fact that some respondents reported receiving assistance even though they did not report seeking it, the vast majority of those who received assistance had reported seeking it. The opposite was also true: the vast majority who sought help reported receiving help. In fact when using our own judgment and encompassing the various sources of assistance, we can find only two cases in which respondents searched in vain for help. Four other guidance-clinic respondents said that they had searched for help and never found it, but we felt that they had received substantial nonagency assistance, and so we classified them as having received assistance (see table 8-3).

In table 8-3 we simply indicated the number of times they had received assistance. Thus if a respondent indicated that the child was given assistance in a psychiatric clinic, we counted that as a single instance of assistance received regardless of the amount of time involved. The same was true if the respondent indicated that she had discussed the child's problem with a friend or relative. When the variable indicating the number of times help was sought by a respondent during the 1963 through 1975-1976 period (range from 0 through 9) was cross-tabulated with the number of times help was received by a respondent (0-9) the Pearsonian r was .72. Thus the more help one sought, the more help one received.

Subsequently we asked respondents how long they had received assistance, whether formal or informal, but without regard to the number of times they mentioned getting that assistance. Table 8-3 shows that almost 90 percent of our respondents gave evidence that they had received assistance of some kind in connection with the child's problem and that, of those not receiving assistance, most had not sought it. Thus it seems clear that

Table 8-3
Frequency Distribution of Number of Times Assistance Received among Guidance-Clinic Respondents

Number of Times Assistance Received	N	%
Sought help in vain	2	00.8
Did not seek help and none received	24	09.8
One	31	12.7
Two	42	17.1
Three or four	69	28.2
Five or more	77	31.4
Totals	245[a]	100.0

[a]Seven cases did not respond.

spontaneous remission is doubtful for most of our subject cases. We seriously doubt, moreover, that any of the helping sources ever asked any of these respondents whether they were in a no-treatment control group.

Knowledge of the nature of the assistance is important. We classified assistance as psychiatric (including psychiatrists, psychologists, and social workers), nonpsychiatric professional, or informal, consistent with the categories presented in table 8-2. We did not include the institutional categories presented in that table (such as prisons and mental hospitals) since these instances seemed to signal largely the end of parental coping efforts and are probably better seen as indications of outcome. These instances also did not seem to involve our respondents as directly in problem-solving behavior as did the other sources of assistance and, this is another reason they were not included among our account of source of assistance. The frequency distributions on these three types of assistance are presented in terms of the number of times (instances) each was received (table 8-4).

Our respondents most often received assistance from nonpsychiatric professionals during the period between our two interviews. Seventy percent received assistance from nonpsychiatric professionals, while the proportions receiving help from psychiatric and informal sources were, respectively, 52 percent and 51 percent. Thus many respondents received help from two or all three sources. The majority of these service contacts, about 70 percent, were made by 1970.

Because many of our respondents contacted more than one source type, we developed a combined index that would identify those who received assistance from a particular source and those who received assistance from a combination of sources. The distribution on this combined index is presented in table 8-5. The combined index is skewed in the direction of com-

Table 8–4

Frequency Distributions of Instances of Assistance Received between 1963 and 1976

	Assistance Received	
	N	%
Psychiatric source		
None	118	48.4
One	64	26.2
Two or three	50	20.5
Four or more	12	4.9
Total	244[a]	100.0
Nonpsychiatric professional source		
None	73	30.0
One	61	25.1
Two	42	17.3
Three or four	49	20.2
Five or more	18	7.4
Total	243[b]	100.0
Informal source		
None	119	49.0
One	52	21.4
Two or three	53	21.8
Four	13	5.4
Five or more	6	2.4
Total	243[c]	100.0

[a]Eight cases no response.
[b]Nine cases no response.
[c]Nine cases no response.

Table 8–5

Combined Index of Sources of Assistance Received

Source of Assistance	N	%
None	26	10.6
Psychiatric only	16	6.6
Nonpsychiatric professional only	43	17.6
Informal only	17	7.0
Any combination	142	58.2
Total	244[a]	100.0

[a]Eight cases did not respond.

Table 8-6
Duration of All Assistance Received

Amount of Time	N	%
Brief (few weeks or less)	42	21.5
Few months or more but less than one year	28	14.4
One year or more but less than two years	69	35.4
Two or more years	56	28.7
Total	195[a]	100.0

[a]Twenty-four cases did not apply for service and did not receive any, eleven cases indicated they could not recall how long they received help, two cases applied but did not receive assistance, and twenty cases either did not respond to this question or indicated that assistance was sought only from officials of justice or rehabilitative institutions.

Table 8-7
Specific Type of Assistance Given

Type of Assistance	N	%
None	26	11.0
Psychotherapy	73	30.9
Counseling	25	10.6
Diagnosis or tests	20	8.5
Educational advice	46	19.5
Physical treatment	4	1.7
Referral or supportive advice	17	7.2
Other	25	10.6
Totals	236[a]	100.0

[a]Eight cases where respondent could not recall type of specific assistance received and eight instances of no response.

binations of helping sources. We conducted a preliminary examination of the various combinations (psychiatric and nonpsychiatric, psychiatric and informal, and nonpsychiatric and informal) as they related to one of our criterion outcome measures and saw few differences among them. Thus we decided not to distinguish among them and to include them together.

Table 8-5 shows that almost 60 percent of our respondents received assistance from a combination of sources and that slightly over 30 percent received assistance from only one of three resource types. Thus the data presented so far clearly show that almost 90 percent of our respondents received assistance between 1963 and 1976. Two-thirds of these received a

Table 8–8
Interrelationships among the Continuous Coping Variables

	1	2	3	4	5
1. Total number of contacts resulting in service	—	0.56	0.66	0.53	0.36
2. Number of instances (programs) of psychiatric service		—	0.21	0.18	0.22
3. Number of instances of non-psychiatric professional service			—	0.03	0.24
4. Number of instances of informal service				—	0.00
5. Duration of assistance					—

variety of types of assistance. Thus it will be difficult to determine which type of service contributes the most to outcome among such cases.

We asked our respondents about the duration of the assistance received in each relevant citation of help given. We added together these various responses in contriving the measure of duration presented in table 8-6. It is notable that so many of our respondents sought and received so much assistance. The assumption that dropouts from one agency or that children in the typical comparison or control groups do not receive substantial assistance, including much psychiatric or nonpsychiatric professional help, is untenable.

Finally we asked the respondents to describe the kind of assistance they had been given apropos of their child's problem. Subsequently we coded the respondent replies (table 8-7). Where multiple responses existed, the coding preference was made in the order in which responses are listed beginning with psychotherapy. Thus a respondent who listed psychotherapy and testing is presented under "psychotherapy." Subsequent response categories are reduced by this procedure. We did this in order to maximize the mental-health-assistance categories.

Relationships among Coping Variables

The Pearsonian r's between pairs of our continuous coping variables are presented in table 8-8. The first variable in the matrix—total number of times service was received—is the one most strongly related to the other coping variables presented. This was expected since it is the one from which the other continuous variables are derived. In spite of the fact that many of the respondents utilized assistance from more than one source type, there is still a good deal of independence among our three source types. When each of these three variables is dichotomized between "none" and "one or more" the two relationships involving psychiatric service versus non-psychiatric professional and informal, respectively, disappear. Moreover, even when not dichotomized, there is no association between nonpsychiatric professional assistance and informal assistance. Consider, for example, the relationship between psychiatric and nonpsychiatric assistance: two-thirds of the 118 respondents who did not receive psychiatric assistance reported receiving nonpsychiatric professional assistance, while almost half of those not receiving nonpsychiatric help got psychiatric assistance. This pattern is similar for the other relationships reported here.

Two matters need to be briefly discussed. The first concerns the relationship of the duration of assistance to the measures of assistance. The last column in table 8-8 reveals that duration is directly related to total number of contacts and to the extent of psychiatric and nonpsychiatric assistance; in contrast, duration is not related to extent of informal assistance. Examination of this latter cross-tabulation revealed a curvilinear relationship; however, those with the most informal contacts reported the shortest duration of assistance. The second matter concerns the cross-tabulation between the combined index of source of assistance and the specific type of assistance received. The later variable maximizes the receipt of psychotherapy (see table 8-9).

The data in table 8-9 reveal the expected—that the mental health workers most often were involved in giving psychotherapy. When respondents had obtained assistance from a combination of sources, which usually involved a psychiatric source, psychotherapy was also frequently, though not always, given. In contrast, the nonpsychiatric professionals and informal sources of assistance did not give psychotherapy; the modal form of assistance given by these sources was educational advice. However, because of the way in which we contrived our typology of assistance and because we know nothing of the type and circumstances surrounding the decision to give psychotherapy, we will not employ it further in this chapter.

Independent Variables Employed in the Analysis of Coping

The list of independent variables employed in our analysis of coping are presented in table 8-10, which also indicates the time during which a given variable was collected. Time I variables are those collected during our 1963 interviews, and time II variables are those collected during our 1975-1976 interviews. The time I variables were described earlier with only two exceptions: respondent's comparison of child's behavior in 1963 with child's

Table 8-9
Cross-Tabulation between Combined Index of Source of Service and Specific Type of Assistance

Combined Index of Source of Service	Psychotherapy		Counseling		Diagnosis or Tests		Educational Advice		Physical Treatment		Supportive or Referral		Other		100% =
	N	%	N	%	N	%	N	%	N	%	N	%	N	%	
Psychiatric	12	85.8	1	7.1	—	—	—	—	—	—	—	—	1	7.1	14
Nonpsychiatric professional	—	—	3	7.5	5	12.5	17	42.5	2	5.0	5	12.5	8	20.0	40
Informal	—	—	—	—	—	—	8	57.1	—	—	2	14.3	4	28.6	14
Combination	61	42.9	21	14.8	15	10.6	21	14.8	2	1.5	10	7.0	12	8.4	142

Note: $N = 210$. Twenty-six cases excluded as no help received, eight respondents could not recall nature of assistance and eight cases did not respond.

behavior in 1962 and respondent's idea of what punishment should consist of when children are disobedient.

Some Hypotheses Relevant to Coping Behavior

Before presenting our hypotheses, it is important to identify the niche our study occupies in relation to some other studies of stress. First, our families already had experienced some initial stress in child-rearing at the time we first interviewed them in 1963. This is indexed by the fact that they had contacted a child psychiatric clinic for assistance. Our interest was in their problem-solving behavior subsequent to their apparent failure to obtain service from the clinic. Because of our interests and the subsequent manner in which the study group was obtained, it is obvious that ours is not a study of the etiology of stress. In contrast, the Midtown Manhattan studies and the Hollingshead and Redlich studies focused on the etiology of mental illness.[3] Our study did not focus on the process leading to the child's problem but on some of the steps that parents took to mediate and cope with a perceived problem. Second, our study is not an evaluation or quasi-experimental study since we did not use the typical treatment-control format. Its strength is that it is relevant to an understanding of stress-coping and stress-outcome processes employed by a group of parents under child-rearing stress. In examining a group that is usually inadequately studied—the no-treatment group—our study is relevant to evaluation research.

Our hypotheses, then, focused on the explanation of some of the coping processes employed by the respondents. The explanatory variables consist largely of the internal and external mediating factors related to the parents' problem-solving efforts.

Although a number of studies have used factors related to the presence of stress, as yet few have attempted to explain problem-solving behavior. Many explanatory variables may be similarly related to both the presence of stress and to the mediation or adaptation response, but there are doubtless a number of factors differentially related to stress and coping. These possible differences will be noted as we rationalize the hypotheses. The hypotheses, finally, focus only on two of our three dependent variables—assistance from psychiatric sources and assistance from informal sources—because we believe these are the sources that will involve the most and the strongest relationships, in part, because of their contrast. This, too, is a hypothesis. Hypotheses, which involve time I independent variables except where otherwise indicated, follow.

1. Social class (indexed by Warner's ISC, chief breadwinner's income, and extent of the mother's education). Middle- and upper-class respondents will be more likely than lower-class respondents to receive service from psy-

chiatric sources, while lower-class respondents will be more likely than their counterparts to utilize the informal support network. This hypothesis is rationalized by a number of studies suggesting that resource availability and the power to manipulate the environment are more often found among middle- and upper-class persons.[4] Moreover, our short-term findings showed that middle- and upper-class respondents were found to be more likely than lower-class respondents to persist in seeking help from psychiatric professionals. We are hypothesizing that this pattern continued in subsequent years.

Table 8-10
Independent Variables Employed in Assessment of Coping

Variables	Code Categories
Time I	
Problem solving and outcome	
Subsequent hlep sought (1962–1963)	1 = none, 2 = nonpsychiatric, 3 = psychiatric
Authority symptoms scale (1963)	1 = no symptoms, 2 = 1 symptom, 3 = 2 symptoms, 4 = 3 symptoms
Neurotic symptoms scale (1963)	1 = no symptoms, 2 = 1 symptom, 3 = 2 symptoms, 4 = 3 symptoms
Demographic and social variables	
Mother's age	1 = 20–29 years, 2 = 30–39 years, 3 = 40–49 years, 4 = 50–59 years, 5 = 60 or more
Mother's race	1 = black, 2 = white
Mother's religion	1 = Jewish, 2 = Protestant, 3 = Catholic, 4 = Other
Mother's marital status	1 = married, 2 = separated, 3 = divorced, 4 = widowed, 5 = never married
Chief breadwinner's income	1 = under $780, 2 = $780–1,299, 3 = $1,300–2,599, 4 = $2,600–3,899, 5 = $3,900–5,199, 6 = $5,200–6,499, 7 = $6,500–7,799, 8 = $7,800–9,199, 9 = $9,200–10,499, 10 = $10,000 plus
Mother's education	1 = some elementary school, 2 = some completed elementary school, 3 = some high school, 4 = completed high school, 5 = some college or more
Warner's ISC	1 = lower class (score of 1, 2, or 3), 2 = middle class (score of 4, 5, or 6), 3 = upper class (score of 7, 8, or 9)
Child's sex	1 = male, 2 = female
Child's age on January 1, 1963 (age at the time of second interview is based on January 1, 1976)	1 = preschooler (1–5 years), 2 = latency (6–10 years), 3 = early adolescence (11–12 years), 4 = middle adolescence (13–15 years), 5 = late adolescence (16–18 years)

Table 8-10 continued

Variables	Code Categories
Respondents' perceptions and attitudinal or personal characteristics	
Blames self for child's problems	1 = yes, 0 = no
Blames relatives for child's problems	1 = yes, 0 = no
Blames child's peers for child's problems	1 = yes, 0 = no
Blames child for child's problems	1 = yes, 0 = no
Focus of blame (combined index)	1 = older generation, 2 = younger generation, 3 = fate
Quick Word Test (index of IQ)	1 = 1st quartile (low), 2 = 2d quartile, 3 = 3d quartile, 4 = 4th quartile
Respondent's comparison of child's behavior in 1963 with child's behavior at time of 1962 clinic application	1 = much better, 2 = somewhat better, 3 = same, 4 = somewhat worse, 5 = much worse
Srole scales:	
Authoritarianism	0 = not authoritarian, 5 = high on on authoritarianism
Anomie	0 = not anomic, 5 = high anomic
Frustration	0 = not frustrated, 4 = high on frustration
Rigidity	0 = not rigid, 6 = high on rigidity
Withdrawal	0 = not withdrawn, 4 = highly withdrawn
Hopefulness for child's future	1 = very hopeful, 2 = mildly hopeful, 3 = not too hopeful, 4 = not hopeful at all
Marital happiness variables	
Respondent's estimate of degree of marital happiness	1 = very happy, 2 = happy, 3 = unhappy
Combined index of respondent's assessment of extent of marital agreement with spouse (includes 11 items)	0 = no agreement, 9 = much agreement
Parental agreement on child-rearing practices (based on 8 items)	1 = nearly always agree, 2 = predominant agreement, 3 = frequent disagreements
Discipline	
Disciplinary measures that should be employed when children are disobedient	1 = whipping, 2 = spanking, 3 = nonphysical
Behavioral index (social participation variables	
Frequency of visits with relatives in month prior to interview	0 = none, 9 = 9 visits
Frequency of attendance at religious services in month prior to interview	0 = none, 9 = 9 times
Social isolation scale (cumulative scale based on visits with friends,	0 = isolate (no visits with friends and no participation in clubs or hobbies), 1 =

Table 8–10 continued

Variables	Code Categories
participation in voluntary associations, and participation in social hobbies)	visits friends but does not participate in clubs or hobbies, 2 = either participates in voluntary associations or social hobbies or both and typically have friends

Time II

Perception related to child
  When did respondent change his or her expectations about the child? — 1 = 1962–1964, 2 = 1965–1967, 3 = 1968–1970, 4 = 1971–1976, 5 = did not change

  Why did respondent stop worrying about child's behavior? — 1 = child was better, 2 = there was a change in circumstances, 3 = child still in trouble so did not stop worrying

Discipline of children
  Form of punishment usually employed for the children — 1 = whipping alone or in combination with other forms of punishment, 2 = spanking, 3 = nonphysical

Life events
  Number of major life events in last 10 or 11 years (based on open-ended question) — 0 = none, 1 = 1, 2 = 2, 3, = 3 or more

Demographic or social
  Number of children in family — 1 = 1, 2 =2, etc., 9 = 9 or more
  Present marital status of respondent — 1 = married, 2 = widowed, 3 = divorced, 4 = separated

  Number of times married — 1 = one, 2 = two, 3 = three
  How long married — Used actual number of years
  Number of times moved since 1963 — Used numbers

Father's role in child rearing
  What was the father's role in child rearing? — 0 = no father in home, 1 = dominant role, 2 = supportive role, 3 = somewhat involved, 4 = weak role, 5 = interfering and destructive

  Did father participate in any aspects of treatment for the child? — 0 = no appropriate, 1 = yes, a lot, 2 = yes, some, 3 = no, 4 = no father in home, 5 = no treatment program involved

Attitude toward child psychiatric clinics
  Given the situation you had in 1962–1963 again, would you contact a guidance center, or the like again? — 1 = yes, 2 = perhaps, 3 = no

2. Intelligence (indexed by the Quick Word Test). Persons of high verbal ability will be more likely than persons of low verbal ability to receive assistance from psychiatric sources, while persons of low verbal ability will

be more likely to utilize informal sources. This hypothesis stems from Hollingshead and Redlich who reported that obtaining good psychiatric care was related to verbal skill.[5] Since it is recognized that education is also related to verbal ability, it would appear that intelligence is, at least in part, class-related. The Dohrenwends have also suggested that verbal ability is related to the manipulation of objective conditions. They consider verbal ability to be a class-related internal mediating factor and have reviewed a substantial amount of literature documenting a relationship between class and verbal ability among children.[6]

3. Marital status. Divorced, widowed, and separated respondents will be more likely to utilize assistance from both psychiatric and informal sources in contrast to married respondents. This hypothesis is not consistent with the stress theory of delinquency, which holds that the reduction of parental roles through divorce or separation is a generating factor in delinquency. The hunch here is that single respondents (usually mothers) will work very hard to find assistance for their children and to prove that they can raise their children without the spouse. The departure of a spouse may actually serve as a problem-producing stressor for the remaining family members; or it might be the key to problem-solving. In either case, the consequence of separation or divorce does not alter the fact that the remaining spouse will want to demonstrate competence in childrearing. Married respondents at least have a spouse as a potential resource and will thereby be less likely to seek external assistance.

4. Number of children in the family (time II variable). The fewer the children, the more likely respondents will be able to find assistance from psychiatric sources and the less likely to utilize the informal support system. This, too, is a class-related hypothesis since lower-class persons have more children and must spread their resources more thinly than do middle-class persons.[7] Families with many other children to be concerned about will not have the resources for seeking and finding psychiatric assistance.

5. Child's age. Respondents whose problems concern younger children will seek and receive more assistance from both psychiatric and informal sources than will respondents with older children. This hypothesis is supported by an assumption that parents typically express more concern about younger children. Moreover, our report on the relationship between age and the clinic's decision to accept for service suggests that psychiatric professionals are also more concerned about younger children.

6. Personality characteristics of respondent: authoritarianism, rigidity, and frustration. Respondents scoring low on these characteristics will seek and receive more assistance from psychiatric sources in comparison with high scorers. In this case, we offer no hypotheses for informal aid. The scale of authoritarianism contains items focused on the need for strong discipline for children and adults, the importance of teaching children to obey their

parents, intolerance for wrongdoing, and the reduction of people to two types, the weak and the strong. Respondents agreeing with several or more of these items are thought to be very controlling and thus not highly receptive to seeking or accepting help from psychiatric sources. Rigidity resembles authoritarianism since these are items focused on doing things "the old way," controlling feelings, not changing one's mind, and intolerance. Rigid people are also not likely to surrender control to others by utilizing their help or assistance. High scores on the frustration scale would appear among those exasperated by life's problems and who think of themselves as failures. Such persons would be too overwhelmed by feelings of inadequacy to be persistent help-seekers.

9. Parental agreement on child-rearing practices (an index based on eight items, including child's doing household chores and allowance money). Parents who agree on child-rearing practices will be more likely to obtain psychiatric and informal assistance than will parents who disagree. It is expected that parents who disagree a lot will be unable to agree on a course of action for the child. Many such parents will not seek assistance; even if they do seek and receive it, it is anticipated that they would be unable to utilize it properly or would not be receptive to it.

10. Disciplinary measures. Parents who use reason and in general are nonphysical in disciplining a disobedient child would be more receptive to and would receive more assistance from psychiatric sources than would parents resorting to physical disciplinary tactics. In contrast, it is expected that the parents who employ physical punishment would more often seek and receive informal assistance than would nonphysical parents. The rationale here is patterned somewhat after that of Lazarus who views stress reactions (emotional reactions) as effects rather than causes and suggests that these effects (such as physical punishment of children) depend on cognitive processes.[8] We suggest that the type of personality who would typically condone the physical punishment of children has located the source of the problems posed by a child in the child himself. Such parents have, in Lazarus's terms, "appraised the threat." We suggest that the nature of such an appraisal is not compatible with an extensive search for psychiatric assistance. This hypothesis is consistent with our hypotheses involving scores on authoritarianism and rigidity.

11. Blame attribution. This hypothesis is directly related to hypotheses 6 and 10 concerning authoritarianism, rigidity, and disciplinary tactics. Thus we hypothesize that respondents who blame the child or his peers (younger generation) will be less likely to utilize psychiatric sources than will respondents who blame relatives or themselves (older generation) or fate for the child's problem. We expect this situation to be reversed with respect to the utilization of informal assistance.

12. Hopefulness for child's future. This is another of the internal mediating factors that the Dohrenwends considered. We hypothesize that

respondents who in 1963 felt hopeless about their children's future will be less likely than hopeful respondents to have sought and received either psychiatric or informal assistance during the subsequent years. The Dohrenwends suggest that "resignation has never proved more than a temporary palliative for the individual" and state that it is the poor who are likely to lack confidence in their power to manipulate life's conditions. They cited a number of studies documenting the relationship of this factor to social class.[9]

13. Social isolation scale (a cumulative scale based on visits with friends, participation in voluntary associations, and participation in social hobbies). Social isolates will be less likely than social participants to receive either psychiatric or informal assistance. In part this hypothesis is based on the common-sense notion that persons who do not interact with others will be unwilling to seek or utilize assistance from others. This hypothesis is also based on the notion that social isolates are not normatively oriented; that is, they do not base their action on broad cultural norms.[10] Such norms, we assume, include the seeking of advice or assistance where the welfare of children is concerned.

14. Number of major life events in last ten or eleven years (time II variable). Respondents who experienced three or more major life events, in contrast to respondents experiencing fewer life events, will be more likely to have received psychiatric and informal assistance. This hypothesis is based on the idea that when a spouse is lost through death, divorce, or illness, the remaining spouse will attempt to replace that loss through the seeking of advice. This should be especially true for respondents still experiencing child-rearing problems.

15. Number of times moved since 1963 (time II). A direct relationship will exist between number of times moved and the extent to which psychiatric resources are utilized; however, an inverse relationship will exist between moving and the utilization of informal assistance. We assume that frequent change of residence, though it may be a response to the child's problem, also involves a loss of potential informal sources of assistance (neighbors, friends, and relatives). When this occurs, we believe the parents become more dependent on professional resources for assistance.

16. Father's role in child-rearing (time II variable). The presence of a dominant or supportive father in child-rearing, in contrast to a weak or destructive father, will be associated with the absence of psychiatric sources of assistance and with the presence of informal sources of assistance. This hypothesis is somewhat paradoxical since it could be expected that strong or supportive fathers might encourage all external assistance. However, we assume that when the father is strong or supportive in the marriage, there is less need for professional psychiatric assistance since such a father would be a constant source of support for other family members.[11]

Although we do not offer hypotheses for all of our forty-two independent variables, we think we have presented enough of them to indicate their interrelatedness to each other and their place in our conception of stress coping. Most of the relationships presented involve independent variables from our 1963 interview and dependent variables from our 1975–1976 interview. These relationships are presented in table 8–11. The measures of association used are Kendall's tau for ordinal variables and Cramer's V for our nominal variables. All tests of significance are of the two-tailed variety. The chi-square test of significance is employed where Cramer's V is presented.

Relationships between Variables

In table 8–11, the measures of association shown involve thirty-two time I variables and ten time II variables for each of the three sources of assistance utilized from 1963 through 1975–1976. Nine time I and four time II variables are significantly related, at the .05 level or better, to the receipt of psychiatric assistance. Few of these relationships are of outstanding strength.

Help-Seeking

Among time I variables related to the psychiatric source, the two strongest predictors involve help-seeking in 1962–1963 (after the 1962 clinic contact) and the number of neurotic symptoms that the child had at the time of our 1963 interview. Of those who had reported not contacting or seeing psychiatric professionals between 1962 and 1963, 40 percent went on to obtain psychiatric assistance during the subsequent years covered by our study. However, of those who had reported contacting or seeing psychiatric professionals earlier, 65 percent obtained psychiatric assistance subsequently. Thus our respondents exhibit a certain consistency in their help-seeking behavior over a substantial period.

Symptoms

The role that symptomatology in 1963 played in the subsequent receipt of psychiatric assistance was impressive. Respondents whose children scored zero, one, two, and three on our 1963 Guttman scale of neurotic symptoms, respectively, reported receiving subsequent psychiatric assistance in the following proportions: 39 percent, 57 percent, 70 percent, and 75 percent.

Our Guttman scale measuring the child's observance of rules of authority was also substantially related to the subsequent receipt of psychiatric assistance. Among respondents whose children scored 0, 1, 2, and 3 on this scale, 39 percent, 52 percent, 64 percent, and 64 percent, respectively, reported receiving psychiatric assistance. Thus more children with neurotic symptoms received help in comparison to children who did not observe the rules of authority. This difference is consistent with the clinics' own report that they more often accept children with neurotic problems compared to antisocial or delinquent problems. Moreover, the higher the neurotic score,

Table 8-11
Association between Coping and Independent Variables

		Psychiatric Service	Nonpsychiatric Professional	Informal
Time I Independent Variables				
I.	Help seeking, 1962-1963 (C)	.22†††	.22††	.17
	Authority symptoms	.12*	.03	.02
	Neurotic symptoms	.24***	−.01	.13**
II.	Mother's age	−.05	−.07	−.05
	Mother's race (C)	.14	.14	.13
	Mother's religion (C)	.18	.15	.10
	Mother;s marital status (C)	.20	.13	.13
	Breadwinner's income	.04	−.04	−.09*
	Mother's education	.07	−.00	−.03
	Social class	.06	−.06	−.08
	Child's sex (C)	.10	.09	.14
	Child's age	−.10*	−.02	−.07
III.	Blames self	.08	−.07	.03
	Blames relative	.08	−.08	.10
	Blames child's peers	.05*	.03	−.05
	Blames child	.03	−.05	−.02
	Focus of blame	.11	.12	.15
	Quick Word Test	−.02	−.04	.04
	Comparison of 1962-1963 behavior of child	.16**	.13*	.04
	Authoritarianism	−.04	.03	.04
	Anomie	−.01	−.03	−.01
	Frustration	.00	.03	.05
	Rigidity	−.10*	−.03	−.02
	Withdrawal	−.05	−.12	.02
	Hopefulness	.13*	.04	.01
IV.	Marital happiness	−.00	−.02	.11*
	Marital agreement	−.01	.05	−.09*
	Agreement on child-rearing	.01	.03	.13***
V.	Discipline	−.07*	−.04	−.02
VI.	Visiting relatives	−.02	−.03	.06
	Church attendance	.01	.03	−.02
	Social isolation	.04	.02	−.04

Table 8-11 continued

	Psychiatric Service	Nopsychiatric Professional	Informal
Time II			
Number of children	− .07	− .01	− .01
Number of life events	.17**	.03	.10*
Discipline	− .10*	− .04	− .12*
Present marital status of respondent (C)	.17	.15	.20†
Number of times respondent married	− .03	.02	− .01
How long married	− .08	.04	− .11*
Number of times moved residence	.03	− .04	.04
Father's child-rearing (C)	.16	.16	.18
Extent father participated in treatment	− .16*	− .11*	− .02
Respondent's inclination to contact clinic again	− .18**	− .02	− .06

Note: Kendall's tau is employed for ordinal variables and Cramer's V (C) for nominal variables. $N = 244$.

    $*p < .05$ Kendall.

   $**p < .01$ Kendall.

  $***p < .001$ Kendall.

     †$p < .05$ chi-square.

    ††$p < .01$ chi-square.

   †††$p < .001$ chi-square.

the more likely respondents were to have received help in two or more instances from psychiatric professionals. (An "instance" is a program of service and does not refer to the precise number of face-to-face contacts.) This is not the case for the authority score, where children with scores of 2 or 3 were less likely to have received help in several instances than were children with a score of 1. Although this difference could reflect a less-extensive search for help from respondents whose children violated the most rules of authority, we believe that psychiatric professionals feel less sure of their problem-solving ability with strongly antisocial children. Still, the fact that almost 60 percent of the children who had one or more antisocial symptoms received their help suggests that many psychiatric professionals were willing to give assistance to such families.

Social Class, Child's Age, and Marital Status

Among the three hypotheses involving the time I demographic variables of social class, child's age, and mother's marital status, only the one involving child's age received substantial support. Our belief that middle- and upper-class respondents would be more apt to receive psychiatric assistance was based in part on other research suggesting that lower-class persons have less resource availability and less power to manipulate the environment than do higher status people. In part the hypothesis was based on our own earlier finding showing that middle- and upper-class persons, in contrast to lower-class persons, had shown more persistence in seeking and/or finding psychiatric assistance between 1962 and 1963. Although this earlier relationship was statistically significant, it was not overwhelming, with 51 percent and 38 percent, respectively, of middle-class and lower-class respondents reporting psychiatric contacts after the 1962 clinic contact. In the long-term interval between 1963 and 1975–1976, 56 percent and 49 percent, respectively, of middle- and lower-class respondents reported receiving psychiatric assistance. A contributing reason for the apparently greater increase in psychiatric assistance for lower-class respondents may be that we lost a few more lower-class persons from the second stage (16 percent to 13 percent) among guidance-clinic respondents. However, in our opinion, this would not be a sufficient number of lower-class cases, even if the bias were adjusted, to provide a significant relationship between social class and receiving psychiatric assistance. We think other factors could explain the lack of a relationship.

First, all of our respondents had voluntarily sought help at psychiatric centers for children in 1962 and represent, in general, a highly motivated group of parents irrespective of social-class level. It may well be that it took lower-class respondents somewhat longer to reapply for psychiatric assistance after the 1962 contact. Supporting this interpretation is our earlier finding that middle- and upper-class persons felt more comfortable in the guidance-clinic setting. A second reason for the greater increase in psychiatric assistance among lower-class persons may be that more psychiatric facilities became available to them. The Community Mental Health Centers Program, begun in 1963, provides one outstanding example of this growth in facilities. In light of these considerations, we believe that it is fair to conclude that parents under child-rearing stress do not differ much by social-class level with respect to seeking and finding professional psychiatric assistance, although it may take lower-class persons a bit longer to do so. This is not to say, however, that the quality, duration, usefulness, and effects of such assistance do not differ by social-class level. At least one important source states that both the quality of service and the availability of needed specialized mental health facilities are less available to the urban poor, to ethnic and racial minorities, to rural communities, to the elderly, and to seasonal workers.[12] Nevertheless we think that the motivation to seek assistance for their children perceived as having problems is as strong among lower-class parents as it is among middle-class respondents.

Supporting this opinion is the finding that breadwinners' income is significantly, and inversely, related to seeking and receiving informal assistance. That is, persons whose earnings were toward the lower and middle levels of the income scale were more likely than upper-level respondents to seek and obtain assistance from informal sources. Perhaps the reason that lower-class persons underutilized psychiatric assistance in the past was their lack of money.

Child's age, as expected, is related to seeking and obtaining psychiatric assistance. We reasoned that both professionals and parents alike would be more concerned about the younger children. Moreover, it has long been held that the child psychiatric treatment culture is better oriented to the service of younger children than to older, adolescent children who would be more likely to present more-persistent and more-antisocial problems. And in Massachusetts, the growth of the court clinics for children may have been based, at least in part, on this notion. Among preschoolers, latency-age children (six to ten years), and adolescents (eleven years and older), respectively, the following proportions were reported as having one or more service episodes with psychiatric professionals: 68 percent, 55 percent, and 46 percent. On the informal service dimension, the relationship was similar, with the comparable proportions being 64 percent, 56 percent, and 45 percent. The latter relationship, however, did not attain statistical significance.

The last of the time I demographic variables that we hypothesized about was marital status. Cramer's V attained a magnitude of .20 when the categories of marital status were not collapsed. When the separated, divorced, and widowed are combined into an unmarried category, the chi-square test is not significant. Fifty-three percent of married women and 43 percent of unmarried women received psychiatric assistance; thus the relationship is not in the hypothesized direction. On the informal dimension, however, the relationship is in the hypothesized direction, with 47 percent of married women and 65 percent of unmarried women receiving informal assistance. These findings, reminiscent of those for social class, may be a bit confusing at first glance. However, on reflection, the findings make sense, just as do those relevant to social class. The commodity that both lower-income families and single parents may lack is money. Certainly in 1962–1963 when most of these respondents had just initiated their help-seeking behavior and when our stressor variables were being collected, people usually required some money before they could acquire psychiatric assistance. All of these respondents had contacted a clinic in 1962. This consideration could account for, or at least be partly responsible for, the subsequent reliance of both poorer families and single parents (separated, widowed, or divorced) on informal assistance. It is not at all clear that such families had a choice with respect to the type of assistance they eventually received, especially since the Community Mental Health Centers Program did not proceed very far until later in the 1960s. Perhaps by the time the mental health centers became available, many of our respondents had already formed their problem-solving strategies or had ceased to worry about these children.

Personality, Perceptions, and Form of Discipline

The hypotheses utilizing these sets of variables are assumed to be inter-related. In our study we utilized the Srole scales as indexes of personality, following other scholars, because we assume that these scales tap the dimensions of authoritarianism, anomia, rigidity, frustration, and withdrawn feelings. We expected persons with low scale scores on authoritarianism, rigidity, and frustration to receive more psychiatric assistance in comparison with high scores. While two of the three hypothesized relationships were in the predicted direction, only one, rigidity, was statistically significant. This was somewhat of a surprise since we had theorized that both rigidity and authoritarianism seemed to focus on feelings of intolerance and established ways of acting. In addition, authoritarianism, but not rigidity, focused strongly on the need for obedience from children and the need for discipline. These items in the authoritarianism measure led us to link it to the respondent's style for disciplining the child when he was disobedient. Finally, we felt that the placing of blame on the child or on his friends would be associated with those cognitive processes generated by authoritarian and rigid personalities. This is now obviously an inadequate formulation, but it had the merit of imposing organization on some of the data. The fact that rigidity, but not authoritarianism, is related to seeking psychiatric assistance forced us to reexamine our rationale. This reassessment suggests that rigidity is not, after all, a parallel measure of authoritarianism. The Pearsonian correlation between the two is .51; although this is a strong association, it means that there is some independence between the two measures. It seems to us that rigidity is tapping self-control in addition to a flexibility dimension, while authoritarianism is tapping control of others in addition to the flexibility dimension. A low score on the rigidity scale probably indicates the presence of self-control and thus allows such respondents to think about their course of action. In contrast, a low score on authoritarianism primarily means that the respondent disavows harsh and primitive methods in controlling others. Although this is speculation, it seems to represent at least a plausible explanation of the fact that respondents with low rigidity scores are more likely to find psychiatric assistance than those with high rigidity scores, by 57 percent to 39 percent.

With respect to the frustration scale, frustration feelings do not appear to inhibit respondents in their search for assistance. Put differently, the stress indicated by a high score on frustration does not mean an absence of stress-reducing behavior in our respondents.

The next of the interrelated hypotheses to be considered involves disciplinary tactics. Our hypothesis stated that parents who used reason in disciplining their children, as opposed to physical measures, would be more receptive to and receive more psychiatric assistance. This hypothesis was directly related to our rationale concerning authoritarianism and rigidity. The hypothesis was not supported; in fact, the relationship, a statistically significant one, is in the opposite direction. Moreover, we asked about forms of punishment during our 1975–1976 interview as well and had similar results. On the time I variable, 40 percent, 33 percent, and 22 percent, respectively, of those who resorted to whipping, spanking, or nonphysical discipline reported receiving assistance from two or more psychiatric professionals. The comparable proportions on the time II measure of punishment were 38 percent, 30 percent, and 22 percent. At least three explanations are possible for this surprising finding. First, guilt feelings may be very strong among parents who whip or paddle their children; such parents realize that something must be done about the situation and so they seek psychiatric assistance for the child. Conversely parents who do not use physical discipline are more apt to feel self-sufficient. A second possibility is that the psychiatric agency is made aware of the physical punishment during the intake process and is more apt to give assistance in such cases. The third explanation, which we prefer, stems from Becker's excellent review of the literature dealing with the consequences of parental discipline.[13] His work suggests that there may be three somewhat independent dimensions of parent behavior (warmth-hostility, restrictiveness-permissiveness, and calm detachment-anxious emotional involvement). While Becker notes that research indicated that physical punishment is associated with hostility variables, the complexity of the dimensional interrelations rules out facile generalizations. He points out that definitions of discipline have varied considerably; for example, some researchers include yelling and threats with physical punishment under the rubric of power-assertive techniques. In spite of the complex nature of the interrelationships, Becker observes that many studies suggest that the power-assertive techniques are correlated with noncooperative, aggressive behavior in children. Now extrapolating from Becker's review, we suggest that there is an interaction between the use of physical discipline and the child's aggression, with continuous looping. The child reacts to physical punishment with noncooperative aggressive behavior, which begets more physical punishment, and so on. With each spiral in this interaction, the parent desperately seeks a solution from external sources; that is, the parent seeks to have psychiatric or other persons present or suggest the answer to the puzzle presented by the child's undesirable, aggressive behavior. The relationship between the child's 1963 score on the authority scale and the measure of discipline is -0.14 ($p < 0.01$), a finding consistent with our explanation. Because the 1975 measure of discipline covers the years after the 1963 authority scores were obtained, we will utilize the 1975 measure of discipline in the regression analysis since we wish to assess the effects of later punishment on both parental coping and the child's adult adjustment. (Incidentally, the r between the discipline scores for the two times was .24.)

Of direct relevance to our hypothesis concerning disciplinary tactics are the quality of the marriage and the extent to which the parents agree on child-rearing practices. We hypothesized that parents who agreed on child-rearing tactics would be more likely to obtain assistance. Our measure of child-rearing was skewed in the direction of agreement with less than one-quarter of the parents reporting any disagreement in this area. The hypothesis was not supported with respect to obtaining psychiatric assistance. Moreover, the relationship involving informal assistance is the opposite of our prediction. When the parents had disagreements in child-rearing, the respondent (usually the mother) reported seeking and obtaining more informal advice than agreeing parents did. In addition, and consistent with this finding, we found that respondents who disagreed in other areas of decision making and who reported marital unhappiness also obtained substantially more informal assistance than did their counterparts (see table 8–11). That parents tend to use their friends and relatives as sounding boards when they have marital and child-rearing differences has important implications for those interested in the coping behavior of parents. Indeed the apparently realistic agency requirement that both parents must be involved before assistance is proffered to the child may discourage some parents who do not wish to discuss tension-provoking subjects. This, of course, is a dilemma for professionals and parents alike since it is possible that the parental disagreement may be at the heart of the child's problems.

Verbal Intelligence

Other researchers have found and/or speculated about an association between verbal skill and obtaining psychiatric aid, and we hypothesized along similar lines. We found no such association. Indeed since verbal skill is considered to be class related, this is not a surprising finding when we consider that class is not related to seeking and finding help among our respondents. However, before the contact with clinics in 1962, a portion of our respondents during the 1963 interview reported earlier help-seeking efforts. For that preguidance-clinic period, we did find that more "intelligent" respondents had been more likely than less "intelligent" ones to have sought assistance. Again our longitudinal analysis leads us to suggest that parents of lower verbal ability do seek and obtain assistance but over a generally longer period of time. They, too, like lower-class respondents, have probably been helped by a growth in the availability of mental health facilities. The relationship between the Quick Word Test scores and social class ($r = .39$) offers some support to this reasoning. Because of this association between class and verbal ability, we shall omit the latter from the regression analyses presented later.

Social Isolation

Contrary to our expectations, social isolation was not related to the utilization of assistance. We surmise that this is due, at least in part, to the relationship between class and social isolation ($r = .36$). This suggests the advisability of omitting social isolation during our later analysis of help-seeking for guidance clinic cases.

Hopefulness for Child's Future

In connection with our hypothesis that respondents who were hopeful about their children's future would be more likely than their counterparts to translate such feelings into coping activities, we had reasoned that people who felt hopeful were confident about their power to manipulate the environment and that a feeling of hopelessness meant surrender. Once again, our hypothesis was not supported, and in the case of psychiatric assistance, the finding was both opposite to our expectations and statistically significant. Parents who felt hopeful about their children's future were much less likely to seek and receive psychiatric aid than were parents who felt hopeless.

It is difficult to know what meanings were attributed to the question by the various respondents. Does being hopeful refer to the aspirations one has for a child's future? Or is the response concerning hope for the future a prediction based on past or recent performance? One clue, we thought, was offered by the fact that respondents' comparison of the child's behavior in 1963 against the child's behavior at the 1962 clinic contact was related to hopefulness. Those parents, in 1963, who thought that the child's behavior had already improved were considerably less likely to utilize psychiatric assistance during the subsequent twelve or thirteen years, in contrast to those who thought the child's behavior was worse (58 percent to 13 percent, in the extreme categories, reported not utilizing any psychiatric assistance). The relationship between hopefulness and the 1962–1963 comparison was then examined in order to shed light on the meaning of hopefulness; the

Pearsonian *r* was .42. The strength of the relationship suggests that, at least for a good portion of the respondents, the extent of hopefulness is derived from the child's recent performance. Other bases of hopefulness, such as aspirations and personality characteristics not included in our study, are probably operating for others of our respondents.

This analysis of hopefulness and of the respondent's comparative assessment of the child's behavior is an important key to the subsequent help-seeking and help-receiving experiences of the parents. This analysis has important implications for the role of spontaneous remission in later adjustment. We know already that only a little more than 10 percent of our respondents reported not receiving any assistance from any source during the 1963 through 1975–1976 period. We also see that parents who perceived their child as having improved by 1963 were less likely than their counterparts to seek psychiatric assistance. The nonpsychiatric professional assistance data in table 8–11 also show that such parents are not as likely to seek nonpsychiatric help. Finally, although we did not present the data in a table, we examined the relationship between the parents' 1963 assessment of improvement and the total number of assistance episodes during the subsequent twelve or thirteen years. Not surprisingly, this relationship is consistent with our discussion ($r = .20$).

Among the 10 percent of cases (twenty-six cases) who did not report any assistance at all during 1963–1976, in only one case did the parent report that the child was worse in 1963. Thus, one could argue that for twenty-five (approximately 10 percent) of all respondents reinterviewed in 1975–1976, a case can be made that adjustment or remission had already taken place and that it is possible that such adjustment was spontaneous—possibly spontaneous because the brief contact at the clinic in 1962 might have been helpful to some parents, allowing them to place their child's behavior within a more acceptable context. The other 90 percent of the parents reported receiving some kind of assistance during the subsequent years, so it would be far-fetched to assume that any subsequent adjustment took place in a vacuum.

So far we have mainly presented findings involving the time I independent variables, those factors that allow us the opportunity for longitudinal analysis. Now we look briefly at a few relationships involving explanatory variables from the 1975–1976 interview. Some of these variables rely on recall, of course, and thus can confound the order of event placement. For this reason we have developed only four predictions involving time II variables, which we believe to be of substantial importance to our study and which we think may be fairly characterized as being representative of antecedent conditions in the analysis of long-term coping. These involve the number of children respondents had had, the number of major life events respondents had experienced over the last ten or eleven years, the number of times respondents had moved their residence over the last twelve or thirteen years, and the role of the father in child rearing.

Number of Children in Family

We had reasoned that people with many children would have fewer mental and material resources for coping with the problems of a family child compared to people with fewer children who could devote more time to problem-solving activities for a difficult child. Thus we hypothesized that people with fewer children would seek and receive more psychiatric assistance than would persons with a large number of children. The test of significance did not reveal a statistically significant relationship ($p < .10$) although the relationship was in the hypothesized direction. Examination of the cross-tabulation revealed a curvilinear relationship; those with fewer children and those with many sought and received more psychiatric assistance than those in the middle category. When number of children was trichotomized into few (one to three), moderate (four to six), and many (seven or more), the proportions reporting having received no psychiatric assistance were 42 percent, 60 percent, and 43 percent, respectively. The fact that there were fewer families with many children accounted for finding an association in the predicted direction. Once again, however, assumptions about coping behavior are not supported by the data in our study. There has been little theory and even less research on the stress-coping process. Even though the poor have more children among our study group (Pearsonian $r = -.27$), and this is consistent with other studies, there is very little support for the prediction that this will negatively affect their child-rearing efforts. The lower-class respondents and those with many children are not apathetic or too burdened with their cares to seek help for children perceived as having problems.

According to our data, the group that bears watching are those with four, five, or six children. We do not know why they are the families who are least likely to seek assistance. One line of inquiry that should be considered by researchers interested in coping is the role of family planning and the extent to which the number of children had is desired. Perhaps those who are most concerned about limiting family size and, thus, more overcome by failure may be found in the middle group.

Number of Times Moved Residence since 1963

We reasoned that families who moved a lot would lose much of their informal support system and thus would become more dependent on professional psychiatric assistance. Our hypothesis was also influenced, in part, by the work of Michael Inbar.[14] Inbar suggests that the latency-age (six to eleven) child who experiences immigration to foreign countries may be at greater risk of future school underachievement (indexed by college admission) than children of other ages. He later suggested that other uprooting experiences, such as residential changes, death, or divorce of parents, may also adversely affect latency-age children. Our data do not permit a test of Inbar's hypothesis since we do not have the required data on the child's age at the precise time such events occurred. However, we reasoned that the more a family moved, the more disruptive this would potentially be for the child. As a result, such families would be required to seek help in coping with the child's subsequent problem.

Our hypothesis is not supported by the data. There is only the slightest tendency for families who move a lot to seek and receive more psychiatric assistance than their opposite numbers. Neither is residential change related to the seeking of other forms of assistance. We now conclude that our data are not refined enough with respect to knowledge about the reasons for residence changes to permit the proper analysis of the relationship between moving and help-seeking.

Number of Major Life Events in Last Ten or Eleven Years

A number of writers have suggested that various life experiences or events, such as a home broken by death or divorce, are related to a variety of emotional problems, including, but not restricted to, delinquency.[15] Since we did not have specific knowledge of the conditions surrounding migration, death, and other life events, we decided to rely only on the number rather than the type of such life events. We hypothesized that respondents who experienced three or more life events, in contrast to those experiencing fewer, would be more likely to have received both psychiatric and informal assistance.

This hypothesis was strongly supported and gives strength to stress researchers who view the family as one of our most vital resources. Its importance is underscored by the activities of our respondents when they were weakened by loss through death or divorce or by other wearing events; they sought help from various available sources.

Father's Role in Child-Rearing

The last coping hypothesis concerned the father's role in child-rearing. We predicted that in situations involving a dominant or supportive father, there would be less resort to psychiatric assistance than in cases where the father was weak or destructive. The relationship was in the predicted direction, but it was not statistically significant. In cases where the father was reported as dominant or supportive, 50 percent of our respondents utilized psychiatric assistance, while in cases involving weak or destructive fathers, 58 percent of the respondents used psychiatric aid. Our data on the father's role are somewhat sparse and do not elaborate in sufficient detail on the complex interplay between the parents for us to speculate on the fathers' contributions to child-rearing. We did find, however, that the more the father participated in the treatment process (without specifying the nature of treatment), the more likely our respondents were to utilize psychiatric assistance. More research needs to be undertaken on the father's role in child-rearing.

Some Higher-Order Relationships Involving Social Class

So far we have presented only the zero-order relationships involving our independent variables and the measures of assistance obtained by respondents. A number of the independent variables were found to be related to the coping variables. Perhaps the biggest surprise was that social-class level was found not to be related to any of the measures of assistance. We surmise that this lack of a relationship is due in part to the fact that ours is a study group of parents who were motivated enough to seek help at a guidance clinic in 1962, and thus the class difference was somewhat reduced through the self-selection process. In addition, the increase in availability of government-supported measures may have reduced the help-finding differential among the various social-class levels.

Because of the theoretical importance of social class in stress-related research, we decided to examine some other relationships while controlling social-class level. Since age of child had been found related to obtaining psychiatric assistance (Kendall's tau $= -.10$) but not to social class (Kendall's tau $= .00$) we examined the three-way relationship.

Table 8–12 shows that social class retains some explanatory power. The zero-order relationship between age and receiving psychiatric assistance resides primarily among families from the upper social-class level. Lower- and middle-class respondents are as likely to receive such assistance for older children as they are for younger children; however, upper-class families are much more likely to find psychiatric assistance for the younger children than for older ones. Moreover, lower- and middle-class families are less likely to find psychiatric assistance for younger children and more likely to find it for older children in comparison with upper-class families.

The zero-order relationship between hopefulness and psychiatric assistance revealed that the less-hopeful parents obtained the most help (Ken-

Table 8–12

Proportions of Respondents Receiving Psychiatric Assistance, by Age of Child in 1963, Controlling Social Class ($N = 237$)

	Proportions Receiving Psychiatric Assistance		
Child's Age in 1963	Lower Class (1–3)	Middle Class (4–6)	Upper Class (7–9)
10 years or under	52% (61)	59% (39)	70% (17)
11–15 years	43 (49)	59 (29)	36 (14)
16–18 years	58 (12)	56 (11)	20 (5)
	Kendall's tau = −.07, ns	Kendall's tau = −.02, ns	Kendall's tau = −.37, $p < .01$

Note: Numbers of children receiving assistance are given in parentheses.

dall's tau = .13); also, upper-class parents were more hopeful (Kendall's tau = −.20). The relationship between hopefulness and psychiatric assistance, with class controlled, was stronger among lower-class respondents (Kendall's tau = 0.13, $p < .05$) than among upper- and middle-class respondents (Kendall's tau = .02, ns). That is, among lower-class persons there was a larger effect, with the hopeful parents being much less likely to obtain psychiatric assistance (46 percent) in comparison to parents who were not hopeful (68 percent). A similar but weaker relationship was found for middle- and upper-class parents.

There is good reason to believe that hopeful feelings arose, in part, from the child's recent behavior. In turn, we could now hypothesize that the parents who obtained the most psychiatric assistance were not only the least hopeful in 1963 but that their children scored higher on our two symptoms scales (observance of authority rules and neurotic behavior) in 1963. Although social class might still show some explanatory power in such an analysis, we suggest that it is less influential than the parents' perceptions of the child's behavior in guiding their problem-solving behavior. Significantly these observations pertain only to the utilization of psychiatric assistance.

In addition to the time I variables mentioned so far in connection with the subsequent utlization of psychiatric assistance, there are other factors, such as respondent personality characteristics, which, if employed in a controlled analysis, might enlighten our understanding of help-seeking. Because of the complexity of the relationships among the variables in our study, demonstrated by the use of social class as a control, it became apparent to us that regression analysis could be of great value in clarifying the coping process. This conclusion is amplified when we see that the differ-

ent types of help received (particularly psychiatric and informal) are influenced by different factors.

Regression Analyses in Connection with Long-term Help-Seeking

A number of factors were interacting in complex ways to influence parental
coping on behalf of the children in this study, so we believed that a higher-
order analysis could be useful in identifying the most relevant variables.
Procedures for the regression analyses presented here are quite similar to
those utilized in chapter 6 in connection with short-term outcome. The primary difference from the earlier regression analysis is that the court-clinic
cases are not included here; thus, only the beta coefficients will be presented
here since this is a within-clinic analysis.

Three dependent measures of long-term help utilization were employed,
with a separate regression analysis performed for each. Two of these—utilization of psychiatric assistance and utilization of informal assistance—were
presented earlier in this chapter in our zero-order analysis. In addition, we
employed our most comprehensive measure of help utilization: total number of times (instances) in which assistance of any type was received (here-
after called "total assistance"). This measure is related to all three of the
sources (types) of assistance, having Pearsonian r's of .62, .50, and .66,
respectively, for psychiatric assistance, informal assistance, and nonpsychiatric professional assistance. Although there is overlap here, there is
some independence between total number of contacts and each of the three
specific sources of assistance. Since total assistance also has the strongest
relationship to duration of assistance among our coping measures ($r = .36$),
we thought it might be the most important of all our measures of coping.

Fifteen independent variables were employed in the regression analyses;
of these, thirteen are time I variables (collected in 1963), and two are time II
data (1975–1976). Three additional time I variables were employed in an
earlier regression analysis but were discarded because they proved to be of
little value in explaining the utilization of assistance. These three were the
social isolation scale, blaming relatives for the child's problem, and blaming
the child's peers. The independent variables included in our analysis were
selected on either empirical or theoretical grounds. All of the variables used
in the regression analysis, dependent as well as independent, are presented
in table 8–13.

The results of our regression analysis (table 8–14) are presented for each
of the three measures of help received. An individual beta coefficient
reflects the explanatory power of one independent variable when the effects
of the other independent variables are controlled. The combined power of
the independent variable is reflected in the postscript at the base of each
column.

Table 8–13
Variables Employed in Regression Analysis of Long-Term Coping

	Code Categories
Dependent variables (time II)	
Psychiatric assistance	Used 0–9 with 0 = none and 9 = 9 or more instances
Informal assistance	Used 0–9 with 0 = none and 9 = 9 or more instances
Total number of times assistance received from all sources	Used 0–9 with 0 = none and 9 = 9 or more instances
Independent variables	
Time I variables (1963)	
Social class (Warner's four-factor ISC)	1–9, with 9 high (upper class)
Child's age on January 1, 1963 (in years)	1–18 with 1 = 1 year and 18 = 18 years
Authoritarianism (Srole's five-item summary scale)	0 = not authoritarian, 5 = most authoritarian
Frustration (Srole' four-item summary scale)	0 = not frustrated, 4 = most frustrated
Rigidity (Srole's six-item summary scale	0 = not rigid, 6 = most rigid
Sought psychiatric assistance between 1962 and 1963	0 = did not seek psychiatric assistance, 1 = sought psychiatric assistance
Sought nonpsychiatric assistance between 1962 and 1963	0 = did not seek nonpsychiatric assistance, 1 = sought nonpsychiatric assistance
Marital status: Respondent separated from spouse?	0 = respondent not separated, 1 = respondent separated
Marital status: Respondent divorced, widowed, or never married?	0 = respondent not divorced, widowed, or never married 1 = respondent divorced, widowed, or never married
Authority symptoms scale score in 1963 (Guttman scale)	1 = score of 0, 2 = score of 1, 3 = score of 2, 4 = score of 3
Neurotic symptoms scale score in 1963 (Guttman scale)	1 = score of 0, 2 = score of 1, 3 = score of 2, 4 = score of 3
Hope for child's future	1 = very hopeful, 2 = somewhat hopeful, 3 = not too hopeful, 4 = not hopeful at all
Parental agreement on child-rearing practices (based on extent of agreement on 8 items)	0 = some or little agreement, 1 = much agreement
Time II variables (1975–1976)	
Number of major life events occurring in last 10 or 11 years	0 = none, 1 = 1, 2 = 2, 3 = 3 or more
Disciplinary measures employed when children were disobedient	1 = whipping, 2 = spanking, 3 = nonphysical

First, a fair amount of the overall variance, r^2, is accounted for by the predictor variables. For two of the three help-receiving measures, the overall F test shows that a statistically significant amount of the variance ($p <$ .001) has been accounted for by our independent variables with the results

Table 8–14

Standardized Regression Coefficients for Three Measures of Long-Term Coping on Fifteen Independent Variables

Variables	Psychiatric Assistance	Informal Assistance	Total Assistance
Time I			
Social class	−.00	−.09	−.08
Child's age	−.04	−.06	−.16*
Authoritarianism	.00	.05	.03
Frustration	−.08	−.05	−.10
Rigidity	−.08	−.08	−.12
Sought psychiatric assistance, 1962–1963	.30***	.08	.36***
Sought nonpsychiatric assistance, 1962–1963	.11	.18*	.23**
Respondent separated	−.08	.07	.00
Respondent divorced, widowed, or never married	−.13	−.03	−.02
Authority symptoms, 1963	−.04	−.11	−.06
Neurotic symptoms, 1963	.19*	.18*	.12
Hope for child's future	.08	−.01	.09
Child-rearing agreement	.04	−.04	.05
Time II			
Number of life events	.19**	.12	.21**
Disciplinary measures	−.16*	−.11	−.17*
	Overall F = 2.97; df = 15/167; $p <$ .001; r^2 = .021; adjusted r^2 = .14	Overall F = 1.23; df = 15/167; $p <$ .10; r^2 = .10; adjusted r^2 = .02	Overall F = 3.42; df = 15/167; $p <$ .001; r^2 = .23; adjusted r^2 = .17

Note: On the F test, significance levels are indicated as follows: *$p <$ .05, **$p <$ .01, ***$p <$ .001.

being more impressive for total assistance. Although the F test is not statistically significant at the conventional .05 level for informal assistance, its approximation to this level is an indication that at least some of the factors relevant to an understanding of informal help utilization for families like ours may have been identified.

Early help-seeking of psychiatric assistance is the best predictor of the long-term seeking and receipt of both psychiatric assistance and total assistance. Thus those who initially seek psychiatric assistance will not only continue to seek it until they find it but they may also be inclined to seek and receive assistance from many and different types of sources. A similar strain of consistency was exhibited by those who sought nonpsychiatric assistance between 1962 and 1963 since the early seeking of such assistance is a strong predictor of the receipt of informal assistance. Although we did not collect data on informal assistance in 1962–1963, it is nevertheless clear that the seeking of nonpsychiatric assistance at the earlier time was a stronger predictor of informal assistance than it was of psychiatric assistance.

Somewhat surprisingly, scores on the neurotic symptoms scale are almost equal in predictive value for both psychiatric and informal assistance. However, the intensity and duration of instances of assistance appear to be greater in the case of psychiatric assistance than in those of informal assistance. Our data, though not conclusive on this issue, support this notion. Thus the duration of assistance is directly related to receipt of psychiatric assistance but not to informal assistance. Offsetting this point, however, is the fact that some respondents received assistance from both source types; this could account, in part, for the fact that the neurotic score is related to both psychiatric and informal assistance. The reason neurotic behavior is not significantly related to total assistance received is apparently due to the absence of a relationship between it and nonpsychiatric professional assistance, the third constituent source type of total assistance.

Notably age is not related to the long-term receipt of psychiatric assistance when the other variables are controlled. Our hunch that both parents and psychiatric professionals would be more concerned with younger children is not supported, although the relationship is in the predicted direction. A similar fate met our prediction that respondents would receive more informal assistance for younger children. But the fact that the direction for all three of the sources of assistance was negative helps to explain the statistically significant relationship between child's age and total assistance, although it does not automatically follow that uniformity of sign direction results in a statistically significant relationship for total assistance. Nevertheless, when all of the occasions of help receiving are summed, it is clear that the younger the child, the greater the amount of assistance received.

The absence of parental agreement in child-rearing practices among predictors was unexpected. Perhaps more rigorous measures of parental agreement are needed.

We were also surprised to observe that respondent hopefulness in 1963 was not significantly related to either receipt of psychiatric assistance or total assistance, although the direction signs are consistent with zero-order relationships. Hopefulness would appear to be more an indication of positive recent change in the child's behavior reported during the 1963 interview than a predictor of respondent's future utilization of external assistance. There is some tendency, nevertheless, for the more-hopeful parents to desist from the use of assistance as indexed by both psychiatric and total assistance.

Our two time II independent variables—number of life events and disciplinary measures—are related to both psychiatric and total assistance. Because of its importance to stress-related research in general and because we have not previously described it sufficiently, we will discuss our rationale for our life-events measure.

Substantial attention has been devoted to the etiological's role that life events play in psychological or psychiatric disorder. Most prior studies of life events have used a matching design involving a set of cases diagnosed clinically and compared with a control group.[16] These have been retrospective studies in that investigators assessed the presence of past life events among clinical cases and their controls, usually finding an excess of stressful life events among the clinical cases. Such studies usually suggest that the stressful life events are etiologically significant. Various students of stress, including the Dohrenwends and Gersten and her associates, have suggested that prospective studies, involving cohorts of subjects who are differentiated by type and extent of stressful life events, may be more useful in etiologic analysis.[17] Gersten and her colleagues caution that other factors such as earlier disturbances and antecedent sociocultural factors should be important components of such cohort studies. These early conditions, they suggest, permit the consideration of other important matters, such as duration.

In our study, we are not pursuing the issue of etiology; instead we are interested in factors related to coping behavior after the perception of a problem. Coping, then, is a theoretically important determinant of the duration of a perceived problem. We hypothesized that subsequent undesirable life events, such as the loss of a spouse through death or divorce, could serve as stimuli for the respondents and lead them to intensify their reach for assistance. Since our own orientation is to view such stimuli as potential stressors, we recognize that such events could also blunt an individual's ability to cope with certain problems, such as child-rearing.[18] Thus we attempted to ascertain the relationship of undesirable life events to coping behavior.

The nature of our interest is relevant to another major issue raised by students of stress, and it concerns the measure of stress employed. Studies focusing on etiology have tended to employ structured indexes. Because we did not assume that we could anticipate all of the possibly stressful life events experienced by members of our study group and because the question of etiology was not a direct question in our study, we decided to pose an open-ended question: "Over the last ten or eleven years, what major changes have there been in your family?" Interviewers were instructed to probe for responses. These were coded into thirteen simple categories; in addition, multiple-response categories were possible. The simple categories were: no major changes, respondent divorce-separation, moved a distance, death in family, remarriage of respondent, decline in living standard, increase in living standard, illness, psychiatric problem, marital problem, legal problem, divorce of a child, and marriage of a child. Death and physical illness were mentioned most frequently and, in fact, among those reporting changes, were the only two categories cited by more than 20 percent of the study group. Respondent's divorce-separation and marriage of a child were next in order of citations, each being mentioned by less than 15 percent of the respondents reporting changes.

In an effort to ascertain the undesirability of any of these changes, we then asked our respondents, "Over the last ten years or so, have there been any major crises or problems in the family?" We then solicited the respondent's list of the problems or crises. By comparing the list of frequency of changes in the last ten or eleven years with the frequency of crises over a similar period, we arrived at a rough indication of desirability or undesirability of the events. The two most frequently cited changes, death and physical illness, were then adduced to be nearly always undesirable. Psychiatric problems, legal problems, divorce of a child, and decline in income were also seen as undesirable by practically all respondents. Respondent's divorce or separation was about equally divided between desirable and undesirable. Somewhat surprisingly, residential moving was not considered undesirable by respondents, a finding that raises the issue of whether moving would be similarly viewed by the children. Higher living standards, remarriage of respondents, and marriage of a child, as a rule, did not appear to be undesirable from the respondent's perspective.

Since we had not employed a prestructured instrument in arriving at a determination of experienced life events and our procedures were not precise, we did not gain some needed information, such as identifying the member of the familiy who died.[19] In addition, our procedures probably resulted in much less information on life changes than would have been the case had we used a structured instrument. Because of these apparent limitations in our data, we decided to use the number of life events as a variable rather than specific events. Although we have added together both desirable and undesirable events, it seems obvious, in view of the frequency distributions, that the numbers include more of the undesirable events.

A comparison of the regression table with the zero-order coefficient presented in table 8-12 shows that the number of life events maintains its strength as a predictor of psychiatric assistance when all other independent variables are controlled; with respect to informal assistance, it also retains the same predictive power.

The second of our time II independent variables, disciplinary measures, gained in predictive power on the measure of psychiatric assistance when other variables were controlled. As in the case of psychiatric assistance, disciplinary practice also predicted total assistance when the other independent variables were controlled. Parents who employ physical punishment, it appears, are searching for assistance, regardless of their conception of causation.

Summary and Conclusions

In this chapter we have employed a variety of help-utilization variables as indicators of parental coping. A traditional measure of coping—parental discipline—was employed as an independent variable in this analysis. Obviously much research remains to be done on the internal styles of coping—those forms that emphasize ways in which parents attempt to cope without the benefit of external assistance.

We began with a series of frequency distributions that revealed widespread help-seeking and help-receiving among the families of our study. Perhaps the most startling of these frequency distributions is the one showing that almost 90 percent of our respondents reported receiving some form of assistance. Slightly more than half of our respondents reported getting psychiatric assistance. Of these, almost two-thirds reported receiving psychotherapy. Since all of our guidance-clinic families had failed to receive the assistance they applied for at psychiatric clinics in 1962, it was gratifying to observe their later success in finding assistance.

A zero-order analysis, using a measure of association primarily, was undertaken in order to locate the apparently relevant independent variables. An attempt was made to use stress-relevant conceptions in the zero-order analysis. Narrowing down the number of independent variables to fifteen, we then employed regression analysis in an effort to locate the best predictors of help utilization. We used three dependent variables in the regression analysis: psychiatric assistance, informal assistance, and total assistance received.

Early seeking of psychiatric assistance was the best predictor of both psychiatric and total assistance. In addition, neurotic scores, number of life events, and disciplinary tactics were each highly useful predictors of assistance. Other predictors of total assistance were seeking early nonpsychiatric help, the child's age, number of life events, and disciplinary measures. Informal assistance was predicted best by the early search for nonpsychiatric assistance and neurotic scores.

Notes

1. See L. Pearlin and C. Schooler, "The Structure of Coping," *Journal of Health and Social Behavior* (March 1978):2–21. T. Langner and S. Michael, *Life Stress and Mental Health* (Glencoe, Ill.: Free Press, 1963).

2. Pearlin and Schooler, "Structure."

3. For the Midtown study, see L. Srole, T. Langner, S. Michael, M. Opler, and T. Rennie, *Mental Health in the Metropolis* (New York: McGraw-Hill, 1962), vol. 1, and T. Langner and S. Michael, *Life Stress and Mental Health* (London: Free Press of Glencoe, 1963), vol. 2. See also A. Hollingshead and F. Redlich, *Social Class and Mental Illness: A Community Study* (New York: Wiley, 1958).

4. See Barbara Dohrenwend and Bruce Dohrenwend, "Class and Race as Status Related Sources of Stress," in Sol Levine and N. Scotch, eds., *Social Stress* (Chicago: Aldine, 1970).

5. August B. Hollingshead and Frederick G. Redlich, *Social Class and Mental Illness* (New York: John Wiley, 1959).

6. Dohrenwend and Dohrenwend, "Class and Race."

7. On this point, see J. Kosa, "The Nature of Poverty," in J. Kosa, A. Antonovsky, and I. Zola, *Poverty and Health,* 1–34.

8. See Richard Lazarus, "Cognitive and Personality Factors Underlying Threat and Coping," in Levine and Scotch, *Social Stress.*

9. Dohrenwend, "Class and Race," pp. 124–125.

10. See James F. Teele, "Suicidal Behavior, Assaultiveness, and Socialization Principles," *Social Forces* (May 1965):510–518.

11. This hypothesis was influenced by a recent work on fathers; see D. Lynn, *The Father: His Role in Child Development* (Monterey, Calif.: Brooks/Cole Publishing Co., 1974).

12. *The Report of the President's Commission on Mental Health* (Washington, D.C.: Government Printing Office, 1978), vol. 1.

13. Wesley Becker, "Consequences of Different Kinds of Parental Discipline," in Martin Hoffman and Lois W. Hoffman, eds., *Review of Child Development Research* (New York: Russell Sage Foundation, 1964).

13. Pearlin and Schooler, "Structure."

14. See Michael Inbar, *The Vulnerable Age Phenomenon* (New York: Russell Sage Foundation, 1976).

15. For example, see J. Teele, "Social Pathology and Stress," in Levine and Scotch, *Social Stress,* 228–256, and S. Croog, "The Family as a Source of Stress," in Levine and Scotch, 19–53.

16. Barbara S. Dohrenwend and Bruce P. Dohrenwend, "Overview and Prospects for Research on Stressful Life Events," in their *Stressful Live Events* (New York: John Wiley, 1974).

17. J. Gersten, T. Langner, J. Eisenberg, O. Simcha-Fagan, "An Evaluation of the Etiologic Role of Stressful Life-Change Events on Psychological Disorders," *Journal of Health and Social Behavior* (September 1977):228–244.

18. See Teele, "Social Pathology and Stress." In a highly relevant and more specific analysis of our life-event data, it was found that within each of the categories of respondent divorce, moving a long distance, and death in the family, there was substantially more help-seeking after 1963 when our respondents had had a face-to-face contact at the clinic in 1962 as opposed to when they had not been seen. See Ann Skendall Teele and James E. Teele, "Subsequent Help-Seeking by Nonsuccessful Applications for Child Psychiatric Treatment" (Paper presented at the 1978 Meetings of the American Psychological Association, Toronto).

19. Langner and Michael, for example, found that the death of the mother was more detrimental to children than the death of the father for lower-class persons, but that among middle-class persons, the death of the father appears more detrimental. *Life Stress,* p. 162.

9

Long-Term Outcome among Guidance-Clinic Cases

We now come to the question of most concern to researchers, parents, and clinicians alike: What are the factors that are of greatest importance to the child's adult well-being? Put differently, How can parents and others who are concerned best help the child to mature into a well-adjusted adult? In the present study it is also appropriate to ask, Among all the variables of our study, which appear to be most relevant to gaining an understanding of the child's adult behavior?

We know now that once parents believe their child has a problem and needs help, they nearly always extend the search for external assistance over a period of years. In many cases, they cannot seem to get enough help. Somewhat paradoxically, the parents who are the least optimistic about their children's future adjustment look for and find the most assistance. Further analysis of the data leads to the conclusion that when children improve, parental optimism grows and the parent is less in need of assistance. Thus as parental expectations changed in response to either the sinking in of early clinic advice or/and the child's changing behavior, such parents dropped out of the help-seeking population, leaving the pessimistic parents as the major help-seekers. Of course, this is only a generality since some parents continued to seek and receive assistance in the face of the child's short-term improvement.

We now wonder if the child's short-term improvement translated into successful adult adjustment; if the parent's earlier pessimism or optimism appears justified in light of adult adjustment; which behavioral, personality, and social factors (including family factors) were relevant in predicting the child's adjustment as an adult; how parental problem-solving behavior and developmental (or maturational) processes operated to influenced the child's adult adjustment.

We have emphasized one aspect of coping: the parents' use of external assistance. We might have concentrated on changes in problem-perception, or change in the parents' philosophy of child-rearing but we offer only limited data on these alternative approaches to coping, choosing to treat certain aspects of these matters only as explanatory variables. Obviously, much research remains to be done on problem-solving behavior.

Measures of Adult Functioning

There are many problems involved in an attempt to construct unidimensional measures of change, even for short periods of time. Such problems are multiplied when more-extended periods of time are considered. In our study, it seemed clear that the construction of change measures was not feasible. The main problem was that the measures of the child's behavior relied on in the assessment of short-term outcome were based on a symptoms checklist administered to respondents in 1963. These symptoms were nearly all relevant to the behavior of children and, in large part, could not be realistically employed for the adult stage. Thus when we were constructing our second-stage design around 1974, we decided to rely on indexes of adult adjustment or functioning rather than attempt to measure change directly. (Of course, this decision does not preclude an effort to employ measures of the child's behavior in the prediction of later adult adjustment.)

Thus in 1975–1976 we collected data that enabled us to employ three measures of the child's adult functioning. These three indexes included one global measure and two measures that tap more limited, specific, areas of adult behavior: instrumental functioning, family involvement, and respondent's view.

Instrumental Functioning

Instrumental functioning refers to the level of performance attained in the conduct of the essential adult tasks of working and carrying on social relationships.[1] Among the various questions asked of respondents in 1975–1976 were the following:

1. "How much satisfaction does _____ get in his/her job at present? (If _____ is still in school, and is not working substitute "school" for "job.") Responses were precoded as "a lot," "some," "little or more," and "don't know."
2. "Is _____ married now?" (If married ask, "How many children does _____ have?")
3. "How satisfying is _____'s social life to him/her?" Responses were precoded as "not at all satisfying," "somewhat satisfying," "very satisfying," and "don't know."

With respect to job satisfaction, we used extent of satisfaction with school for those not working, whether in college or technical school. All females who were neither in school nor working but who were married and had children were then assigned to the high-performance category on the job-satisfaction measure.[2] There were only nine cases of this type. At the time of the interview, we also had one case in prison, another case in a half-way house for mental patients, and two cases in schools for the retarded. The respondents reported each of these children to be performing poorly on each component of performance. Eighteen of the 252 guidance-clinic cases reinterviewed either did not know how their child was performing or were unwilling to share this information.

We then cross-tabulated our job- or school-satisfaction measure against the social-satisfaction measure; the two three-point measures produced nine cells (table 9–1). The numbers in parentheses are the scoring categories into which the cells were placed. When the cells are summed as indicated in table 9–1, the distribution shown in table 9–2 results. While there is some skewing toward the high-adjustment category, a sizable number of children are not adjusting very well.

Since we realize that this measure of instrumental functioning is based in large part on the respondent's judgment, it is important to add here that the instrumental measure is strongly related to the actual number of years of schooling that the child had completed ($r = .32$). Thus we are fairly confident that this index of instrumental functioning is a reasonable one.

Family Involvement

Although many social scientists have long emphasized the importance of understanding instrumental behavior in our society, relatively few have undertaken research on the role of the affective dimension of human life. In an odd twist in our society, we probably tend to think of family relations as being important to instrumental or achievement-oriented behavior far more often than as an end in itself. Indeed the very nature of the family (and of

Table 9–1
Measure of Adult Adjustment: Instrumental Functioning

	Extent of Satisfaction with Social Activities			
Extent of Job or School Satisfaction	Not at All	Somewhat	Very Satisfying	
A lot	17 (3)	34 (2)	90 (1)	141
Some	17 (4)	12 (3)	39 (2)	68
Little or none	8 (4)	11 (4)	6 (3)	25
	42	57	135	234[a]

Note: The scores assigned to cases in each cell are in parentheses.
[a]Insufficient information in eighteen cases.

Table 9–2
Distribution of Measure of Adult Adjustment

Score	N	%
1 (high)	90	38.5
2	73	31.1
3	35	15.0
4 (low)	36	15.4
Total	234	100.0

the male-female relationship) is changing as women join men in the attempt to wrest fulfillment and self-actualization from the pursuit of instrumental goals. This pursuit is perhaps strong evidence that our society has long undervalued the importance of the roles of wife and mother, seeing them as "only" aids to males in a male-dominated society. Perhaps developing societies in today's world have no alternative but to emphasize instrumental performance and thus to reduce the difference between men and women with respect to task assignment. The problem has to do with whether the affective dimension of life will become even more undervalued in the future and the effects of such undervaluing should it occur.

When women suggest that men should take more time with their children, they are sometimes acknowledging the importance of the affective dimension as well as the need for more balancing of instrumental and affective pursuits between the sexes. It is an acknowledgment that the nuclear family is a social form or institution of overbearing importance with unique tasks. The survival importance of the affective role may not be clear at the moment since the family has always more or less, as we moved from the extended to a nuclear unit, seen to its performance. However, an unpublished paper by Robert Helmreich, John Wilhelm, and Thomas Runge of the University of Texas at Austin, discussing the implications of their study of space flight, suggests that expressivity (the affective dimension), considered to be a feminine trait, may be more crucial to the future survival and well-being of human life than instrumentality and thus points up the role of the family.[3] They found that the ability to get along with others was a critical element in space flight and facilitated working with others, while competitiveness interfered with task performance. Their study is not definitive, but it suggests the importance of the family and the need for more study of both the instrumental and affective tasks.[4]

We have made this brief detour in order to underscore two matters. First, our measure of instrumental functioning in fact combines job and school satisfaction (what social scientists call instrumental) with satisfaction in social relationships (closer to the meaning of expressivity). Thus it is more appropriate perhaps to call it a combined index of instrumental-expressive adjustment. The second reason was to provide some background for the discussion of our measure of family involvement. To be more specific, our measure of family involvement concerns the extent to which our adult children stay in touch with their parents. The measure is not as good as we would like it to be, but we think that it will buttress our measure of instrumentality and point to an area in need of further research. Our underlying assumption is that adult children who do not stay in touch with their parents are commenting negatively on the quality of the parent-child relationship and probably are alienated from their parents. It is, of course, arguable as to whether family involvement should be considered as an indication of adult adjustment. After all, it is not a foregone conclusion that a child who avoids his parents is making or has made a poor adjustment. In fact they may have been able to make a good adjustment only because they avoided their parents. Our own orientation and judgment strongly suggest, however, that an important component of adulthood is missing when children fail to communicate over extended periods with their parents and that this component lies within the expressive mode.

During our 1975–1976 interview with respondents, we asked a series of questions designed to tap the extent to which the child stayed in touch with his parent(s):

1. "In what city does _____ live?"
2. "How often do you see _____ ?" Precoded response categories were "once a week," "once a month," "once a year," and "seldom or never."
3. [This question was directed at those who responded "once a year" or "seldom or never" to the preceding question.] "How often do you talk with _____ on the telephone?" Precoded response categories were "often," "sometimes," and "seldom or never."

The first of these three questions, bearing on the present whereabouts of the child, allowed us to determine how far away from home the child lived. We found that 23 percent of the children still lived in the parental home, 22 percent lived in the same town or city as their parents, and another 22 percent lived in the same metropolitan area (Boston or Worcester primarily). Thus two-thirds of our adult children either resided with or close to their parents. Of the remaining children, approximately 20 percent lived in a different metropolitan area or elsewhere on the East Coast, and 13 percent lived a substantial distance away from their parents, including some on the West Coast and a few living abroad.

When we cross-tabulated the adult child's distance from home against the frequency with which they saw their parents, we found, not unexpectedly, a very strong relationship ($r = .73$). We then assessed the frequency with which those who saw their children only yearly or less often spoke with their child on the telephone. (Since seeing the child was strongly related to where the child lived, we decided to exclude the child's place of residence from our measure). Thus we developed an index of the child's involvement with his parents based on the extent to which the child saw and/or conversed on the phone with parents. The distribution of the adult children on the measure is heavily skewed (table 9–3). Because of the necessity of using a collapsed interview, we had some slippage in our measure of family involvement. This measure of family involvement is skewed in the direction of frequent visiting, due in part to the fact that some adult children still live close to or with their parents. We included them anyway since they are involved with their parents. Moreover, some children lived close by and still rarely saw or called their parents.

Respondent's View

This is a global measure of outcome, based on a question designed to elicit the parent's assessment of how the subject child was performing at the time of the 1975–1976 interview: "Just how is your child _____ doing these days? Please tell me about him/her." [The interviewer was asked to probe but to be sensitive to the respondent's feelings if the child is not doing well]. Since this was an open-ended question, we coded responses later into one of the following categories: "very well," "fairly well," "poorly," and "very poor." There were only eleven guidance-clinic cases who were in the

Table 9–3
Frequency Distribution of Adult Children on Extent of Family Involvement

Extent of Involvement	N	%
Visits at least weekly	125	58.4
Visits at least monthly	46	21.5
Rarely visits parents but telephones often	19	8.9
Rarely visits or telephones	24	11.2
Totals	214[a]	100.0

[a]Of the 252 guidance-clinic cases involved in the second-stage interviewing, there was insufficient information on family involvement in 38 cases, or for 15 percent of the cases.

"very poor" category so we combined them with those doing poorly. The distribution is presented in table 9–4.

As with our other two outcome measures, this one is also skewed in the direction of satisfactory performance or adjustment. It is most interesting, however, that the proportions of those making satisfactory adjustments in adult life is similar to such proportions in studies emphasizing either or both treatment effects and spontaneous remission. Thus we think it is fair to say again that the present study is relevant to these other concerns.

At this stage in the consideration of long-term outcome measures, we think it appropriate to assess the interrelationships among them. These are presented below; the measure of association employed is Kendall's tau: instrumental functioning versus family involvement, .02; instrumental functioning versus respondent's view, .54; and family involvement versus respondent's view, .14.

It is obvious that the measure of instrumental functioning is independent of family involvement. This is not surprising since previous research on social participation suggested that participation with relatives was independent of participation with friends, and an item on friends is part of our measure of instrumental functioning.[5] In contrast to the lack of relationship between instrumental functioning and family involvement is the strong association between the measure of instrumental functioning and the respondent's more-global assessment of the adult child's adjustment. Also there is not much overlap between involvement with family and the respondent's global assessment. These differences in magnitude of association among the three measures of outcome offer hope that we are on the right track in searching for various dimensions of adjustment, an approach suggested by Strupp and his associates.[6] We suspected, however, that the absence of a relationship between instrumental functioning and family involvement was due in part to the fact that many of our older adult children were living away from home and functioning as adults, while many of the younger adults were living at or close to home and naturally had closer

Table 9–4
Distribution of Adult Children on Respondent's Assessment of Outcome

Respondent's Assessment	N	%
Very well	136	54.4
Fairly well	58	23.2
Poor or very poor	56	22.4
Totals	250[a]	100.0

[a]Two respondents indicated that they did not know how their children were faring.

ties with their parents. The fact that instrumental functioning is more strongly related to the respondent's global view, in contrast to the weak relationship between family involvement and the global assessment, suggests that parents attach greater importance to their child's holding a job and to other indications of adult adjustment than they do to direct contacts with their children, especially during the child's young adult years. We cannot test this hunch directly with our data, but we can examine the extent to which our three outcomes measures involve the same, or different, predictive factors.

Relationships between Independent Measures and Indicators of Adult Adjustment

The independent variables employed in this chapter include all forty-one of those presented in table 8–10 in connection with parental coping behavior. In addition, the predictor variables presented here include the six coping variables viewed as the dependent variables in chapter 8. The code categories and frequency distributions for these six variables are presented there in tables 8–3, 8–4, 8–6, and 8–7. The distribution regarding the specific type of assistance given has been dichotomized to whether psychotherapy was given; no psychotherapy is indicated by "0" and psychotherapy given is indicated by "1." The remaining five external coping variables are coded here precisely as they were in tables 8–3, 8–4, and 8–6. Finally, the independent variables include one new variable: those respondents who indicated that they were no longer worried about the child's behavior were asked to state when (in what year) they changed their expectations or ceased worrying about him. Their responses were coded so that the low ("1") end of the variable meant that they changed expectations a relatively long time ago (by 1964) and the high end ("4") meant that they changed rather recently (between 1971 and 1975 or 1976). The zero-order relationships between each of our forty-eight independent variables and the three outcome measures are presented in table 9–5.

Instrumental Functioning (Zero-Order Relationships)

Ten of the independent variables were related to this index of adjustment; these include four time I and six time II variables. Two of the time I variables described the child and two described the responding parent. More specifically, older children and children who did not have problems obeying authority rules in 1963 made better instrumental adjustments than did their counterparts. Parents who expressed hopefulness for the child's future and who scored high on the measure of rigidity in 1963 had children who made

Table 9–5
Associations between Outcome and Independent Variables

Independent Variables		Instrumental Functioning	Family Involvement	Respondent's View
Time I variables				
I.	Help-seeking, 1962–1963	.12	.08	.09
	Authority symptoms	.11*	−.02	.20***
	Neurotic symptoms	.05	.02	.14**
II.	Mother's age	−.06	.05	−.05
	Mother's race (C)	.16	.03	.06
	Mother's religion (C)	.16	.17	.17
	Mother's marital status (C)	.09	.17	.10
	Breadwinner's income	−.02	.00	−.10*
	Mother's education	−.02	−.05	−.13**
	Social class	.02	−.03	−.07
	Child's sex (C)	.05	.06	.14
	Child's age	−.19***	.09	−.04
III.	Blames self	−.07	−.08	.00
	Blames relatives	−.04	.07	.05
	Blames child's peers	−.03	.01	−.01
	Blames child	−.02	.08*	.01
	Focus of blame (C)	.13	.14	.04
	Quick Word Test	.00	.01	−.03
	Comparison of 1962–1963 (behavior of child)	.04	.16**	.14**
	Authoritarianism	.02	−.05	.13*
	Anomia	−.04	−.04	.03
	Frustration	.02	−.01	.07
	Rigidity	−.11*	.05	−.03
	Withdrawal	.00	.02	−.02
	Hopefulness	.16**	.13*	.18****
IV.	Marital happiness	−.01	.02	.06
	Marital agreement	.05	−.05	.01
	Agreement on child rearing	−.01	.01	.09
V.	Ideas on discipline	.01	−.04	−.10*
VI.	Visiting relatives	.03	−.08	−.03
	Church attendance	−.06	−.08	−.10*
	Social isolation	.01	−.04	−.08
Time II variables				
	Number of children in family	−.05	−.06	−.02
	Number of life events	−.02	.15**	.12*
	When changed expectations	.21***	.11*	.34****

Table 9–5 continued

Independent Variables	Instrumental Functioning	Family Involvement	Respondent's View
Actual discipline	.06	− .05	− .02
Present marital status of respondent (C)	.18	.16	.15
Number of times respondents married	− .05	.12*	− .00
How long married	− .12*	.03	− .09
Number of times moved residence	.04	.17***	.10*
Father child rearing (C)	.14	.17	.20
Extent father participates in treatment	.08	.03	− .06
Psychiatric sources, 1963–1976	.10*	− .02	.21****
Nonpsychiatric sources, 1963–1976	.16**	− .08	.18***
Informal sources, 1963–1976	.07	.05	.18***
Total number times received help	.21***	.00	.29****
Psychotherapy or not	.06	− .04	.09
Duration of assistance	.18**	.01	.17**

Note: Kendall's tau for ordinal and Cramer's V (C) for nominal variables.
  *$p < .05$ Kendall's tau.
 **$p < .01$ Kendall's tau.
 ***$p < .001$ Kendall's tau.
****$p < .0001$ Kendall's tau.

better instrumental adjustments as adults. We suggested in chapter 8 that the rigidity scale is probably tapping a dimension better thought of as self-control. No matter what we call this scale, it seemed to us that its content and its relationship to instrumental functioning strongly suggest that parental consistency and persistence in child-rearing contribute positively to the instrumental performance level attained by their adult children.

Among variables collected in 1975–1976, four of the coping measures were significantly related to instrumental performance. Parents who received the most assistance, in contrast to those who reported receiving less assistance, consistently had proportionately more children who can be described as performing poorly in the instrumental area. This is true for each of the four coping measures found significantly related to instrumental adjustment. The picture, however, is more complex. When the question is put as to whether those who received no help, subsequent to 1963, performed the best, the answer is no; it was those who received service in one instance only, whether from psychiatric or nonpsychiatric professionals, who were generally performing the best in the instrumental area. Examination of these relationships suggests that the next best thing to receiving limited external assistance is receiving no external assistance. Such a statement, however, is inexact since it clouds sequential considerations. There is reason to believe that the children who received no assistance after our 1963 interview began to conform to parental expectations more quickly than did those who received aid. The statistically significant relationship ($p < .001$) between year of change in parental expectations and instrumental functioning in 1975 or 1976 supports this reasoning since the relationship suggests that the earlier the child's behavior changed, the less the need for external assistance and the better the child's instrumental performance as an adult. We thus attempted a fuller explication of this view of events and found further support for our explanation. The earlier the respondent stopped worrying, the less likely the child was to be in any type of trouble and, also, the earlier the parent's expectations changed, the less likely they were to seek and receive aid. For example, among parents who changed expectations between 1962–1967 and 1968–1975, we found that 62 percent and 32 percent, respectively, did not seek or receive any psychiatric assistance. We believe that these data supported the rather common-sense notion that the parents who seek and receive the most help do so out of greater need, but we will wait until more evidence is presented before drawing firm conclusions. In the meantime, although it does not seem unreasonable to emphasize that children of those who sought no help did, in fact, appear to make good adjustments, it is also important to emphasize that only twenty-six cases (about 10.6 percent of the study group) were in this category. Based on the evidence presented here, it seems fair to state that this proportion represents the upper limit of those who experienced spontaneous remission.

The last variable that we found related to instrumental performance was the length of time the respondent had been married. It was found that respondents who had been married the longest tended to have more children with superior performance levels as adults, in contrast to parents with fewer years of marriage. Although the relationship between number of years married and number of times married is strong ($r = -.67$), these two variables are not mutually exclusive; some can report an impressive number of married years because they have been married several times. Regardless of this caveat, the more years respondents are married, the better off the children, generally, in the instrumental area.

Family Involvement (Zero-Order Relationship)

Seven of the independent variables are related to family involvement; three are time I and four are time II variables. None of the external coping (help-finding) variables is related to involvement with the parental family. Parents may not encourage their children to come home by searching widely for help, but it does not seem to hurt either.

What does seem to affect whether the adult children stay in touch is the degree of parental optimism about the child that was expressed in 1963. At that time, the parents were asked to compare the child's behavior in 1963 with the behavior about a year earlier. During the same interview, we also asked parents to indicate the extent to which they felt hopeful about the child's adult future. The parents who thought that their child was better in 1963 (compared to 1962) were more likely than their counterparts to have children who stayed in touch with them. Also parents who were the most hopeful were likelier than less-hopeful parents to have children who remained involved with the family in adulthood.

The third of the time I variables that is significantly related to family involvement—blaming the child—seems to fit in with this picture. Respondents who, in 1963, blamed the child for his problem, in contrast to those who placed the blame elsewhere, had substantially fewer weekly visits from the adult child in 1975–1976: 41 percent versus 62 percent. Although these three zero-order relationships are statistically significant, they are not very strong, yet they do seem to present a pattern. This pattern involves the message that was probably communicated to the child over a period of years. If the parents indicated to the child in some way that the child was improving, that they were optimistic about the future, and that the child was not to blame for his problem, then that child, as an adult, was likelier to feel loved and to want to see them; when parents communicated a negative message, the child was less likely to find it convenient to stay in touch.

Among the time II variables, three of the four independent variables that were found related to family involvement had not been found associated with instrumental adjustment. These three were number of significant life events, number of times moved residence, and number of times respondent married. Although there is some overlap among these variables since getting married and changing residence were cited by some respondents as being critical or important events (along with death, illness, and divorce, for example), a pattern seems to adhere in this case also. The three variables are all indications of possible or actual stress experiences; while these potential stress experiences did not, in general, impede the child's instrumental functioning as an adult, they did seem to result in the appearance of strain in the child's family relationship. Thus a certain type of stress mastery might have been gained at the expense of another important component of adult adjustment: attachment.

The fourth, and last, of the time II variables related to family involvement is the year when respondents changed their expectations. The earlier the parents stopped worrying about the child and their expectations changed, the greater the adult child's involvement with them. This finding is consistent with the message that the respondents may have transmitted to their children.

Respondent's Global Assessment (Zero-Order Relationship)

By far the largest number of independent variables were significantly related to the respondent's global assessment of adjustment: nine time I and eight time II variables. There are seven new variables which were related to the respondent's assessment but not to the other two outcome measures: the neurotic scale, income, mother's education, authoritarianism, attitude on discipline of children, respondent's attendance at church, and seeking informal assistance. Only two of the independent variables were related to all three outcome indexes: respondent's hopefulness and the time the respondent changed expectations. This adds to the notion that the three outcome measures are tapping somewhat different areas of behavior, with family involvement being the most independent of the outcome variables.

The pattern of relationships on this adjustment measure suggests that not only by definition is this outcome measure directly subjective, but also the respondent's view is more subjective in the sense that more of the respondent's attitudes, views, and beliefs seem to be related to the responding parent's assessment (for example, ideas about discipline and church attendance are not related to the other two outcome measures); also, the respondent's view really is global (and in that sense, perhaps more objective) in that it seems to be based on more data. It seems a bit elliptical to observe that this measure of outcome is global because more variables are related to it, but perhaps this is preferable to calling a variable global when it is not related to anything. Moreover, it seems to us that if anybody is entitled to a global view of children's behavior, it is the parents.

Perhaps the major surprise in terms of the variables associated with the respondent's view is that the child's age is not among them. Thus, on two of the three outcome measures, the child's age is not a significant predictor of adjustment. When we found the child's age directly related to level of instrumental functioning, we thought that this was a case of maturation at work and that the maturation process would also be evident when we considered the other two outcome variables. Such is not the case. Although maturation undoubtedly plays a role in the area of instrumental functioning, it has little influence on the respondent's more-global assessment or with the child's inclination to stay in touch with his parents.

The most powerful time I predictors of the parent's global assessment are the child's score on the authority symptoms scale and the degree of hopefulness for the child's future as expressed by respondents. Two other independent variables are also very noticeable: the child's score on the neurotic symptoms scale and the respondent's comparison of the child's behavior in 1963 with the child's behavior at the time of application at the source clinic in 1962. If the child's behavior was acceptable, as indexed by the two scales, and also if the child showed general improvement during that first year after application, then the long-term outcome was much better than if the contrasting conditions existed. The parent's hopefulness appears to be realistically based since it is highly correlated with their evaluation of the change in the child's behavior between 1962 and 1963 ($r = .42$).

Although Warner's four-factor ISC continues to be unrelated to the outcome measures, the mother's education has a significant association with the respondent's global view, as does breadwinner's income. We have no explanation with respect to these relationships and suggest only that more highly educated mothers may be able to see strengths in their children that are not reflected in our other two measures of adjustment.

Among the six coping variables, all but one—"psychotherapy or not"—were found significantly related to the global measure of adjustment. The direction of each of these relationships is very similar to the case reported for instrumental functioning; parents who received the most assistance, in contrast to those who received none or limited assistance, tended to have proportionately more poorly adjusted children (table 9-6). Moreover, when the global assessment variable is dichotomized between "well" and "poor," the following proportions of cases, respectively, were doing poorly among those receiving psychiatric services "not at all," "once," in "two or three" instances, and in "four or more" instances: 20 percent, 11 percent, 40 percent, and 50 percent. This J-shaped relationship appears consistently when the assistance variables are tabulated against both instrumental functioning and the global measure of adjustment. However, because many of the parents received help from various sources over the years, it is difficult to attribute the child's later success or failure in adjustment to any one source. Indeed this fact may point to why the "psychotherapy or not" variable was not related to any of the outcome measures. That is, in most cases, the receipt of psychotherapy was accompanied by many other sources of assistance, and these additional sources of aid may have neutralized the therapy, or, they may have helped it. We have, in fact, not emphasized the lack of relationship between psychotherapy and outcome since we did not have data on the quality of the therapy, the type of therapy, or the length of therapy.[7] In spite of these shortcomings in our data or perhaps because of them, we made an effort to separate out those respondents who only received help from one type of service from those who received assistance from a combination of sources. While the largest

Table 9-6
Total Number of Instances in Which Service Was Received and Respondent's Global Assessment in 1975-1976 (N = 241)

Global Assessment	Number of Instances of Services Received										
	None		One		Two		Three or Four		Four or More		
	N	%	N	%	N	%	N	%	N	%	
Child is well	20	77.0	21	70.0	23	54.8	37	56.1	26	33.8	127
Child is fairly well	5	19.2	8	26.7	10	23.8	16	24.2	19	24.7	58
Child is doing fairly poorly	1	3.8	1	3.3	9	21.4	13	19.7	32	41.5	56
100 % =	26		30		42		66		77		

Kendall's tau = 0.29; $p < .0001$

number of respondents (58 percent of the total of 240 cases) received a combination of types of aid, there were the following numbers of cases in single categories: psychiatric only, 15 cases; nonpsychiatric professionals only, 42 cases; and informal only, 17 cases. In addition, 26 cases received no assistance. Among the respondents seeing psychiatric professionals, 13 indicated that psychotherapy was administered to their children. Since 73 respondents altogether indicated that psychotherapy had been rendered, this means that 60 of them were in the combined service category. Perhaps this is yet another indication of why it is so difficult to evaluate psychotherapy fairly.

Our data do suggest that when the child and/or his family receive assistance only from a psychiatric professional (and such assistance usually includes some psychotherapy), the child is likely to make a good adult adjustment. Among cases receiving "no assistance," "psychiatric service only," "nonpsychiatric professional service only," "informal assistance only," and "assistance from a combination of sources," the following proportions of poorly adjusted adult children were found: 4 percent, 0 percent, 21 percent, 29 percent and 29 percent. Thus yet another measure of coping seems to suggest that, in general, limited assistance is more effective than a lot of assistance. Yet it is also important to note that approximately half of the respondents who reported their children well adjusted had indicated receiving help from a combination of sources, which typically included psychiatric sources.

Our data also provide evidence suggesting that the parents who persisted in their help-seeking efforts were doing so because their children continued to pose problems for them. Once again the earlier the parents changed their expectations and stopped worrying, the more likely the child was seen to be a well-adjusted adult. In fact, this relationship was the strongest one yet found. Parental hopefulness and optimism in 1963 seemed to be a strong indication that the child was showing positive signs and did not require them to launch a constant search for aid.

While the debate will continue as to which type of problem and which type of client will benefit the most from a particular mode of therapy, the task in the current study is to help clear up some of the surrounding static. We think we are doing that. We have stated that the sources of confusion have included lack of information on selection and history, with researchers being especially derelict with regard to coping behavior. This void was filled by debates over spontaneous remission. A service was performed by Eysenck, Levitt, and others in making researchers and clinicians aware of the weakness of their claims of success. We are demonstrating that parents employ many resources in their child-rearing tasks. Moreover, we have shifted the focus to a study of the family, parental characteristics and beliefs, parental behavior, and the child. In the future, we expect that researchers will have to pursue more rigorous study of selection and history, in addition to all the other research considerations, if they wish to evaluate properly the effects of intervention with children or with adults.

Higher-Order Analyses: Controlling Social Class and Child's Sex

Our measure of social class (Warner's ISC) was not related to any of the indexes of adult adjustment. Since sex, another important human characteristic, was also unrelated to adjustment at the zero-order level, we decided to examine certain relationships while using these variables as controls. Although a fairly sizable number of variables are available for our study, we are limited with respect to the number of three-way analyses we can reasonably present here. Thus we report on the regression analysis undertaken in an effort to identify the more-powerful predictors among our independent variables. We viewed the three-way analyses, however, as a preliminary step to the regression analysis.

Since child's age was strongly related to instrumental functioning (Kendall's tau was $-.19$) and sex and age have been found related in important ways in various other studies, we decided to use the child's sex as a control here.[8] When we did so, we found that the statistical relationship between age and instrumental functioning was similar among members of both sexes. The Kendall's tau measure of association was significant at the .01 level for males and females alike, with the older adult children making better adjustments. Significance levels aside, however, there is an interesting difference that appears when we examine the cross-tabulations: the age difference seems stronger for females (table 9–7). The table, although abbreviated, suggests that fewer females than males with childhood problems adjust before age twenty-three in the instrumental area but that after age twenty-three the females have an edge. We do not wish to overemphasize this matter, since so many other factors could account for this appearance and also because the number of females in our study is fairly small. Moreover, the direction and strength of the relationship between age and functioning appears relatively unchanged when sex is controlled.

We then examined the relationship between child's age and instrumental functioning while controlling the family social-class level. Kendall's tau yielded magnitudes of $-.30$, $-.12$, and $-.04$ for the age and adjustment relationship, respectively, for lower-, middle-, and upper-class respondents. Thus, although class is not related to instrumental functioning, it does appear to mediate the relationship between age and instrumental functioning. However, the persistence of the age influence is somewhat obscured by the coefficients shown. When the cells are combined, the class-related age differences do not appear very large (table 9–8). The table shows that there

Table 9-7

Child's Age and Proportion Performing Satisfactorily or High on Instrumental Functioning, at Follow-Up, Controlling Child's Sex

	Proportion Performing Satisfactorily or High at Follow-Up			
	Males		Females	
Child's Age at Follow-up (in years)	%	100% =	%	100% =
15–23	66.3	86	50.0	28
24–31	75.3	85	80.0	35

is not a major age difference among class levels, although there are fewer upper-class adult children functioning at a satisfactory level than there are for the other class categories. On balance then, it seems that age is a persistent predictor of instrumental functioning when either sex or social class is controlled.

Some variables may cancel out the effects of others. Although we have both theoretical and empirical bases for attempting to guess which variables are most important in predicting outcome, we thought that regression analysis would be an important tool in the process of identifying these variables and assessing their relative and combined power.

The Regression Analysis

Our regression analysis was designed to identify those variables showing the most promise as predictors of long-term outcome. We were interested both in the individual power of the independent variables, as well as in their combined utility in accounting for variation in our various measures of adjustment. Since we are confining our analyses here to guidance-clinic cases, we are presenting beta coefficients (standardized regression coefficients).

Eighteen independent variables are employed in the analyses, chosen either because lower-order analyses indicated predictive power and/or because of their theoretical relevance in the study. In any such selection, possibly useful variables are omitted, and we are sure that this is true here. This statement, of course, is limited only to the variables excluded among those available; naturally there are other relevant variables, which we never included. The eighteen independent variables include five so-called dummy variables, two each derived from the nominal variables: marital status and

Table 9-8
Child's Age and Proportion Performing Satisfactorily or High On Instrumental Functioning, Controlling Social Class

Child's Age at Follow-Up	Proportion Performing Satisfactorily or High at Follow-Up					
	Lower Class (1–3)		Middle Class (4–6)		Upper Class (7–9)	
	%	100% =	%	100% =	%	100% =
15–23	61.0	59	67.6	37	56.3	16
24–31	77.6	58	79.5	39	68.4	19

help-seeking between 1962 and 1963 and agreement on child rearing. The independent variables are presented in table 9–9.

The results of this regression analyses are presented in table 9–10. First, for two of our three outcome variables, a fair amount of the overall variance (r^2) is accounted for. For both instrumental functioning and respondent's global assessment, the overall F test indicates that a statistically sig-

Table 9–9
Independent Variables Used in Regression Analyses of Long-Term Adjustment

Variables	Code Categories
Time I	
Warner's ISC	1–9 with 9 high
Child's age, Jan. 1, 1963	1–18 years (numbers)
Child's authority symptoms (Guttman scale) score, 1963	no symptom = Guttman score of 1, 1 symptom = Guttman score of 2, 2 symptoms = Guttman score of 3, 3 symptoms = Guttman score of 4
Child's neurotic symptoms (Guttman scale) score, 1963	no symptom = Guttman score of 1, 1 symptom = Guttman score of 2, 2 symptoms = Guttman score of 3, 3 symptoms = Guttman score of 4
Respondent authoritarianism (five-item summary scale)	0 = not authoritarian, 5 = high on authoritarianism
Respondent frustration (four-item summary scale)	0 = not frustrated, 4 = high on frustration
Respondent rigidity (six-item scale)	0 = not rigid, 6 = high on rigidity
Husband-wife agreement on child rearing	0 = some or no agreement, 1 = much agreement
Respondent's hope for child's future	1 = very hopeful, 2 = somewhat hopeful, 3 = not too hopeful, 4 = not hopeful at all
Respondent's comparison of child's behavior in 1963 with behavior in 1962	1 = much better, 2 = somewhat better, 3 = the same, 4 = somewhat worse 5 = much worse
Respondent is separated?	0 = no, 1 = yes
Respondent is divorced, widowed, or never married?	0 = no, 1 = yes
Respondent sought psychiatric help for child	0 = no, 1 = yes
Respondent sought nonpsychiatric help for child	0 = no, 1 = yes
Time II	
Respondent's usual disciplinary practice	1 = strongly physical ("whipping"), 2 = spanking, 3 = nonphysical
Number of family events (changes or crises) over past 10 or 11 years	0 = none, 1 = 1, 2 = 2, 3 = 3 or more
Number of times (courses) in which psychiatric aid was received since 1963	0 = none, 7 = 7 (courses)
Total number of times in which aid was received since 1963 (psychiatric, nonpsychiatric professional, and informal)	0 = none, 9 = 9 or more

nificant amount of variance is accounted for by the independent variables ($p < 0.001$ for each). In contrast, the r^2 is substantially less for family involvement and the significance level does not reach .05, although $p < .10$.[9]

Instrumental Functioning

More of the overall variance is accounted for on instrumental functioning in comparison with the other outcome measures; in addition, it has the highest number of statistically significant predictor variables on the F test: five. Each of these five variables accounts for a significant amount of the vari-

Table 9-10
Standardized Regression Coefficients of Adult Child's Long-Term Outcome on Eighteen Independent Variables

Variables	Instrumental Functioning	Family Involvement	Respondent's Global Assessment
Time I			
Social class (ISC)	.05	− .05	.02
Child's age	− .21**	.08	− .04
Child's authority symptoms score	.10	− .09	.18*
Child's neurotic symptoms score	− .04	− .03	.01
Respondent's authoritarianism score	.06	− .13	.08
Respondent's frustration scale score	.01	− .12	.01
Respondent's rigidity scale score	− .11	.14	− .05
Husband wife agreement in child rearing	.01	− .05	.07
Respondent's hope for child's future	.23**	.11	.18*
Comparison of child's 1962 and 1963 behavior	− .09	.23**	− .03
Respondent separated	− .06	.05	− .04
Respondent divorced, widowed, never married	.07	.09	.03
Respondent sought psychiatric help	− .08	.05	− .12
Respondent sought nonpsychiatric professional help	− .23**	− .04	− .12
Time II			
Respondent disciplinary practices	.16*	− .13	.07
Number family events or crises last 10 years	− .07	.09	.06
Number times psychiatric aid received	− .04	− .03	.08
Total number of times aid received (all)	.30**	− .07	.29**
	Overall $F =$ 2.94, df = 18/164, $p <$ .001; $r^2 = .24$; adjusted $r^2 = .16$	Overall $F =$ 1.52; df = 18/164, $p <$ .10; $r^2 = .14$; adjusted $r^2 = .05$	Overall $F =$ 2.69; df = 18/164, $p <$ .001; $r^2 = .23$; adjusted $r^2 = .14$

Note: On the F test, significance levels indicated as follows: * $p = < .05$, ** $= p < .01$.

ance in instrumental functioning when the other independent variables are controlled. The five are child's age, hopefulness, seeking nonpsychiatric professional help in 1962–1963, disciplinary practices, and total number of times assistance was received during the interval between our two interviews (1963–1976).

Child's age was strongly related to instrumental functioning at the zero-order level, and it remained strong when either social class or child's sex was controlled. When all of the other independent variables are controlled, once again the older children in the study are making better adult adjustments than the younger ones as indexed by instrumental functioning. It would seem almost automatic that the maturation process is at least partly responsible for adult instrumental performance. Two considerations, however, guard against our taking the simplistic stance of asserting that the older the child, the better the instrumental functioning. First, there are only thirteen instances, 5 percent of our cases, in which the study group child was under 18 years of age at the time of follow-up. Thus, even if this measure of adjustment tilts toward favoring those old enough to have finished school or to have a job, there are not very many cases at the youngest follow-up age level of 15 to 17 years. The second caution involves the fact that the zero-order relationship showed a downward trend in instrumental functioning for the oldest age group. Thus, among groups of children aged 15–18, 19–23, 24–28, and 29–31 years at follow-up, the following proportions, respectively, were found to be functioning at the highest level (score of "1"): 14 percent, 31 percent, 51 percent, and 41 percent. We suggest, then, that while maturation (as indexed by age) appears to be operating to some extent, the existence of curvilinearity cautions against an assumption that age or maturation operates continuously on functioning without interference or influence from other, perhaps unincluded, factors. The complexity of this relationship is not reduced when we recall that in 1963 the oldest children were making the best adjustment. The regression hypothesis, while difficult to test here since we are employing different outcome criteria for the two occasions, does not explain the lack of movement for the younger age groups. Finally, when the attrition factor is considered, it would seem that the level of adjustment would decline further among the older adult children. Thus, we believe that our finding of a performance decline among older children is in part a reflection of the attrition factor; if the older children had remained in the study, it seems certain that the strength of age as a predictor would decline somewhat.

Other researchers have focused on the important and complex relationship between age and adjustment. The thirty-year follow-up study of Lee Robins appears to be marginally comparable to our study, although there are substantial differences in method as well as in the substantive issues considered by the two studies. [9] Robins focused primarily on the relationship between childhood symptoms and the presence of either adult antisocial behavior or other adult psychotic diagnosis; our primary emphasis is on the relationship between parental problem-solving behavior and the child's subsequent behavior, involving both short-term and long-term outcomes. The procedures of the two studies are just as different. Robins, for example, combined court referrals with those who reached the municipal clinic in St. Louis through more typical avenues, while, in our case, practices at the Massachusetts clinics permitted us to undertake separate analyses of court clinics and guidance-clinic cases throughout. The nature of Robins's study involved an important distinction that is relevant to the comparison of age-related differences; Robins had a thirty-year follow-up period that allowed her to assess the functioning of her subjects at more advanced ages than is currently possible in our study. With these differences, and others, between the two studies, it is wise not to assume comparability between them. Still, it may be important to recognize the many differences existing between studies and to plan future studies with some awareness of factors that may limit comparability. With this caveat, it is of interest that Robins found improvement possible for all ages among sociopathic cases, with the median age of improvement being 34.5 years for this group. The median age of improvement for her other diagnostic categories was 35 years. Since the oldest age in our study was 31 years, we cannot draw firm parallels or differences between the two studies. Nevertheless, the two studies seem similar in the finding that the relationship between age and outcome is not linear. Robins's study seems clearer in this regard, and this suggests that the relationship between age and outcome in our study group will become more complex with advancing age. Other researchers who undertake long-term prospective studies, it is hoped, will pay particular attention to age-related experiences among their subjects as they advance from childhood into various adult stages.

The second of the strong predictors of instrumental functioning is the extent of hopefulness for the child's future expressed by respondents during the 1963 interview. We have characterized this factor as an internal mediator. A number of social scientists have theorized about the role of expectations and feelings of powerlessness or resignation on performance. Although the variety of both the measures of hopefulness and of research designs used makes it difficult to draw comparisons among studies, it seems likely that expectations and attitudes of powerlessness, apathy, and hopefulness about goals are tapping a similar content area, which may be called "outlook." Outlook may, however, be most difficult to account for. It may be the result of reality testing or of personality; indeed it is likelier that it is a result of some mix of realism and of personal qualities. Whatever it is that accounts for outlook, it seems that it is a powerful predictor of outcomes. Freeman and Simmons, for example, found it related to the posthospital performance of ex-mental patients in the community, while others have found teacher expectations related to school performance.[11] In all of these cases, expectations were generally consistent with observed performance. More recently, Pearlin and Schooler, in their cross-sectional study, found that the best mode of response for parents in minimizing parental stress is not resignation but a conviction on the parent's part that he or she can exert influence over the child.[12] Consistent with these other findings showing the general power of expectations or outlook, we find in our own study that the parent's hopefulness, assessed thirteen years earlier, is one of the most powerful predictors of instrumental functioning. Not only at the zero-order level but also in the regression analysis, hopefulness stands out as an important predictor of subsequent adult functioning. Clinicians and researchers who have an interest in problem-solving behavior would do well to pay close attention to the role of prophesy and of expectations as they relate to the behavior of others.[13]

None of the Srole personality scales, also viewed as internal stress mediators, is related to instrumental functioning. Rigidity, the only one of the Srole scales related to functioning at the zero-order level, comes closest to being statistically significant on the F test and also has the greatest beta weight among the three Scrole scales employed in the regression analysis. The direction of the relationship involving rigidity is different from the other two scales; thus the more rigid the respondent, the more likely the adult child is to perform well in the instrumental area. This relationship seems to support our suggestion that rigidity is not a close parallel of authoritarianism but is tapping another dimension, which we labeled self-control; a better term may be persistence. In any event, it seems that more work on some of the Srole scales is needed in order to clarify their meanings and to heighten their research utility.

The third of the independent variables that is significantly related to instrumental functioning is the respondent's report of the usual disciplinary tactics employed in the home. Respondents who reported using physical punishment, in comparison with respondents reporting the sole use of non-physical discipline, were more likely to have adult children performing at the highest level as indexed by our measure of instrumental functioning. This is a most interesting finding since it brings to mind the old adage, "Spare the rod and spoil the child," but it repels many who look with disfavor on the physical punishment of children. The fact that we do not know just where the line was drawn with respect to the severity of physical punishment should alert human-service workers to the variability in physical punishment and to the need to protect parents from unwarranted charges of child abuse, as well as to protect children from unwarranted physical abuse.[14]

Several additional observations should be considered in attempting to understand this relationship. The first is that since there was no significant zero-order relationship bètween disciplinary practice and instrumental functioning, some of the remaining independent variables were masking the relationship that emerged when these other variables were controlled. This appears to be the case since the following variables were observed to be significantly related to discipline at the zero-order level: social class, separation status, parental agreement about child rearing practices, child's symptom scores in 1963, and receiving assistance between 1963 and 1975–1976. More specifically, parents resorting to physical discipline were, at the zero order level, likelier to be lower class, to be separated, to disagree with their spouses about child rearing, to seek and receive psychiatric and informal assistance and to have children who scored high on the two symptoms scales, in contrast to their counterparts. The second observation is that disciplinary practices may be considered to be one of a repertoire of coping steps available to parents whose children present them with problems. Our procedure in treating style of discipline as an explanatory variable involved a different analytic intention but it does not mean that disciplinary tactics must continue to be viewed that way.[15] As noted above (and also in chapter 8), the parents who resorted to physical punishment were also substantially more likely to seek and receive psychiatric and informal assistance. The same is true with respect to the measure of total assistance. Thus it appears that parents who employ physical discipline as a coping mechanism have heavy doubts about their practice or about the child, or both, and, in consequence, are likelier to seek external assistance than are parents who employ nonphysical discipline. Whatever the process is that involves the use of physical discipline, it bears notice that the children involved are likelier to perform at higher instrumental levels than their counterparts.

The remaining two of the five independent variables which were found significantly related to instrumental functioning when all other variables were controlled are (a) whether or not respondents had sought nonpsychiatric professional assistance during the 1962–1963 period and (b) the total number of occasions on which assistance was received during the period 1963–1975 or 1976. In a nutshell, (1) respondents who sought early 1962–1963 nonpsychiatric professional assistance (from school personnel, clergymen and physicians) were more likely than those who sought no such early help (includes "none" and "psychiatric professionals") to have adult children who scored high on instrumental performance; respondents who sought and received a lot of assistance after 1963, typically involving two or more different source types, were more likely in contrast to those whose children received either limited or no treatment, to have adult children who scored low on instrumental functioning. These findings bear restating. When all other independent variables are controlled, respondents who sought help early from specialized, nonpsychiatric sources reported better instrumental adjustment for their children than did parents who either sought no early help or who sought help from psychiatric professionals. When all other independent variables are controlled, among those seeking and receiving any assistance of any type between 1963 and 1976, there are progressively higher proportions of adult children functioning poorly as the number of occasions of assistance-receiving increases beyond one.

We could not evaluate the effects of psychotherapy in this study. Our findings indicate the difficulty in attempting to evaluate psychotherapy without proper attention being paid to the sources of invalidity. Thus it is clear that other types of assistance—informal and nonpsychiatric professional—also contribute to desirable adult functioning when used sparingly. Finally, it seems that when a battery of different types of aid is used and used often, the poorest outcomes result. Psychotherapists cannot assume that theirs is the best part of the battery since our data show that others can also make that claim. We are not choosing any particular type of assistance as best since there are other relevant factors not addressed in this study. What we are doing is making it clear that coping behavior is very widespread and very important to the parents and children in our study and that it should be of central interest to clinicians, researchers, and policy makers alike.

Family Involvement

This is the only one of the three long-term outcome variables for which the overall F is not statistically significant; an insufficient amount of the variance is accounted for. We suspect that either our measure of family involvement is not sound enough or that we have not involved some of the variables that are relevant to the analysis, or both. We lean to the notion that the measure of family involvement is the main problem. There are several omissions from this index that should be considered by researchers with an interest in this dimension. They include the fact that we neglected to ascertain if absent adult children wrote letters home and the frequency with which they did so. It would have been valuable, too, if we had ascertained the duration and quality of contacts that the parents had with children who visited them. Thus a long and enjoyable visit with one's child is not the same as several miserable visits over a stated period. In view of these inadequacies, we urge caution in the interpretation of our findings regarding family involvement. We present these findings since there is interest in this dimension. We refer here to those who warn us that love and support are vital elements in child-rearing and family life and should not be totally ignored as we exhort our children to succeed in the world of work.

Observing the column of beta coefficients under family involvement in table 9-10, it is of substantial interest that none of the variables measuring external help-seeking is related to involvement with family members when the other variables are controlled. Indeed, only one of the independent variables is significantly related to the adjustment index when the other independent variables are controlled: the respondent's comparison of the child's behavior in 1963 with the child's behavior in 1962 (at the time of contact with the clinic). On the F test, this relationship was satistically significant at the .01 level. Three other predictors are noted although they did not attain the conventional .05 level of significance: respondent's disciplinary practice and two of the Srole scales, rigidity and authoritarianism. The directions or signs for these four variables suggest that the following conditions help to predict later strong family involvement for adult children: the respondent believed that the child had shown improvement in his behavior over the year preceding the interview in 1963, the respondent did not use physical punishment on the children in the family, the respondent scored low on the rigidity scale in 1963, and the respondent scored high on authoritarianism in 1963.

In assessing these findings, it might be helpful to review our discussion in chapter 8 in which we considered the possible meanings of rigidity and authoritarianism. We suggested that rigidity might be tapping a dimension of flexibility, while authoritarianism seemed to be tapping control of others. This reasoning helps to rationalize the fact that the beta weights for family involvement show rigidity and authoritarianism with different signs. Also of interest is the fact that at the zero-order level, rigidity is not related to type of discipline ($r = .00$) but authoritarianism is related to discipline type ($r = -.12$, $p < .05$); that is respondents who are authoritarian are more likely than their counterparts to resort to physical punishment in disciplining their children. Generally the regression coefficients on family involvement indicate that in addition to the strong tendency for children to reward an early show of optimism in parents by staying in frequent contact, there is also a tendency, less strong, for children to avoid harsh and punitive parents and to favor flexibility in their parents. Offsetting this, however, is a tendency for authoritarian parents to maintain involvement with the children.

The last, but not insignificant, observation to be made about family involvement is the frequency with which different signs appear among the beta coefficients when family involvement is compared with instrumental functioning. For example, of the ten negative signs in that column, only three are also negative for family involvement. The more interesting variables having contrasting signs are the comparison of the child's behavior between 1962 and 1963 and respondent's disciplinary practices. Parents who indicated lack of optimism, believing the child's behavior had deteriorated over the year 1962-1963, and who employed physical punishment, in comparison with their counterparts, more often had adult children who were performing well in the instrumental area; however, the same two conditions increased the likelihood that the children, as adults, rarely contacted their parents.

These observations not only reinforce the view that both short- and long-term outcome measures are needed in assessing behavior but also that we need to develop outcome measures that tap different dimensions of behavior.

Respondent's Global Assessment

As indicated in table 9-10, the overall F test indicates that a statistically significant amount of the variance in global assessment is accounted for by the independent variables. In addition, three independent variables have predictive power and are significantly related to the global adjustment variable when all other variables are controlled. Two of these three—respondent hopefulness and the total number of times aid was received—were similarly related to the index of instrumental functioning. As was the case for instrumental functioning, none of the variables that attained statistical significance on the global measure was so related for family involvement. The unique feature for this variable is that the child's score on the authority symptoms scale in 1963 is one of its strong predictors. While the score on authority symptoms (observance of rules of authority) is in the same direction for instrumental performance, it is a much stronger predictor when the question of the adult child's behavior is put directly to the respondent. More specifically, children who had a low score (absence of symptoms) on the scale in 1963 were much more likely than high scorers to be seen by respondents as adjusting well in adulthood.

In contrast to the case for the authority symptoms score, the child's age declines in predictive strength as we move from the instrumental performance area to the global assessment. Assuming that the child's symptomatic behavior remains somewhat stable over the intervening years, the parents appear to be influenced more by the social behavior of the child than they are by the child's age progress. Of more than passing interest also is the fact that the child's 1963 neurotic symptoms score—controlling all other independent variables—has no predictive power at all with respect to the global assessment of adult behavior. This finding suggests that helping agents should focus more attention on antisocial children.

Somewhat surprising, perhaps, is the finding that the respondent's assessment of short-term improvement (comparison of 1962 with 1963 behavior) has virtually no independent power to predict the respondent's long-term global assessment of the adult child. Once again the need for longitudinal research is demonstrated.

Respondent hopefulness, the second of the stronger predictors of global assessment, was discussed earlier in this chapter in the analysis of instrumental functioning. The latter outcome measure is strongly related to the global assessment (Kendall's tau = .54). What was said earlier about the importance of parental outlook in connection with later instrumental performance of the child also applies to the global assessment. In short, parents who are hopeful about their child's future apparently have the ability to help realize their hopes, while pessimistic parents more often have children who fulfill their prophecy.

The last and strongest of the major predictors of global assessment is the total number of occasions on which assistance was received between 1963 and 1975–1976. As was the case for instrumental performance, respondents whose children received either limited or no assistance, in contrast to respondents whose children received a great deal of assistance, more often reported their children's making good adult adjustments when other factors were controlled.

The seeking of help early (1962–1963) from nonpsychiatric but specialized sources is not statistically significant in its relationship to global assessment. This, of course, is a departure from the case for instrumental performance. Indeed, seeking early psychiatric help has about the same predictive power as seeking early nonpsychiatric help with respect to the parent's global assessment. In this case, at least, seeking either type of early assistance is beneficial in terms of the child's adult adjustment. Our controlled analysis clearly indicates that parents who seek help early for their children are increasing the chances that their children will make good adult adjustments. On the other hand, our data strongly suggest that seeking a lot of help, from a variety of different sources, over an extended period is a signal that the child is doing poorly and is in substantial danger of making a poor adult adjustment.

A Case Study

Data such as we have been presenting lead to generalizations that do not necessarily describe individual cases. This is a fair caveat since our guidance-clinic study group, at stage II still contained 250 cases. However, because case studies have a value of their own and may help to place our study in clearer perspective, we are presenting a case description, based on clinic records and data from our two interviews with the parent. The real name is not employed, and one or two pieces of identifying data have been altered so as to protect our family. The case was chosen simply because it illustrates certain aspects of parental coping behavior. It is understood that every child in the study group has idiographic features and that our case selection is arbitrary. We hope only that readers will thereby not only appreciate the uniqueness of individuals but also will recognize the common roads we travel.

When she was eleven years old, in 1962, Claire was depressed and talked about suicide. Her mother was deeply distressed and discussed the problem with her minister. He suggested that she call a psychiatric clinic. Mrs. A did so and made an appointment to take Claire there. Soon after—for reasons unclear but probably having to do with Mr. A's view that Claire did not have any problems—Mrs. A called the clinic and cancelled the appointment. The clinic, however, did not let the matter drop and sent someone to the house to speak with Mrs. A. The clinic representative according to Mrs. A "seemed disappointed that we didn't want to follow through, but didn't press it." At this point, Mrs. A said that her husband "was furious that I looked for help."

Since Claire was intelligent, Mrs. A felt very hopeful that her daughter would overcome her problems. Her husband, a mechanical engineer, simply assumed that his children—there were three, and Claire was the oldest—would go to college and do at least as well as he had done.

Mr. A was a very harsh father who physically abused all three of the children and was the most severe with Claire. Mrs. A did complain to her own nearby parents about her husband's harsh discipline, the only reported area of disagreement in her marriage, but her parents "were down on him and were not very helpful to her." He was so abusive, in fact, that at one point the usually undemonstrative Mrs. A "told him that I would call the police if he ever hit Claire again. He never did." Mrs. A earlier said during the 1963 interview that her husband "had lost his own mother at age five and was now mistrustful of women," including his eleven-year-old daughter.

After our 1963 interview, Claire was still having behavior problems although she managed to get good grades in high school. After the 1962 clinic contact, no further professional help was sought until 1969 when things got much worse. Around that time, when she was seventeen years old, Claire started talking about suicide again, was burning her hands with cigarettes, and was also using drugs. This led Mrs. A to discuss Claire's problems with the family's physician, who referred her to a private psychiatrist. Mrs. A accompanied Claire to the psychiatrist's office and reported to us, in our 1975 interview, that "it was not a good experience." Both Claire and her mother got defensive and joined forces against the psychiatrist. Shortly thereafter, Mrs. A contacted a psychiatric social worker. The relationship with the social worker lasted several months but was also negatively evaluated; she, too, "was not a successful contact." Mrs. A seemed offended that the social worker felt that Claire's sister Alice had problems (used drugs and chose friends unwisely) and observed that "Mr. A was hostile." Claire did not trust the social worker, claiming that she did not respect confidentiality since the worker "would turn in kids to the police if they used drugs." When this association ended, Mrs. A sought no further professional help.

Shortly thereafter, Claire graduated from high school and enrolled in college. When she was nineteen, she dropped out of college and took a job as an art assistant in a department store. Mrs. A reports that Claire received several promotions on this job and kept this job until she married and moved to North Carolina at age twenty-two. Her mother says that she is happily married. She has a baby, is back at work, is well liked by her coworkers, and is doing quite well all around. The parents both feel that she could have a better job if she finished college, but Mrs. A is no longer worried about her. Claire stays in close touch on the telephone and comes home about twice a year to visit her family.

When Mrs. A was asked, "What happened to influence Claire's present adjustment?" she said, "I don't know. She just worked it through by herself. Her husband has helped a lot. Also, getting approval from a lot of people and seeing that people are fond of her has finally made her feel secure." Although Mrs. A did not seem to like either of the clinicians who attempted to give assistance and did not credit them with having a hand in Claire's subsequent improvement, it is quite possible that they contributed a great deal and helped Claire to gain valuable insight about her situation. We have no additional clarifying information about the nature of Claire's contacts or about the quality of the clinician-patient relationship.

Two additional matters impress us about this case. The first concerns the fact that Mrs. A probably could have obtained assistance earlier from the clinic she contacted in 1962. To its credit, that agency sent a worker to call on her when it discovered the parents' reluctance to keep the first appointment. It was unfortunate for the family that Mr. A was probably allowed to derail this earlier opportunity. However, Mrs. A's explanation for not having continued contact with the clinic in 1962 was that "Claire would be picked on by other children if she went to a psychiatrist." Possibly Mrs. A shared her husband's resistance to professional psychiatric help. She may have been protecting her husband by rejecting the clinic outreach in 1962. Also, Claire did not see a psychiatrist until she was seventeen. Indeed when Claire reached college age, she chided Mrs. A, saying that her mother "didn't stand up for her enough."

The second impression concerns the fact that Mrs. A eventually took a strong stand against the child-abusing father. He apparently ceased his abusive behavior when Mrs. A threatened to call the police. This revelation appeared during our 1975 interview, and we cannot pinpoint the precise time at which Claire's mother made her protective threat. Evidence in each interview, however, implies that he resorted to physically abusing Claire over a considerable number of years. Again, then, it seems that Mrs. A should have acted earlier since it appears that Mr. A's behavior contributed to Claire's depression, as well as her reported anger at Mrs. A for not intervening earlier.

The case is valuable in illustrating some of the family dynamics that affect children and parents, and it shows some consistency with our general findings—for example, that obtaining early help leads to an earlier end to parental worrying. In this case, Mrs. A did not begin to relax about Claire until about 1973 when Claire was twenty-two years old and married. It is also consistent with our finding that physical punishment is related to later instrumental functioning. Perhaps such harshness drives children away, forcing them to become independent. With respect to family involvement, however, our findings are only partly consistent with the aggregate results. In our regression analysis, we noted a tendency for physical punishment to be related to low family involvement. Claire, however, married and living in North Carolina, comes home on visits once or twice a year and, according to Mrs. A, telephones often. Our hunch would be that Claire stays in touch for the sake of her mother and siblings; however, we do not have clarifying data on this matter. We note only that there is no indication of a rapprochement between Claire and her father.

In sum, then, Claire appears to be making a good adjustment as indexed on all three of our outcome measures. However, a better test of her adjustment would come when her own parenting could be observed.

Summary

In this chapter, we presented data on factors related to three measures of long-term adjustment: instrumental functioning, family involvement, and respondent's global assessment. Forty-eight independent variables were included in a zero-order analysis of each outcome measure. Later, based on theoretical or empirical relevance, eighteen of these independent variables, predominantly from stage I, were employed in separate regression analyses for each outcome measure. For both instrumental functioning and global assessment, a statistically significant amount of the overall variance was accounted for. It was felt that family involvement was, perhaps, inadequately measured and that this might have accounted in part for its lower r^2 value.

The largest number of predictors found in the controlled analyses involved instrumental functioning, which had five; in contrast, family involvement had only one efficient predictor. Only two of the independent variables were found to be predictive for at least two of the outcome measures: hopefulness and the total number of times aid was received between 1963 and 1975-1976, with each being significantly related to both instrumental functioning and respondent's global assessment when all other independent variables were controlled. Respondents who held little early hope for their children's future accurately predicted a dim outcome on each of these two measures. In addition, respondents who sought and received assistance from a large number of helping agents reported fewer satisfactory outcomes on these two measures than did those receiving either limited or no assistance.

Further, it was found that early help-seeking from specialized nonpsychiatric professionals, in contrast to an absence of such early help-seeking, more often resulted in satisfactory instrumental performance in adulthood when all other factors were controlled. Other independent predictors discussed with respect to one of the three outcomes included the child's age, respondent's disciplinary practices, child's earlier score on the authority scale, and the respondent's comparison of the child's behavior in 1962 with his behavior in 1963. A case study was also presented, in order to demonstrate the complexity of family dynamics.

We used the presented hypotheses in chapter 1 primarily as an organizing or heuristic device. Still, readers may wish to know whether we think any of the general hypotheses are tenable. In our opinion, our findings generally support a couple of the hypotheses, with some qualifications.

The first hypothesis stated that parental expectation would be more strongly related to adult outcome than would type of problem. A perusal of the regression analysis presented in this chapter generally supports this hunch with respect to all three types of outcome measures. However, an earlier indication of antisocial behavior is also predictive of the respondent's global assessment. Our second general hypothesis stated that resource availability such as family strength and middle-class status would be related to outcome. Our data do not support this hypothesis, possibly because all of the guidance-clinic cases had already initiated a search for help. Whatever the reason, however, other factors were far better predictors of outcome than marital or social status. The third general hypothesis states that the nature of the parental use of resources would be related to outcome. We further suggested, however, that persistence would pay off. While our findings suggest that a focused and limited use of external sources of aid is rewarding in terms of adult outcome, they certainly suggest also that a persistent (extensive) use of multiple sources of aid is related to a poor adult outcome. This hypothesis requires more specificity.

The hypotheses, partially derived from a stress model, served a useful function in helping to give some direction to the presentation of data. The model has proved useful and should continue to be valuable in stress-related research.

Notes

1. For a model measure of instrumental performance, see H. Freeman and O. Simmons, *The Mental Patient Comes Home* (New York: John Wiley, 1963), pp. 57–61. Countless other scholars have considered job performance and engagement in social relationships to be the crucial adult tasks in our society.

2. Although it was not a prerequisite for being included in the high-job-performance category, these women were all reported to be happily married.

3. Cited by Howard Muron, *Psychology Today* (June 1980):14.

4. Sociologists, because of their traditional interest in the family, have long emphasized the importance of both dimensions to the social system. For one example, see Talcott Parsons and Robert Freed Bales, with J. Olds, M. Zelditch, Jr., and P. Slater, *Family, Socialization and Interaction Process* (Glencoe, Ill.: Free Press, 1955).

5. For example, see James E. Teele, "Measures of Social Participation," *Social Problems* (Summer 1962):31–39.

6. See Hans Strupp, Suzanne Hadley, Beverly Gomes, and Stephen Armstrong, "Negative Effects in Psychotherapy: A Review of Clinical and Theoretical Issues Together with Recommendations for a Program of Research" (unpublished paper, May 1976).

7. On some of these issues, see D.F. Ricks, "Supershrink: Methods of a Therapist Judged Successful on the Basis of Adult Outcomes of Adolescent Patients," in D.F. Ricks, M. Roff, and A. Thomas, eds., *Life History Research in Psychotherapy* (Minneapolis: University of Minnesota, 1974).

8. For example, see M. Inbar, *The Vulnerable Age Phenomenon,* (New York: Russell Sage Foundation, 1976.

9. The correlation coefficients on which this analysis is built are based on fluctuating n's with the lowest n of 185 resulting from attrition on the punishment variable. Most of the n's involved 273 or more cases.

10. Lee Robins, *Deviant Children Grown Up* (Baltimore: William & Wilkins, 1966).

11. Howard E. Freeman and Ozzie Simmons, *The Mental Patient Comes Home* (New York: John Wiley, 1963), pp. 175–183. See also Robert Rosenthal and Lenore Jacobson, *Pygmalion in the Classroom* (New York: Holt, Rinehart & Winston, 1968); and Pamela Rubovits and Martin Maehr, "Pygmalion Black and White," *Journal of Personality and Social Psychology* (February 1973):210–218.

12. Leonard Pearlin and Carmi Schooler, "The Structure of Coping," *Journal of Health and Social Behavior* (March 1978).

13. The seminal contribution of Robert Merton to this whole discussion should be clear. See especially his analysis of the self-fulfilling proph-

ecy in *Social Theory and Social Structure* rev. ed. (New York: Free Press, 1957), chap. 13.

14. This caution does not apply in the too-numerous cases where infants and a small children are involved and there is no excuse for physical discipline.

15. Indeed Leonard Pearlin and Carmi Schooler did treat discipline as a coping tactic in their study, although their measure involves the "threat of punishment." See their "The Structure of Coping," *Journal of Health and Social Behavior* (March 1978):9, 10.

10 Conclusions and Implications

There is wide disagreement over the demonstrated efficacy of intervention, including psychotherapy, for children with emotional problems. Much has been said about this matter and there has been a proliferation of intervention techniques, but there has also been a dearth of rigorous and relevant research. One of the more general shortcomings has been the absence of long-term research. Other problems are more specific. They include the lack of attention paid by researchers to problems of selection and of history, not only the history of problems that children have but the history of the parents' problem-solving efforts. This book has reported research on these problems in long-term as well as short-term perspective. Table 10–1 summarizes our findings.

Conclusions

Selection

We described the clinics' applicant population, the different problems represented, and the disposition or selection of applicants and then analyzed the factors differentiating those accepted for service from those not accepted by clinic personnel. Two-thirds of those applying did not receive the help they sought. This fact would not disturb us if we had not subsequently found that 90 percent of those we followed up kept searching for help during the ensuing years. While service delivery in mental health programs for children has improved since 1962, there was a lot of room for improvement. We found too many anguished parents who did not know where to turn in their efforts to solve their problems, or, if they did have an alternative coping strategy, were angry with the mental health delivery system that focused on what to them were secondary considerations, such as the ability to pay.

An analysis of the factors related, or unrelated, to the guidance-clinic decision suggests some of the causes of this parental distress. First, the clinics were more likely to give service to the younger children (under eleven years of age) than to those between eleven and eighteen years of age. This relationship held when type of presenting problem was controlled. Since serious rule-violative behavior is known to increase up to about fourteen

Table 10-1
Summary Description of Independent Factors Related to Positive Outcome, Guidance Clinics

Short-Term Outcome (1963)		Long-Term Outcome (1975–1976)	
Authority score	Neurotic scale	Functional	Global
Not blaming relatives	Older age	Older age	Low score on authority scale in 1963
Low authoritarianism	Low frustration	Hopeful outlook	Hopeful outlook
Low frustration	Low neurotic score in 1962	Early nonpsychiatric professional help	Selective or no later help
Not seeking help		Physical discipline	
Low authority score in 1962		Selective or no later help	

years of age, this drop in clinic services could only increase the stress of the affected parents. Moreover, the importance of age in the client-selection process is heightened in light of our discussion of the relationship between age and adult instrumental functioning. The relationship was not linear, and there was a downturn in performance for the oldest age group, the group that was least often served in 1962.

The other selection factor that we wish to consider here involves the broad type of presenting problem. Type I was believed to be of greater concern to parents, if not to clinicians, since it included law-violative and life-threatening behavior, while type II included neurotic problems primarily. We found that the clinic decision to accept for service was not related to type of presenting problem. Indeed there was a tendency, not statistically significant, for the clinics more often to give service to type II clients. Our suggestion that the parents may have been more distressed by type I behavior received some support in our data on long-term outcome. Our regression analysis showed that the authority scale score, based on the child's rule-violative behavior, is related to the parent's global assessment of the adult child's behavior when all the other independent variables are controlled. More specifically, childhood antisocial behavior was an efficient predictor of poor adult adjustment from the responding parent's perspective. Clearly the clinic's selection practices appear to have both immediate consequences, in terms of bringing stress to parents, and long-term consequences for the children.

Although our study seems to be unique in focusing attention on the long-neglected population of worried parents, it was the absence of a relationship between case selection and presenting problem that suggested that it was similar in important respects to the typical clinic control group. In addition, no relationships were found between case disposition and either child's sex or father's occupation. Moreover, only a small proportion (10 percent) of those not served resembled dropouts or defectors. Thus, paradoxically, our study of client selection by the clinics produced an ideal opportunity to focus on the subsequent experiences of an "untreated" group of problem children.

History

History of Problems: In brief our study of the history of the children whose parents called a guidance clinic in 1962 indicated that a majority of these children had earlier problem manifestations. Since many of the parents had waited over a year before contacting the clinic, it is likely that many of them were fairly worried by the time they took this action. This notion is strengthened by the fact that the available evidence indicated that a number of parents perceived the childrens' problems as having gotten worse during the interval. Even given the possible limitations of parental data, the need to investigate the history or background of a problem is crucial for clinicians and researchers. Indeed it seems likely that the type of early problem manifestations may be less important to the subsequent mental health of parent and child alike than the historical aspects of the problem, for two reasons. One is that a number of our children changed from type II (neurotic) to type I (antisocial) behavior by the time the parents called the clinic. The second reason is that childhood antisocial symptoms, and not neurotic symptoms, were related to parental perception of adult adjustment problems in their children. Until we learn more about the paths that childhood symptoms take, it seems important that clinicians take parent initiatives seriously.

History of Problem-Solving Behavior: The help-seeking behavior of our families was quite substantial and at times awe inspiring. Our data place the long and often acrimonious debate over spontaneous remission in a new perspective. A part of this debate has concerned the definition of the term *spontaneous.* Some believe that the term means the improvement of neurotic patients without the benefit of psychotherapy. Others, like ourselves, prefer the Bergin-Lambert usage, which is consistent with Webster's clarity: *"spontaneous,* having no external cause or influence."[1] It would, no doubt, be perplexing for parents who have worked and worried over the problems of child-rearing to hear the successful results attributed to spontaneous remission. We will not belabor this point. The evidence is clear and runs throughout this book: there is not much evidence in support of the argument for spontaneous remission. Indeed some of the children might have been better off if their parents had not worked so hard at helping them. Most of our parents received help from multiple sources; however, those who sought limited and focused aid had the most success with respect to their children's adult behavior. In addition, it now seems clear that early help-seeking is far more effective than a protracted course of action, although these effects may not appear until much later. The emphasis on early intervention, made by clinicians and researchers alike, is supported by our results.

Outcomes

Depending on the criterion of outcome employed, between 70 percent and 80 percent of the guidance children in our study made successful adjustments in adulthood. Early help was important to this adjustment. Although these figures are impressive, there is obviously a great deal of room for improvement; from the clinical, parental, or societal perspective, a 20 percent to 30 percent poor adult adjustment rate is high. These figures are probably not reflective of adult adjustment rates for the general population, but it is extremely important to remember that all of our families had sought help long ago and thus presented opportunities for intervention.

Change and growth, and deterioration, will continue to take place among the children and parents of our study. Thus the outcome study presented here, long term as it is, is only a partial contribution to the knowledge we should be seeking.

Implications

Research Implications

The process of growth from infancy to adulthood is complex, with a number of hazards along the way for both child and parent. As the family structure evolves, as the external or societal conditions change, and as unforeseen problems emerge, it must seem as though we will never reach the goal of providing children and parents with the knowledge and opportunities needed for healthy growth. Yet the effort ought to be made.

Our research has focused mainly on the coping processes parents who are experiencing stress in child-rearing employ. A vast number of important and relevant research questions remain. For example, what are the dominant cognitive processes that operate among parents as they identify or define problems in their children? In a relevant and perceptive piece,

Richard Lazarus sees "threat and coping with threat as the consequences of cognitive processes."[2] He emphasizes that the term *cognitive* implies only that thought processes are involved and not the quality or type of thought. Clearly a whole range of stress-related research should result from Lazarus's conception. To take one example, why do some parents view childhood enuresis as threatening and react aggressively to it while other parents see it simply as a developmental problem that the child will out-grow? This difference in appraisal and in coping, in Lazarus's terms, is cog-nitive; perhaps these cognitive differences bear as much study as do their effects. Indeed Lazarus further suggests that the child's disturbed reaction to parental aggression should be seen as effect rather than cause. Our own finding—that parental outlook, especially as indexed by hopefulness for the child's future, was strongly predictive of later adult adjustment—indicates the importance of studying the cognitive processes.

In a relevant assessment of the research on the effects of psycho-therapy, Parloff suggests that while various therapies seem "more effective than . . . the mere passage of time [there is] the question of whether the effects are due primarily to a placebo, for example, suggestion, expectation, cajolery."[3] As Parloff notes, it is difficult to control for placebo effects since the knowledge about how they work is usually missing. In our study with its indication of the power of expectations, whether positive or nega-tive, we do not know the reasons for these expectations, though we had some evidence that they were related to prior changes in behavior of the subject children.

A second area requiring research bears on the age-relevant experiences related to the identification of childhood problems and to the sequelae. Erikson's work has suggested that a failure of development at one stage can lead to problems at a later stage.[4] The issue of how early problems change, both within childhood and as the child grows into adulthood, requires much study.

A third area in which more research is needed, and which is especially related to age-related research, concerns parental coping styles. A large number of problem-solving techniques are being offered to parents; which do they select, if any, and why? Given the apparent rise in adolescent stress in the United States, for example, what types of coping styles and strategies should parents be considering?[5] Changes in family structure, including an increase in the number of single-parent homes, increase the urgency of the need for research on coping. The availability of resources and the responses of external sources of assistance are, of course, central to this concern. Thus a need for research that builds on the findings reported here is obvious.

With respect to our own data, there are further problems that we will pursue. We intend, for example, to take a small sample of families that had similar presenting problems, such as suicidal threats or attempts, and pursue the interrelation of family process and coping behavior in dealing with the problem. Further and more purposive contacts with these families will be required. Another area for research suggested directly by our work concerns the fate of children referred to but not accepted for treatment at the court clinics. No one can rest easily over our decision to postpone further consideration of the court-clinic cases at this time. We did so because of the depressing outcomes for these cases, a situation that requires a different set of analytic intentions. We hope that the analysis to be done will enable us to suggest some of the directions for research on such families.

The final area of research concerns the need not only for better evaluation research on psychotherapy effects but also on all major types of therapy. Moreover, efforts should be made to assess the effects of professional nonpsychiatric intervention as well.

Researchers are indebted to Eysenck and to Levitt, in particular, for focusing attention on the need to evaluate the effects of intervention with children. They must heed now the warning of Barrett and his colleagues that more evaluation research must be undertaken on the effects of intervention with children.[6] They note, too, the need to integrate such research with issues of parenting and a more general assessment of the family.[7]

Implications for Clinical and Governmental Policy

Our advice to child psychiatric clinics is to do as much as possible for every applicant, including children, as soon as they call or apply for help. Often the clinics have not been given the credit they are due for in many cases they have provided the major source of aid and reassurance for distressed parents. Often they have done this in a very brief time; they should continue to do this and to try to do it better. Finally, they should cooperate as much as possible in research designed to assess the effects of what they do.

Government at all levels should continue to provide for as much early intervention as possible. In Massachusetts, a state law, chapter 766, provides for early professional assessment of children thought to be at risk for behavioral or learning problems. This assessment, available to both parents and teachers on request, has provided reassurance to many parents and teachers who otherwise might not know where to turn in their quest for help. This program includes diagnostic services for children of all ages and preschool screening. Parents must participate in and approve of the service recommendations.

Programs such as the one provided for by chapter 766 in Massachusetts and others, like Headstart, that provide early intervention should be constantly monitored. The governmental policies that make them possible should also ensure that appropriate evaluation follows, including long-term outcome studies.

As far as other policies are concerned, such as third-party payments for child psychotherapy, there is reason for administrators to proceed cautiously and to ask for sound evidence that children and families will benefit and that positive results will stand the test of time.

Notes

1. See especially Allen Bergin and Michael Lambert, "The Evaluation of Therapeutic Outcomes," in Sol Garfield and Allen Bergin, eds., *Handbook of Psychotherapy and Behavior Change,* 2d ed. (New York: John Wiley, 1978), chap. 5.

2. Richard Lazarus, "Cognitive and Personality Factors Underlying Threat and Coping," in M. Appley and R. Trumbull, eds., *Psychological Stress* (New York: Appleton-Century-Crofts, 1967); reprinted in S. Levine and N. Scotch, eds., *Social Stress* (Chicago: Aldine, 1970).

3. Morris Parloff, "Can Psychotherapy Research Guide the Policy-maker?" *American Psychologist* 34 (April 1979):298.

4. Erik H. Erikson, *Childhood and Society* 2d ed. (New York: W.W. Norton, 1963).

5. Dr. Beatrix Hamburg of NIMH, at a recent NIMH conference on stress and adolescence, noted that adolescence is the only age group in this country in which the death rate is rising, "due to suicide, homicide, drug abuse, and alcohol-related automobile accidents." See *ADAMHA News* 6 (October 1980):1.

6. See C. Barrett, I.E. Hampe, and L. Miller, "Research on Child Psychotherapy," in Garfield and Bergin, *Handbook*.

7. For a discussion of an impressive list of limitations in research on child care see A. Clarke-Stewart, *Child Care in the Family* (New York: Academic Press, 1977), pp. 68–74. For a discussion of parent education see Orville Brim Jr., *Education for Child Rearing* (New York: Russell Sage Foundation, 1959).

Appendix A:
Distribution, by Sex, of Court-Clinic Cases on Convictions, 1964–1976

Number of Convictions in Massachusetts	Males		Females		Total
	N	%	N	%	N
0	6	14.6	7	13	
1	7	17.1	3	21.4	10
2–4	4	9.8	2	14.4	6
5–9	5	12.2	1	7.1	6
10–19	11	26.8	—	—	11
20 or more	8	19.5	1	7.1	9
Totals	41	100.0	14	100.0	55

Source: Massachusetts Probation Department.

Note: Among those convicted, the year of last charge in Massachusetts was 1970 or later in thirty-one of the fourty-two relevant cases. Among cases with no Massachusetts record, some may have records in other states and women who married may have convictions under other names.

Appendix B:
Validity and Reliability
of Measures

On Validity

Validity of Short-Term Adjustment Measures: Authority Relations and Neurotic Symptoms

The assumptions attached to particular scaling practices are varied; they involve the universe of responses or judgments and the universe of relevant questions. The assumptions affect or determine the sampling or selection practices, which, in turn, affect the scales produced. All of these considerations enter into the observers' assessment as to whether a scale measures what it purports to measure. The nature of the present study group—for example, the manner in which it was selected and its size—affected research procedures and the type of scales employed. Clearly we have made a number of assumptions, some of which may not be justified, in deciding that the unidimensionality of our two measures of short-term outcome was the crucial criterion of validity.

We employed Guttman's scale analysis in constructing the time I outcome measures. One of the goals of this technique is to determine whether the behavior being analyzed (the universe of content) actually involves only a single dimension. The main estimate or index of unidimensionality, then, is the extent to which a cumulative scale is produced. Our decision to attempt to develop two such scales was determined, in part, by an invariable practice or convention among clinicians and researchers in the children's field to give primary consideration to "antisocial" and "neurotic" problems. These, admittedly, are sometimes vaguely or broadly conceived; thus it was decided to make an attempt to refine them. In doing so, we excluded other dimensions of behavior that might have been produced from our research data.

In chapter 6 we employed Guttman's criteria in selecting the items that went into our scales. Three dichotomized items went into each scale, and zero-cell analysis was utilized in the determination of error. The following statistics on reproducibility (error in reproducibility) and scalability resulted when the selected items were analyzed for two relevant time points (1962 and 1963):

1. Observance of rules of authority in 1962
   Coefficient of reproducibility, 0.90
   Minimum marginal reproducibility, 0.66

      Coefficient of scalability, 0.70
2.   Neurotic behavior in 1962
      Coefficient of reproducibility, 0.88
      Minimal marginal reproducibility, 0.65
      Coefficient of scalability, 0.66
3.   Observance of rules of authority in 1963
      Coefficient of reproducibility, 0.92
      Minimum marginal reproducibility, 0.67
      Coefficient of scalability, 0.77
4.   Neurotic behavior in 1963
      Coefficient of reproducibility, 0.88
      Minimum marginal reproducibility, 0.62
      Coefficient of scalability, 0.69

The conventional standard suggests that the coefficient of scalability should be above 0.6 if a scale is cumulative and unidimensional. A level of 0.9 or above is the desired standard for the coefficient of reproducibility. The authority scale is the stronger of the two types of scales, although both scales appear to be both cumulative and unidimensional. Future researchers in this area could benefit from efforts to sharpen these scales further.

The Social Isolation Scale

My earlier attempts to develop a cumulative scale of social isolation were based on the same items and procedures employed in this study. The results were the same; a partially cumulative scale was all that could be attained. Those at the active end of the scale "either participate in voluntary associations or social hobbies or both, and typically have friends." There are, no doubt, too few items here to offer a real opportunity to develop a cumulative measure meeting scaling requirements. Perhaps current theorizing and research on social networks will eventuate in or allow improved measures of social participation in the future. Some readers may believe that the absence of a stronger index of social isolation might amount for the measure's failure to predict short- or long-term outcome for guidance-clinic cases. Paradoxically, however, this measure was a strong predictor of short-term outcome among court-clinic cases. It would seem that theorists and researchers ought to continue to develop this concept.

On Reliability

Reliability is closely related to validity in its concern with distortion. When validity of a measure is uncertain, which is often the case, it is useful to know whether a measure is dependable.

It is, important to know that research instruments give consistent and repeatable results. We employed Cronbach's alpha, where appropriate, as a measure of reliability. A number of our measures, such as our index of instrumental functioning, could not be submitted to this test because of the way they were constructed; in such instances, we usually resorted to other tactics in assessing the soundness of a variable.

The variable for which we obtained reliability coefficients using Cronbach's alpha were the five scales developed by Leo Srole and the combined index of marital agreement based on eleven "yes-no" items derived from the work of Burgess and Wallin. The coefficients for these six variables are presented in table B-1.

The reliability coefficients are quite acceptable for at least two of the Srole scales—authoritarianism and anomia—and borderline or less for the remaining scales. The marital agreement index is the most reliable of these six variables. These results, perhaps, reflect the amount of work that social scientists have put into the refinement of these scales. It will ve important for researchers to work toward the improvement of the measures we use.

Table B-1
Reliability Coefficients for Six Variables

Measures	Cronbach's Alpha	Standardized Item Alpha
Authoritarianism	0.70	0.70
Anomia	0.66	0.67
Frustration	0.56	0.57
Rigidity	0.45	0.46
Withdrawal	0.38	0.39
Marital agreement	0.81	0.81

Appendix C:
1963 Interview Schedule

Person to Be Interviewed _____

Child Clinic Study
Attention: James Teele
Judge Baker Guidance Center
295 Longwood Avenue
Boston, Massachusetts

Schedule No._____

Name of Interviewer_____

Name of Child_____

Source Agency_____

Name and Relationship
of Person Interviewed_____

_____

Interviewer: Use the following introduction where appropriate, as, for example, when you have not been able to telephone the respondent before arriving. If you have set up the appointment in advance, use a "convenient" introduction.

Hello, I'm _____ from Children's Hospital (show ID). We are trying to learn how hospitals and social agencies can do a better job in providing services to children. We know that some time ago you were in touch with the _____ clinic about your (son, daughter, niece, nephew), _____. We would be grateful if you would help us by cooperating in our study. Any information you give us will be strictly confidential, and will be used only in helping children who need help.

First, I'd just like to know some simple facts about your family. I know it is sometimes difficult to remember exact dates and other facts, so just give me your best guess if you are not sure about any of the things I would like to know.

Interviewer: Be sure at this point to indicate if the person you are about to interview is the informant named on cover sheet. Also verify the kin relationship of the informant to the child. If the desired informant is not present, interview the closest adult female relative.

1. First, I would like to have some information about your child or children living with you here. (If the informant is not a parent or guardian of the child, obtain information about the child's brothers and sisters).

Name of Child	Sex	Date of Birth	Grade in School	Fill in only if not in school: Employment or not?
1				
2				
3				
4				
5				
6				

(Interviewer: Skip 1a if informant is not the child's parent.)

1a. Do you have any other children, not living with you? __1 Yes __2 No
    If yes, complete the following:

Name of Child	Sex	Date of Birth	Grade in School	Where is this child now?
1				
2				
3				

Interviewer: If informant is not the child's mother or father, ask questions 2-4 about the child's mother.

2. What is your present marital status? (That is, are you married, separated, etc.) (02:12)

_____ 1 married at present   _____ 3 divorced   _____ 5 never married
_____ 2 separated   _____ 4 widowed   _____ X DK or NA

If never married, skip 2a

2a. How long have you been married (separated, divorced, or widowed? (2:13-14)

_____ years   _____ 0 not married   _____ X DK

Now, I would like some information about you and your spouse. (Interviewer: If informant is not a parent or guardian of the child in the study, ask question 3 about the child's parents or guardians. If information is not known, write in DK for each category.)

(02:15-32)

3.

	Age	Usual Occupation	Highest grade completed (Circle one)	Religion	Nationality	Birthplace: City, Country
Mother			1,2,3,4, 5,6,7,8, 9,10,11, 12,12/			
Father			1,2,3,4, 5,6,7,8 9,10,11, 12,12/			

4. Before the _____ Clinic was contacted, were any of the follow-

ing persons or agencies contacted about (his) (her) problems?
(For court clinic cases:) Before _____ came to the attention of
the court, were any of the following persons or agencies contacted?

(02:33–56)

	Yes	No	If Yes, Why	If Yes, How long ago (in years)
Clergymen	____1	____2	_____	
Psychiatrists	____1	____2	_____	
Social Workers	____1	____2	_____	
Probation or Police Officers	____1	____2	_____	
School Teachers	____1	____2	_____	
Child Guidance Centers	____1	____2	_____	
Family Service Agencies	____1	____2	_____	
Other	____1	____2	_____	

5. Whose idea was it to contact the _____ Clinic?
    (For court clinic cases:) Whose idea was it to contact the court clinic
    (or psychiatrist)?

    _____

6. In your opinion, what or who caused _____'s problem? (02:58)

    _____

7. When was the problem first noticed (month and year)?____ (02:59–62)

8. Was _____ in school at the time the _____Clinic was
    contacted?   (02:63)

    _____1 Yes   _____2 No   _____X DK

9. If _____ *was* in school, how well was he getting along with his
    teachers at school at the time you (or caller) were (was) in contact with
    the _____ Clinic?   (02:64)

    _____1 Yes   _____3 not too well _____4 poorly
    _____2 fairly well   _____5 not in school_____X DK

10. If _____ *was not* in school, ask: Was he employed at the time
    you (or caller) were (was) in touch with the _____ Clinic?
                                                                  (02:65)

    _____1 Yes   _____2 No   _____X DK

10a. *If Yes*, ask: How was he getting along on the job?   (02:66)

_____1 very well   _____2 fairly well   _____3 not too well

_____4 poorly   _____X DK

11. How was _____ getting along at home with other members of the family about the time you (or caller) were (was) in touch with the Clinic?   (02:67)

_____1 very well   _____2 fairly well   _____3 not too well

_____4 poorly   _____X DK

Lots of kids do things at home or in the community which their parents worry about. I will mention some of these things.
Now, would you please think back to around the time before contact with the _____ clinic.

12. Would you please indicate how frequently—never, rarely, sometimes, or often—_____ did the following things occur around the time you (caller) called the clinic: (03:12-34)

	Never	Rarely	Some-times	Often	DK	NA
a. kept bad company	___1	___2	___3	___4	___X	___Y
b. got into fights	___1	___2	___3	___4	___X	___Y
c. stayed out too late	___1	___2	___3	___4	___X	___Y
d. had bad dreams	___1	___2	___3	___4	___X	___Y
e. told lies	___1	___2	___3	___4	___X	___Y
f. was sad or unhappy	___1	___2	___3	___4	___X	___Y
g. was a truant from school	___1	___2	___3	___4	___X	___Y
h. took things that did not belong to him	___1	___2	___3	___4	___X	___Y
i. was disobedient at home	___1	___2	___3	___4	___X	___Y
j. destroyed things	___1	___2	___3	___4	___X	___Y
k. used swear words	___1	___2	___3	___4	___X	___Y
l. made you lose your patience	___1	___2	___3	___4	___X	___Y
m. had failed to pass an exam	___1	___2	___3	___4	___X	___Y

n.	stayed by himself	___1	___2	___3	___4	___X	___Y
o.	cried a lot	___1	___2	___3	___4	___X	___Y
p.	misbehaved at school	___1	___2	___3	___4	___X	___Y
q.	set fires	___1	___2	___3	___4	___X	___Y
r.	masturbated or played with himself	___1	___2	___3	___4	___X	___Y
s.	had problems with opposite sex	___1	___2	___3	___4	___X	___Y
t.	wetting problem	___1	___2	___3	___4	___X	___Y
u.	feeding problem	___1	___2	___3	___4	___X	___Y
v.	soiling	___1	___2	___3	___4	___X	___Y
w.	threatened suicide	___1	___2	___3	___4	___X	___Y
x.	Other:_____	___1	___2	___3	___4	___X	___Y

13. How difficult did you (the caller) find it to talk to the people at the _____ Clinic about _____'s problem?   (03:35)

_____1 not difficult   _____2 slightly   _____3 fairly
      at all   difficult   difficult

_____4 very difficult_____X DK

If 3 or 4: why did you (the caller) find it difficult?   (03:36)

_____

_____

14. How helpful did you (the caller) feel the person(s) was (were) with whom you (he, she) spoke about _____'s problem?   (03:37)

_____1 very helpful _____2somewhat   _____3 slightly
                      helpful   helpful

_____4 not helpful _____X DK or NR
      at all

15. How understanding did you (the caller) feel the person(s) was (were) with whom you (he, she) spoke about _____'s problem? (03:38)

_____1 very   _____2 somewhat   _____3 slightly
      understanding   understanding   understanding

_____4 not under-   _____X DK or NR
      standing at all

16. How comfortable did you (the caller) feel in talking about _____'s problem to Clinic personnel?   (03:39)

_____1 very   _____2 somewhat   _____3 slightly
      comfortable   comfortable   comfortable

_____4 not comfor- _____X DK
      fortable at all

(For guidance-clinic cases) Let me read you a list of things which child guidance clinics have said to callers who have contacted the clinics about children. Please indicate if the clinic said or did any of the following things: (03:41–49)

	Yes	No	DK or NR
a. The clinic could not take on any new cases, as it was overloaded	____1	____2	____X
b. A private psychiatrist should be consulted	____1	____2	____X
c. The child should be sent away for his own good	____1	____2	____X
d. Wait a few months and call back if necessary	____1	____2	____X
e. The clinic would call back in a few weeks or months	____1	____2	____X
f. The problem was not a big one and would probably "pass"	____1	____2	____X
g. It would be a good idea if another clinic which had had experience with this kind of problem were contacted	____1	____2	____X
h. The child was too old for this clinic	____1	____2	____X
i. The child did not live in the area covered by this clinic	____1	____2	____X

17. (For court-clinic cases) Let me read you a list of things which people in the court clinics may say to people about their children. Please indicate if the clinic said any of the following things: (03:41–49)

	Yes	No	NR
a. The clinic could not take on any new cases, as it was overloaded	____1	____2	____X
b. A private psychiatrist should be contacted	____1	____2	____X
c. It might be better for the family if the child were sent to a detention center	____1	____2	____X
d. It would be better for the child if he were sent to a detention center	____1	____2	____X

e. If his family promised to cooperate, the clinic would try to help   _____1   _____2   _____X

f. The family should try to get the child into a different school   _____1   _____2   _____X

g. It would be a good idea if he got a job   _____1   _____2   _____X

h. Another clinic or agency should be contacted   _____1   _____2   _____X

i. Other (indicate): _____   _____1   _____2   _____X

18. How did you (or caller) feel about the advice given by the people at the _____ Clinic? (Probe)   (03:50)

_____

_____

19. Were you (or caller) referred to any other clinic or agency?   (03:51)

_____1 Yes   _____2 No   _____X DK

(*If No or DK,* go to question 21)
(*If Yes,* ask questions 19a, b, c and 20)

19a. Where were you (or caller) referred? _____(03:52)

19b. Were you (or caller) just told to call or did the Clinic arrange the referral for you (telephone, letter, etc.)?   (03:53)

_____1 told to call   _____2 arranged by   _____X DK
                        the Clinic

19c. Did you (or caller) call? _____1 Yes _____2 No _____X DK (03:54)

If Yes: (1) About how long did it take before you (or caller) were able to call?   (03:55)

_____

(2) What happened when you (or caller) called? (Probe) (03:56)

_____

_____

If No: Why didn't you (or caller) follow the Clinic's suggestion? (Probe)   (03:55)

_____

_____

_____

Skip 20 if the informant is not the person who contacted the clinic.

20. Here are some things people have said about how they *felt* when they were told by the clinic to go elsewhere. Would you please tell me if you felt any of the following things:

	Yes	No	NR	NA
a. I didn't really know exactly where I was to go or what I was to do	1	2	X	Y
b. I did not feel comfortable in talking to any new people about the problem	1	2	X	Y
c. I felt going elsewhere would cost more money than I could afford	1	2	X	Y
d. I didn't like the clinic's suggestion in the first place	1	2	X	Y
e. I felt that following the clinic's suggestion would upset the child	1	2	X	Y
f. I felt I would be able to handle the problem by myself	1	2	X	Y
g. I felt the problem would really take care of itself after a while	1	2	X	Y
h. I just felt I didn't have the time or energy to follow the advice	1	2	X	Y
i. Please indicate what other feelings you had when you were told to go elsewhere:	1	2	X	Y

_____

_____

21. Now, please indicate how frequently _____ has been doing any of these things in recent months (if child is in a detention center or rehab. center, enter NA):   (04:12–34)

Symptoms	Never	Rarely	Some-times	Often	DK	NA
a. kept bad company	1	2	3	4	X	Y
b. got into fights	1	2	3	4	X	Y

		1	2	3	4	X	Y
c.	stayed out late	___1	___2	___3	___4	___X	___Y
d.	had bad dreams	___1	___2	___3	___4	___X	___Y
e.	told lies	___1	___2	___3	___4	___X	___Y
f.	was sad or unhappy	___1	___2	___3	___4	___X	___Y
g.	truanted	___1	___2	___3	___4	___X	___Y
h.	took things	___1	___2	___3	___4	___X	___Y
i.	was disobedient at home	___1	___2	___3	___4	___X	___Y
j.	destroyed things	___1	___2	___3	___4	___X	___Y
k.	used swear words	___1	___2	___3	___4	___X	___Y
l.	made you lose your patience	___1	___2	___3	___4	___X	___Y
m.	failed an exam	___1	___2	___3	___4	___X	___Y
n.	stayed by self	___1	___2	___3	___4	___X	___Y
o.	cried a lot	___1	___2	___3	___4	___X	___Y
p.	misbehaved at school	___1	___2	___3	___4	___X	___Y
q.	set fires	___1	___2	___3	___4	___X	___Y
r.	masturbated or played with himself	___1	___2	___3	___4	___X	___Y
s.	had problems with opposite sex	___1	___2	___3	___4	___X	___Y
t.	feeding problem	___1	___2	___3	___4	___X	___Y
u.	wetting	___1	___2	___3	___4	___X	___Y
v.	soiled self	___1	___2	___3	___4	___X	___Y
w.	threatened suicide	___1	___2	___3	___4	___X	___Y
X.	Other: _____	___1	___2	___3	___4	___X	___Y

22. In general, compared with _____'s behavior at the time of the contact with the _____ (court clinic), do you think _____'s behavior is: (04:35)

_____1 much better   _____2 somewhat better

_____3 somewhat worse   _____4 much worse   _____X DK

23. Do you think he would have gotten better if he had had regular contact with the _____ Clinic?   (04:36)

_____1 Yes   _____2 No   _____X DK

24. Is _____ in school now?   (04:37)

   _____1 Yes   _____2 No   _____X DK

   If Yes: How well is he getting along with his teacher?   (04:38)

   _____1 very well   _____3 not too well   _____5 not in school

   _____2 fairly well   _____4 poorly   _____X DK

25. Is he employed at present?   (04:39)

   _____1 Yes   _____2 No

   If Yes: How is he getting along on the job?   (04:40)

   _____1 very well   _____2 fairly well   _____3 not too well

   _____4 poorly   _____X DK

26. How is _____ getting along at home with other members of the
   family   (04:41)

   _____1 very well   _____2 fairly well   _____3 not too well

   _____4 poorly   _____X DK

27. Since the contact with the _____ Clinic, has _____ been
   involved in trouble with legal authorities?   (04:42)

   _____1 Yes   _____2 No_____X DK

   If Yes: (a) When did the trouble occur (year and month)?   (04:43-46)
            (b) What was the trouble about?

   Interviewer: Specify the act which led to legal involvement, such as stealing
   an automobile.

   _____

   _____

   _____

28. As you know, ther are various people and agencies which have contact
   with children who have problems. Generally speaking, who do you feel
   would be helpful to children with problems? (Probe)   (05:12&13)

   _____

   _____

   _____

   _____

29. Since the contact with the _____ Clinic, have you or any other

member of the family seen any of the following persons or contacted any of the following agencies with respect to _____'s problems?

(05:14–21)

	Yes	No	DK
A Clergyman	___1	___2	___X
A Psychiatrist	___1	___2	___X
A Child Guidance Center	___1	___2	___X
A Social Worker	___1	___2	___X
A Probation Officer	___1	___2	___X
A Court Clinic	___1	___2	___X
A Family Service Agency	___1	___2	___X
A School Teacher	___1	___2	___X

30. Whether you have seen any of these people or not, in general, how helpful do you feel any of the following would be: (05:22–29)

	Very Helpful	Somewhat Helpful	Not Too Helpful	DK
Clergymen	___1	___2	___3	___X
Psychiatrist	___1	___2	___3	___X
Child Guidance Centers	___1	___2	___3	___X
Social Workers	___1	___2	___3	___X
Probation Officers	___1	___2	___3	___X
Court Clinics	___1	___2	___3	___X
Family Service Agencies	___1	___2	___3	___X
School Teachers	___1	___2	___3	___X

Interviewer: In question 31 below, first go down the list and get responses regarding likelihood of family seeing each of the persons or agencies. After completing this, ask "why not" for each of the persons or agencies for which category 3 or 4 is checked.

31. If _____'s problem returns or gets worse, how likely would the family be to do any of the following: (05:30–45)

	Very Likely	Fairly Likely	Not Too Likely	Not Likely At All	Not?	Why
see a minister	___1	___2	___3	___4	___X	_____
see a psychiatrist	___1	___2	___3	___4	___X	_____

call a guidance center	___1	___2	___3	___4	___X _____
call a law officer	___1	___2	___3	___4	___X _____
call a family agency	___1	___2	___3	___4	___X _____
see his teacher	___1	___2	___3	___4	___X _____
handle it alone	___1	___2	___3	___4	___X _____
do nothing	___1	___2	___3	___4	___X _____

Other: (specify) _____

---

32. In general, do you feel that _____'s problems are _____3, more serious than those of other children his age; _____, the same as those of other children his age; _____3, less serious. than those of other children his age; _____X DK.   (05:46)

33. How hopeful do you feel about _____'s chances of developing into a normal adult?   (05:47)

    _____1 very hopeful   _____2 somewhat   _____3 not too
           hopeful   hopeful

    _____4 not hopeful   _____X DK
           at all

    (Skip question 34 if _____ does not have a sibling.)

34. How hopeful do you feel about (name of sibling closest to _____ in age)'s chances of developing into a normal adult?   (05:48)

    _____1 very hopeful   _____2 somewhat   _____3 not too
           hopeful   hopeful   hopeful

    _____4 not hopeful   _____X DK
           at all

Ask Questions 35 to 41 only of informants who are child's parents or guardians and who are or have been married.

Now I would like to ask you a few things about yourself:

35. Were you married more than once?   (05:49)

    _____1 Yes   _____2 No   _____X NR

If respondent has been married more than once, ask questions 36 to 41 regarding most recent marriage.

36. Every marriage has its agreements and disagreements. We would like to

know whether you and your spouse have generally agreed about the
following things: (05:50–60)

	Yes	No	DK
a. Handling family finances or money matters	___1	___2	___X
b. How to spend leisure time	___1	___2	___X
c. Religious matters	___1	___2	___X
d. Amount of time that should be spent together	___1	___2	___X
e. Amount of time that should be spent with children	___1	___2	___X
f. Choice of friends	___1	___2	___X
g. Dealing with in-laws	___1	___2	___X
h. On bringing up the children	___1	___2	___X
i. Where to live	___1	___2	___X
j. Way of making a living	___1	___2	___X
k. Household chores	___1	___2	___X

37. Everything considered, would you say that your marriage is (was)
                                                           (05:61)

_____1 very happy   _____2 somewhat   _____3 somewhat
         happy   unhappy

_____4 very unhappy _____X DK

38. How many children did you want to have when you first got married?
_____   (05:62)

39. How many did your spouse want? _____   (05:63)

Interviewer: Ask 40 only if there was disagreement between questions 38
and 39.

40. Was the number of children you hoped to have a problem between you
and your spouse?   (05:65)
_____1 Yes   _____2 No

41. With regard to bringing up the children, do you (have you) and your
spouse agree(d) always, agree(d) most of the time, agree(d) some of the
time, or agree(d) little of the time about the following things: (05:66–73)

	Agree(d) always	Agree(d) most of the time	Agree(d) some of the time	Agree(d) very little of the time	DK
a. How late the child(ren) stay(s) up	___1	___2	___3	___4	___X
b. How late they can stay out in the street or on dates	___1	___2	___3	___4	___X
c. Clothes for the child(ren)	___1	___2	___3	___4	___X
d. Ways of punishing or disciplining them	___1	___2	___3	___4	___X
e. Household chores	___1	___2	___3	___4	___X
f. Their schooling	___1	___2	___3	___4	___X
g. Teaching them good manners	___1	___2	___3	___4	___X
h. Allowance money	___1	___2	___3	___4	___X
i. Other (specify)_____	___1	___2	___3	___4	___X

42. What do you think punishment should be when _____ is very disobedient?   (05:74)

_____1 he should be scolded   _____2 he should be whipped

_____3 he should not be given any privileges, such as money to spend

_____4 the police should be   _____X DK
        called

43. What does (did) your spouse think the punishment should be when _____ is very disobedient?   (05:75)

_____1 he should be scolded   _____2 he should be whipped

_____3 he should not be given any privileges, such as money to spend

_____4 the police should be   _____X DK or NR
        called

44. Do you like the neighborhood you live in?   (06:12)

_____1 a lot   _____2 some   _____3 a little   _____4 not at
                                                                      all

45. To which of the groups do you feel closest?   (06:13)

_____1 working class   _____2 middle class

_____3 upper class   (_____ X DK)

46. When you left school what particular kind of occupaton or life work was it your ambition to achieve some day?   (06:14)

_____

47. How many times did you visit with friends (at your home or theirs) in the last month? _____   (06:15)

48. Do you have any hobbies?   ____1 Yes   ____2 No   (06:16)

    If Yes: (a) What is your chief hobby? _____   (06:17)

        (b) How many hours a week do you spend at your hobby? ____

49. How many times did you visit with relatives (at your home or theirs) in the last month? _____   (06:19)

50. How many times did you attend religious services in the last month?
    _____   (06:20)

51. Are you a member of any clubs, unions, lodges, or other organized groups?   (06:21)

    _____1 Yes   _____2 No

    _____   _____

    If Yes: (a) Which ones? _____   (06:22)

        (b) Do you attend their meetings   (06:23)

    _____1 rarely   _____2 sometimes   _____3 regularly

52. How much money does the person who is the chief breadwinner of _____'s family earn?   (06:24)
    (Before taxes) (Use Card 1)_____

_____

Week	Month	Year
____1 if under $15	Under $25	Under $780
____2 if 15–24	65–99	780–1299
____3 if 25–49	100–199	1300–2599
____4 if 50–64	200–319	2600–3899
____5 if 65–99	320–429	3900–5199
____6 if 100–124	430–539	5200–6499
____7 if 125–149	540–649	6500–7799
____8 if 150–174	650–749	7800–9199
____9 if 175–199	750–859	9200–10,499
____10 if 200 plus	860 plus	10,500 plus

53. Does _____'s family receive any pension or welfare money?

(06:25)

_____1 Yes   _____2 No   _____X DK

If Yes: Approximately how much is this per month? _____   (06:26)

54. Now tell me whether you agree or disagree with the following:

	Agree	Disagree	(NR)	
a. If you want to keep your health, go to sleep at the same time every night	___1	___2	___X	(06:27)
b. On the whole, life gives you a lot of pleasure	___1	___2	___X	(06:28)
c. You sometimes can't help wondering whether anything is worthwhile anymore	___1	___2	___X	(06:29)
d. What young people need most of all is strict discipline	___1	___2	___X	(06:30)
e. There are two kinds of people in this world, the weak and the strong	___1	___2	___X	(06:31)
f. Any good leader should be strict with people under him in order to gain respect	___1	___2	___X	(06:32)
g. Prison is too good for sex criminals; they should be publicly whipped, or worse	___1	___2	___X	(06:33)
h. The most important thing to teach children is absolute obedience to their parents	___1	___2	___X	(06:34)
i. Nowadays a person has to live pretty much for today and let tomorrow take care of itself	___1	___2	___X	(06:35)
j. In spite of what some people say, the problems of the average man are getting worse, not better	___1	___2	___X	(06:36)
k. It's hardly fair to bring children into the world with the way things look for the future	___1	___2	___X	(06:37)
l. These days a person doesn't really know whom he can count on	___1	___2	___X	(06:38)
m. A person has moments when he feels he is a stranger to himself	___1	___2	___X	(06:39)

n. Nothing ever turns out for me the
   way I want it to   ___1   ___2   ___X   (06:40)

o. There's little se writing public
   officials because they aren't really
   interested in the problems of the
   average man   ___1   ___2   ___X   (06:41)

55. Now, we would like to know whether you would say yes or no to the
following:

a. Whatever you do must be done
   perfectly. Would you give your
   child such advice?   ___1   ___2   ___X   (06:42)

b. One drink is too many. Would you
   give your child such advice?   ___1   ___2   ___X   (06:43)

c. Never show your feelings to others. ___1   ___2   ___X   (06:44)

d. Once your mind is made up, don't
   let anything change it.   ___1   ___2   ___X   (06:45)

e. Very often, the old way of doing
   things is the best way.   ___1   ___2   ___X   (06:46)

f. When you go out, do you usually
   prefer to go by yourself?   ___1   ___2   ___X   (06:47)

g. Do you feel somewhat apart even
   among friends?   ___1   ___2   ___X   (06:48)

h. To avoid arguments do you
   usually keep your opinions
   to yourself?   ___1   ___2   ___X   (06:49)

i. Do you feel you have had
   your share of good luck in
   life   ___1   ___2   ___X   (06:50)

56. Now, I have just one more thing to ask you to do. (Hand respondent
    Card No. 2.)

Interviewer: Questions 57–63 are to be asked only if this case is a withdrawn
case.

57. How many visits did you (or caller) make to the _____ Clinic?
                                                              (07:12)

    _____ (use numbers) _____ X DK.

58. Whom did you (or caller) see there? (Position or title) _____

    _____ X DK.   (07:13)

59. What did you (or caller) talk about? _____ (07:14)

_____

60. All in all, what did you (or caller) like most about the _____
    Clinic? _____ (07:15)

61. All in all, what did you (or caller) like least about the _____
    Clinic? _____ (07:16)

62. Why did you (or caller) withdraw from the clinic? (Probe) _____
    _____ (07:17)

63. Some people stop going to the clinic for different reasons. Did you (or
    caller) withdraw for any of the following reasons?

		Yes	No	DK	
a.	It was hard to keep appointments	__1	__2	__X	(07:18)
b.	The people there were not friendly	__1	__2	__X	(07:19)
c.	It was felt that the clinic did as much as it could for _____.	__1	__2	__X	(07:20)
d.	The clinic just wasn't helping ____.	__1	__2	__X	(07:21)
e.	_____ was upset by having to go there.	__1	__2	__X	(07:22)
f.	_____'s problems just seemed to go away by themselves	__1	__2	__X	(07:23)
g.	Members of my family did not like the idea of _____'s going there.	__1	__2	__X	(07:24)
h.	The family could not afford the expense	__1	__2	__X	(07:25)
i.	It was decided to look for help elsewhere.	__1	__2	__X	(07:26)
j.	The waiting time was too long.	__1	__2	__X	(07:27)

Card 2

As you know words have a different meaning to different people. Here is a list of 40 words. Please look at those in capitals in the left hand column and decide which *one* of the four words to the right comes closest to the having the same meaning as the one in CAPITALS.

Take only one line at a time. Just tell me the number of the one of your choice.

A.	WEIRD	1. tire	2. bore	3. note	4. eery
	TWIST	1. onto	2. game	3. warp	4. whip
	STERN	1. rear	2. glum	3. rage	4. shop
	QUOTA	1. cite	2. part	3. read	4. atom
	FLESH	1. fast	2. lard	3. glit	4. pulp
B.	GREET	1. vast	2. live	3. like	4. hail
	WRATH	1. veil	2. mask	3. race	4. rage
	IRATE	1. rant	2. lift	3. ired	4. like
	PEACE	1. fear	2. rule	3. gain	4. pact
	ELIDE	1. omit	2. dash	3. bump	4. trod
C.	GRIME	1. smut	2. poem	3. fool	4. best
	DRAFT	1. draw	2. wood	3. reef	4. hero
	ABYSS	1. rule	2. duet	3. urge	4. gulf
	GRAVE	1. rant	2. deep	3. dirt	4. tomb
	FLOUT	1. hurt	2. jeer	3. fool	4. drop
D.	CANAL	1. duck	2. duct	3. rer	4. wade
	COUNT	1. rely	2. main	3. rich	4. faze
	INANE	1. loco	2. pert	3. void	4. wise
	WHARF	1. dock	2. bark	3. warp	4. blow
	CAPER	1. romp	2. ness	3. wrap	4. roll
E.	CEASE	1. bend	2. open	3. stop	4. hire
	WAVER	1. sway	2. disk	3. abet	4. abut
	STORM	1. wild	2. wash	3. dead	4. rave
	PETAL	1. foot	2. leaf	3. bike	4. tend
	CLOUD	1. gray	2. haze	3. rain	4. soft
F.	FLUNK	1. fail	2. bite	3. drop	4. dolt
	VISTA	1. call	2. doze	3. idle	4. view
	ARDOR	1. zeal	2. iron	3. gilt	4. vine
	POUND	1. oval	2. beat	3. lead	4. hear
	BLANK	1. shot	2. espy	3. area	4. void

G.	PADRE	1. rope	2. peal	3. boat	4. monk
	FACET	1. pain	2. turn	3. side	4. easy
	QUACK	1. fake	2. duck	3. lack	4. slap
	PRICK	1. fool	2. hair	3. dirt	4. spur
	MURKY	1. fend	2. gray	3. scum	4. dark
H.	TEMPT	1. sexy	2. lead	3. time	4. wear
	THINK	1. muse	2. shit	3. nick	4. know
	GROSS	1. bulk	2. oily	3. ream	4. vile
	PRIMP	1. look	2. fuss	3. dent	4. evil
	COVET	1. envy	2. coat	3. rill	4. love

Interviewer Ratings

1. *House Type* (Check One):

   _____1. Excellent houses. This includes only houses which are very
             large single-family dwellings in good repair and sur-
             rounded by large lawns and yards which are landscaped
             and well cared for. These houses have an element of osten-
             tation with respect to size, architectural style, and general
             condition of yards and lawns.

   _____2. Very good houses. Roughly, this includes all houses which
             do not quite measure up to the first category. The primary
             difference is one of size. They are slightly smaller, but still
             larger than utility demands for the average family. Exclu-
             sive apartment buildings, large apartments, servants.

   _____3. Good houses. In many cases they are only slightly larger
             than utility demands. They are more conventional and less
             ostentatious than the two higher categories. Apartment
             houses with medium to large apartments, well kept but no
             fancy display.

   _____4. Average houses. One and a half to two-story wood-frame
             and brick single-family dwellings. Conventional style, with
             lawns well cared for but not landscaped. Small apartments
             in clean but plain buildings, strictly utility.

   _____5. Fair houses. In general, this includes houses whose condi-
             tion is not quite as good as those houses given in 4 rating.
             It also includes smaller houses in excellent condition.
             Apartments in deteriorated buildings, often converted
             from large homes, and public housing projects.

   _____6. Poor houses. In this, and the category below, size is less
             important than condition in determining evaluation.
             Houses in this category are badly run down but have not
             deteriorated sufficiently that they cannot be repaired. They
             suffer from lack of care but do not have the profusion of
             debris which surrounds houses in the lowest category.

   _____7. Very poor houses. All houses which have deteriorated so
             far that they cannot be repaired. They are considered
             unhealthy and unsafe to live in. All buildings not originally
             intended for dwellings, shacks, and overcrowded
             buildings. The halls and yards are littered with junk, and
             many have an extremely bad odor.

2. *Dwelling Area* (Check One):

_____1. Very high. The best houses in town are located in such an area. The streets are wide and clean and have many trees.

_____2. High. Dwelling areas felt to be superior and well above average but a little below the top. There are fewer mansions and pretentious houses in such districts than in the first. However, the chief difference is one of reputation.

_____3. Above average. A little above average in social reputation and the eye of the scientific observer. This is an area of nice but not pretentious houses. The streets are kept clean and the houses are well cared for.

_____4. Average. These are ares of workingmen's homes which are small and unpretentious but neat in appearance.

_____5. Below average. All the areas in this group are undesirable because they are close to factories, or because they include the business section of town, or are close to the railroad.

_____6. Low. These areas are run down and semi-slums. The houses are set close together. The streets and yards are often filled with debris, and in some of the smaller towns some of the streets are not paved.

0_____7. Very low. Slum districts, the areas with the poorest reputation in town, not only because of unpleasant and unhealthy geographical positions; for example, being near a garbage dump or a swamp; but also because of the social stigma attached to those who live there.

_____x. Did not see dwelling area.

Interviewer Ratings of Respondent

Please use the following ten-point scales and rate each respondent on the degree to which the statements listed below describe characteristics of the respondent. Thus, for example, if the informant *is extremely active,* you would rate her (him) closer to 9 than you would to 0.

Is very active	0	1	2	3	4	5	6	7	8	9
Shows solidarity and friendliness	0	1	2	3	4	5	6	7	8	9
Intelligence	0	1	2	3	4	5	6	7	8	9
Is very tense	0	1	2	3	4	5	6	7	8	9
Initiative	0	1	2	3	4	5	6	7	8	9
Makes others feel he understands them	0	1	2	3	4	5	6	7	8	9
Rationality and logic	0	1	2	3	4	5	6	7	8	9
Gets upset easily	0	1	2	3	4	5	6	7	8	9
Makes many suggestions	0	1	2	3	4	5	6	7	8	9
Likeability	0	1	2	3	4	5	6	7	8	9
Clear-mindedness	0	1	2	3	4	5	6	7	8	9
Tends to be nervous	0	1	2	3	4	5	6	7	8	9
Assertiveness	0	1	2	3	4	5	6	7	8	9
Emotionality	0	1	2	3	4	5	6	7	8	9

Appendix D:
1975–1976 Interview
Schedule

Child Clinic Study (Follow-up)
Return to: James E. Teele
Sociology Department
Boston University
96 Cummington Street
Boston, Ma. 02215

Person to be interviewed _____

Relationship of Interviewee to Child_____

Schedule No. _____

Name of Initial Interviewer in 1963_____

Name of Follow-up Interviewer in 1976 _____

Name of Child _____

Source Agency _____

Date of Interview _____

Date on which consent was obtaned for participation in the study _____

(check one) Consent obtained: Via telephone_____

Via letter _____

Address: _____

Telephone: _____

Instructions for Interviewer to follow when telephoning for an appointment:

Hello, I'm _____ from Boston University. I work with Professor Teele, a professor of Sociology at Boston University. _____, his assistant, contacted you recently so that we could discuss how you now feel about the experiences and problems you had in raising _____. I am calling for an appointment at your convenience.

CONSENT FORM (TO BE COMPLETED AT RESPONDENT'S HOME PRIOR TO THE INTERVIEW)

I, _____, have been informed of the purpose of a study by Dr. Teele (or _____) of Boston University. It is my understanding that this study is designed only to explore the problems which parents encounter in searching for help for their children and the steps which parents take to solve developmental problems of their children. I have been promised complete confidentiality. If there is any question I care not to answer, that question will be omitted. I have given my consent to be interviewed for the purposes described above.

Name: _____

Date: _____

1. Ten or eleven years ago, when you sought help at the _____ clinic, you apparently did not receive the help you sought at that time. Do you recall contacting the _____ clinic around 1962 re _____'s problem?

   Yes _____ No _____

2. Just think back and try to recall why you sought help at that time for _____. (Probe)

3. What was (he) (she) doing at that time that was a source of concern for you? (Probe into the child's exact *behavior* ten or eleven years ago. If this material was obtained in question 2, go on to question 4.)

4. Can you recall how you felt about your child's behavior back in 1962 or 63? (Probe)

5. Can you recall your participation in this study (through an interview with one of Dr. Teele's associates) back in 1963?

   _____ Yes, definitely   _____ Not sure   _____ No

6. In 1963, you said that you thought _____ was the cause of your child _____'s problem. Did the clinic or anyone say anything or do anything to change or confirm this feeling? (Probe)

6a. How would you now explain you child's behavior (in 1962)?

6b. What disagreements were there among family members about the causes of _____'s behavior?

7. What advice were you given at the clinic when you contacted them in 1962?

7a. How did you feel about the advice you were given at the clinic?

8. In 1963, can you recall what kind of adult you thought _____ would become?

8a. [*If appropriate, ask* the following] Did you think your child had an excellent, good, fair, or poor chance of growing up into a well-adjusted adult?

9. Did you, after that time, (1963), change your expectations about your child _____'s future possibilities? (If yes, ask why and when they changed, in addition to the nature of the changed expectation. Probe, especially as to *when* they changed expectation, and as to *if* and *when* they stopped worrying about the child's future.)

Interviewer introduction to question 10: We would like to review with you now your experiences subsequent to our contact with you in 1963, covering both earlier experiences in 1963 or 64 as well as any later ones you had in connection with your child's problems.

10. After our contact with you in 1963, can you recall the various relatives, persons unrelated to you, or agencies that you contacted for assistance with reference to the child's problem at that time? (Interviewer, just list all the persons or agencies contacted and appropriate date. If no person or agency was contacted, go on to question 13.)

Person or Agency Contacted	Date of Contact	Source of Referral
(1)		
(2)		
(3)		
(4)		
(5)		
(6)		

10a. What did your child know about any of this effort on your part (Probe)

11. *Interviewer*, now say: "Let's go over the list of persons or places you contacted. Would you please try to tell me *why* you contacted them and *what* advice or assistance they gave you and what you thought about the advice or assistance, and what you did?" (Probe please)

1st contact: _____ *Why?*

   Advice or assistance given:

   What you thought about the assistance:

   What did you do about it:

2nd contact: _____ *Why?*

   Advice or assistance given:

   What you thought about the assistance:

What you did about it:

3rd contact: _____ *Why?*

Advice or assistance given:

What you thought about the assistance:

What you did about it:

4th contact: _____ *Why?*

Advice or assistance given:

What you thought about the assistance:

What you did about it:

5th contact: _____ *Why?*

Advice or assistance given:

What you thought about the assistance:

12. Please try to think of anyone else you talked to about this problem, like a minister or relative not mentioned before regardless of when you contacted them. (Interviewer, probe)

13. If no one contacted as per question 10, ask: Why was that? (Probe)

14. Were there any other manifestations of this earlier problem?

14a. Can you think of any other problems that you had with your child _____ other than the one you contacted the clinic about in 1962?
Yes _____ No _____ (If no, skip to 17)

15. If *yes to 14,* ask: *What* were these other problems, *When* did they occur, and what did you *do* about them?

Problem	*Date of Problem*	*Action Taken*
1.		
2.		
3.		
4.		
5.		

15a. If *yes* to 14, ask: Were the subsequent or later problems more difficult for you to deal with than earlier problem? more (   ) less (   )

15b. Why was that? (Probe)

16. If *yes* to 14, ask: For these subsequent problems, who or what did you find especially helpful in coping with each of them? Who or what was discouraging about each of them?
Problem 1 (a) (state problem)

    (b) (person or agency contacted)

    (c) (helpful action)

    (d) (discouraging experience)

Problem 2 (a) (problem)

    (b) (person or agency contacted)

    (c) (helpful action)

    (d) (discouraging experience)

Problem 3 (a) (problem)

    (b) (person or agency contacted)

    (c) (helpful action)

    (d) (discouraging experience)

Problem 4 (a) (problem)

    (b) (person or agency contacted)

    (c) (helpful action)

    (d) (discouraging experience)

Problem 5 (a) (problem)

    (b) (person or agency contacted)

    (c) (helpful action)

    (d) (discouraging experience)

17. Was there a time when you stopped worrying about (his) (her) problems? Why was that?

18. Just how is (your child) _____ doing these days? Please tell me about (him) (her). (Probe, note to interviewer: please be sensitive to respondent's feeling if the child is not doing well.)

18a. Did _____ complete high school? _____ attend college _____ Years of ed. _____

18b. What about _____'s job or career? Please describe it. Does he/she like this type of work?

18c. How much satisfaction does _____ get in his/her job at present?
(1) _____ a lot (loves the job)   (2) _____ some
(3) _____ little   (4) _____ none (hates job)
(9) _____ don't know

18d. How much friction does _____ experience with other people at work?
(1) _____ very little or none   (2) _____ some
(3) _____ a lot   (9) _____ don't know

18e. Is _____ married now? _____

18f. *If married ask:* "How many children _____ have?" _____

18g. Is _____ happily married? _____

18h. How much friction does _____ experience in marriage?
(1) _____ very litle or none   (2) _____ some
(3) _____ a lot   (9) _____ don't know

18i. How satisfying is _____'s social life to him/her?
(1) _____ is not at all satisfying   (2) _____ somewhat satisfying
(3) _____ very satisfying   (9) _____ don't know

18j. How much of _____'s time does he/she spend with friends other than spouse)?
(1) _____ little or none   (2) _____ some
(3) _____ a lot   (9) _____ don't know

18k. In general, how outspoken would you say _____ is with others?

   (1)_____very quiet   (2)_____about equally quiet and outspoken

   (3)_____very outspoken(9)_____don't know

18l. What happened to influence your child's present adjustment? (Probe into whether school or relatives or other adults affected the child's development, whether good or adverse).

19. When was the last time you saw _____ ?

19a. In what city does _____ live? _____

19b. How often do you see _____?

   (1)_____once a week   (2)_____once a month

   (3)_____once a year   (4)_____seldom or never

19c. If respondent sees _____ "seldom or never," ask how often they talk on the telephone.

   (1)_____often   (2)_____sometimes   (3)_____seldom or never

20. Do you have other children? Yes_____ No_____ Number_____

   If yes, what are their names and ages? If no, skip to question 26.

Names of Additional Children	Ages	Sex	Last Seen
_____	_____	_____	_____
_____	_____	_____	_____
_____	_____	_____	_____
_____	_____	_____	_____
_____	_____	_____	_____
_____	_____	_____	_____

20a. Was this like the combination of girls and boys that you had hoped for? Yes _____ No _____

   Comments, if any:

20b. How many children did you want initially?_____

21. *If yes to 20,* ask: Did you have any problems with your other (child) (children)? Yes _____ No _____

22. *If yes to 21,* ask: What kind of problems did you have with your other (child) (children) and at what age? (Interviewer, please obtain information on problems for each additional child beginning with the oldest.)

Child's Name   *Problem*

_____

_____

_____

_____

23. *If yes to 21,* ask: What did you do about the problems your other children had? (Probe especially who they sought/and got assistance from.)

24. *If yes to 21,* ask: Was it easier to deal with problems your other children had? Yes _____ No _____

24a. Why was that?

25. What form of punishment did you usually employ for your children when they were very disobedient?

(Note any distinctions made)

26. Over the last 10 or 11 years what major changes have there been in your family? (Probe)

27. Over the last 10 years or so, have there been any major crises or problems in the family? Yes _____ No _____

27a. If *yes* to 27, ask: What were these problems and can you also tell me what you did about them?

1st crisis and what was done:

2nd crisis and what was done:

3rd crisis and what was done:

4th crisis and what was done:

5th crisis and what was done:

28. Given the situation that you had back in 1962–63 with _____,
    just what would you do if you had the chance to do it again?

29. Given the situation of 1962–63 again, would you contact a child psychi-
    atrist, a guidance center, or the like again?

30. If someone close to you were in that situation now (e.g., your child),
    what advice would you give them?

31. [*Interviewer:* refer back to question 16] With respect to each subequent
    problem which you had with your child, _____, what do you
    now think would have been the most helpful action?

I just have a few more questions and we'll be through.

32. What is your present marital status? _____
    If married, how long? _____

33. Could you tell me your usual occupation now?_____

34. What is your (husband's, wife's) usual occupation now?_____

35. How much money does the family's chief breadwinner earn (before
    taxes)? (Interviewer, use card 1.)_____

36. How many times have you changed your residence during the last ten
    years? _____

37. Do you like the neighborhood you live in?
    _____1 a lot,   _____2 some,   _____3 a little,   _____4 not at all

38. Are you a member of any clubs, lodges, etc.? _____ Yes _____ No

38a. *If yes,* which ones?

38b. Do you attend their meetings?
    _____1 rarely   _____2 sometimes   _____3 regularly

Card 1
Income

Week	Month	Year
_____1 if under $15	Under $65	Under $780
_____2 if 15–24	65–99	780–1299
_____3 if 25–49	100–199	1300–2599
_____4 if 50–64	200–319	2600–3899
_____5 if 65–99	320–429	3900–5199
_____6 if 100–124	430–530	5200–6499
_____7 if 125–140	540–649	6500–7799
_____8 if 150–174	650–749	7800–9199
_____9 if 175–199	750–859	9200–10,499
_____10 if 200–250	860–1,000	10,500–11,999
_____11	1,000–1,250	12,000–14,999
_____12	1,250–1,666	15,000–20,000
_____13	1,666–plus	20,000–plus

39. How many times did you visit with friends (at your home or theirs) in the last month?_____

40. How many times did you visit with relatives in the last month? _____

41. How many times did you attend religious services in the last month?

_____

42. To which of the following groups do you feel closest?

_____1 working class   _____2 middle class

_____3 upper class   _____x don't know

43. Please answer if your child _____ has had any of the following conditions in the past 6 months. If yes, did the condition limit hes/her usual activity?

   a. Cough any time during the
      day or night for about three
      weeks?   Yes_____ No_____ Act. Limited____
   b. Sudden feelings of weakness
      or faintness?   Yes_____ No_____ Act. Limited____

c. Getting up some mornings
    exhausted even with a usual
    amount of rest   Yes_____ No_____ Act. Limited____

d. Feeling tired for weeks at a
    time for no special reason?   Yes_____ No_____ Act. Limited____

e. Frequent headaches?   Yes_____ No_____ Act. Limited____

f. Skin rash or breaking out on
    any part of body?   Yes_____ No_____ Act. Limited____

g. Diarrhea (loose bowel
    movements) for four or five
    days   Yes_____ No_____ Act. Limited____

h. Shortness of breath even after
    light work?   Yes_____ No_____ Act. Limited____

i. Waking up with stiff or
    aching joints or muscles?   Yes_____ No_____ Act. Limited____

j. Pains or swelling in any joint
    during the day?   Yes_____ No_____ Act. Limited____

k. Frequent backaches?   Yes_____ No_____ Act. Limited____

l. Unexplained loss of over ten
    pounds in weight?   Yes_____ No_____ Act. Limited____

m. Repeated pains in or near the
    heart?   Yes_____ No_____ Act. Limited____

n. Repeated indigestion or upset
    stomach?   Yes_____ No_____ Act. Limited____

o. Repeated vomiting for a day
    or more?   Yes_____ No_____ Act. Limited____

p. Sore throat or running nose
    with a fever as high as 100
    degrees for at least two days   Yes_____ No_____ Act. Limited____

q. Nose stopped up, or sneezing,
    for two weeks or more?   Yes_____ No_____ Act. Limited____

r. Unexpected bleeding from any
    part of the body not caused
    by accident or injury?   Yes_____ No_____ Act. Limited____

s. Abdominal pains (pains in the
    belly or gut) for at least a
    couple of days?   Yes_____ No_____ Act. Limited____

t. Any infections, irritations, or
    pains in the eyes or ears?   Yes_____ No_____ Act. Limited____

u. Toothache?   Yes_____ No_____ Act. Limited____

v. Bleeding gums   Yes_____ No_____ Act. Limited____

w. Severe pain anywhere on your
   body on a regular basis?   Yes_____ No_____ Act. Limited____

x. Regularly coughing up phlegm
   (sputum)?   Yes_____ No_____ Act. Limited____

z. Please list any diseases or
   conditions that _____
   had diagnosed by a doctor
   in the last 6 months.

_____

_____

_____

44. What was the father's role in childrearing? For example, did he gener-
    ally express his opinions about the children's behavior?_____

    Did he talk with the children frequently?_____

    Did he participate in any aspects of treatment (if any was obtained)?

_____

    Which child/children did he spend most time with?_____

_____

45. Think of the pleasures and problems that exist in life in your family
    these days.
    Think of each of the following moods and rate each of these moods
    from "1" to "10" with "1" being "not at all" and "10" being "most
    strongly."

    frustrated _____   neglected _____
    generally supported   loved and cared about _____
    _____
    worried _____   listened to _____
    happy _____

46. Please indicate whether you talk to other people about the following
    items:

                                    *Family
                                    Members   Others   No one*

    1. My personal opinions about
       religion   _____   _____   _____

2. What I believe is attractive
to men and women . . .   _____   _____   _____

3. What I would appreciate most
for a present. . .   _____   _____   _____

4. What I enjoy *least* in my
daily work   _____   _____   _____

5. What I feel are my shortcomings in the performance
of my activities . . .   _____   _____   _____

6. What I feel are my special
strong points and skills. . . _____   _____   _____

7. How I budget my money . . . _____   _____   _____

8. Whan I feel good about
myself . . .   _____   _____   _____

9. When I feel bad about
myself . . .   _____   _____   _____

47. Please put these four feelings in the order in which you believe it's ok
for a child to express. Give "1" to the one that's *most ok*, etc. Also, do
this for your spouse the way you believe he/she would presently order
them.

	Self				*Spouse*	
	Present		*Present*		*1962*	
	Boy	*Girl*	*Boy*	*Girl*	*Boy*	*Girl*
Anger						
Fear						
Joy						
Sadness						

Interviewer Ratings

1. *House Type* (Check One):

_____1. Excellent houses. This includes only houses which are very large single-family dwellings in good repair and surrounded by large lawns and yards which are landscaped and well cared for. These houses have an element of ostentation with respect to size, architectural style, and general condition of yards and lawns.

_____2. Very good houses. Roughly, this includes all houses which do not quite measure up to the first category. The primary difference is one of size. They are slightly smaller, but still larger than utility demands for the average family. Exclusive apartment buildings, large apartments, servants.

_____3. Good houses. In many cases they are only slightly larger than utility demands. They are more conventional and less ostentatious than the two higher categories. Apartment houses with medium to large apartments, well kept but no fancy display.

_____4. Average houses. One and a half to two-story wood-frame and brick single-family dwellings. Conventional style, with lawns well cared for but not landscaped. Small apartments in clean but plain buildings, strictly utility.

_____5. Fair houses. In general, this includes houses whose condition is not quite as good as those houses given in 4 rating. It also includes smaller houses in excellent condition. Apartments in deteriorated buildings, often converted from large homes, and public housing projects.

_____6. Poor houses. In this, and the category below, size is less important than condition in determining evaluation. Houses in this category are badly run down but have not deteriorated sufficiently that they cannot be repaired. They suffer from lack of care but do not have the profusion of debris which surrounds houses in the lowest category.

_____7. Very poor houses. All houses which have deteriorated so far that they cannot be repaired. They are considered unhealthy and unsafe to live in. All buildings not originally intended for dwellings, shacks, and overcrowded buildings. The halls and yards are littered with junk, and many have an extremely bad odor.

2. *Dwelling Area* (Check One):

_____1. Very high. The best houses in town are located in such an area. The streets are wide and clean and have many trees.

_____2. High. Dwelling areas felt to be superior and well above average but a little below the top. There are fewer mansions and pretentious houses in such districts than in the first. However, the chief difference is one of reputation.

_____3. Above average. A little above average in social reputation and the eye of the scientific observer. This is an area of nice but not pretentious houses. The streets are kept clean and the houses are well cared for.

_____4. Average. These are ares of workingmen's homes which are small and unpretentious but neat in appearance.

_____5. Below average. All the areas in this group are undesirable because they are close to factories, or because they include the business section of town, or are close to the railroad.

_____6. Low. These areas are run down and semi-slums. The houses are set close together. The streets and yards are often filled with debris, and in some of the smaller towns some of the streets are not paved.

_____7. Very low. Slum districts, the areas with the poorest reputation in town, not only because of unpleasant and unhealthy geographical positions; for example, being near a garbage dump or a swamp; but also because of the social stigma attached to those who live there.

_____x. Did not see dwelling area.

Interviewer Ratings of Respondent

Please use the following ten-point scales and rate each respondent on the degree to which the statements listed below describe characteristics of the respondent. Thus, for example, if the informant *is extremely active,* you would rate her (him) closer to 9 than you would to 0.

Is very active	0	1	2	3	4	5	6	7	8	9
Shows solidarity and friendliness	0	1	2	3	4	5	6	7	8	9
Intelligence	0	1	2	3	4	5	6	7	8	9
Is very tense	0	1	2	3	4	5	6	7	8	9
Initiative	0	1	2	3	4	5	6	7	8	9
Makes others feel he understands them	0	1	2	3	4	5	6	7	8	9
Rationality and logic	0	1	2	3	4	5	6	7	8	9
Gets upset easily	0	1	2	3	4	5	6	7	8	9
Makes many suggestions	0	1	2	3	4	5	6	7	8	9
Likeability	0	1	2	3	4	5	6	7	8	9
Clear-mindedness	0	1	2	3	4	5	6	7	8	9
Tends to be nervous	0	1	2	3	4	5	6	7	8	9
Assertiveness	0	1	2	3	4	5	6	7	8	9
Emotionality	0	1	2	3	4	5	6	7	8	9

Name Index

Abeles, Gina, 148
Antonovsky, Aaron, 139, 189
Appley, M., 233
Armstrong, Stephen, 139, 224

Bacal, Howard, 12
Bales, Robert Freed, 224
Balfour, Frederick, 12
Barrett, C., 232, 233
Barron, Milton, 41
Baum, Rainer, 41
Beavin, J., 62
Becker, Wesley, 174, 189
Bergin, Allen, 5, 6, 12, 88, 233
Blake, Phyllis, 148
Borgatta, E.F., 11, 88
Bott, Elizabeth, 139
Brim, Orville, 233
Burgess, Ernest, 97, 139

Caplan, Gerald, 88
Clarke-Stewart, A., 233
Corsini, R.J., 88
Croog, Sydney, 10, 13, 56, 63, 189
Cumming, C. Randolph, 12
Cumming, J., 12

DeVinney, L., 13
Dohrenwend, Barbara, 10, 13, 63, 165,
   166, 167, 186, 189
Dohrenwend, Bruce, 10, 13, 63, 165,
   166, 167, 186, 189

Eckland, Bruce, 148
Eisenberg, J., 189
Empey, Lamar, 11
Ericson, Maynard, 11
Erikson, Erik, 231, 233
Eysenck, H.J., 2, 3, 5, 11, 12, 89, 139,
   206, 232

Freeman, Howard, 213, 214

Gardner, George, 38
Garfield, Sol, 12, 88, 233
Gersten, J., 186, 189
Goffman, Erving, 123, 139
Gomes, Beverly, 139, 224
Guttman, L., 92–93

Hadley, Suzanne, 139, 224
Hamburg, Beatrix, 233
Hampe, I.E., 233
Heath, Sheldon, 12
Helmreich, Robert, 194
Hoffman, Lois, 189
Hoffman, Martin, 189
Hollingshead, August, 39, 161, 189
Howard, Alan, 13

Inbar, Michael, 179, 189, 224

Jackson, D., 62
Jacobson, Lenore, 9, 10, 13, 224
Johnson, Norman, 40
Jones, Wyatt, 11

Kadushin, Charles, 12
Kathovsky, Walter, 2, 11
Kiesler, Donald, 5, 12
Kissel, Stanley, 12
Koos, Earl L., 40, 88
Kosa, John, 139, 189
Kuhn, Thomas, 7, 12

Lambert, Michael, 5, 6, 12, 233
Langner, Thomas, 13, 63, 149, 188,
   190
Lazarus, Richard, 166, 189, 231, 233
Levine, Sol, 13, 63, 189, 233
Levitt, E.E., 2, 3, 5, 11, 12, 89, 102,
   139, 206, 232
Lynn, D., 189

Maehr, Martin, 224

Subject Index

About the Author

James E. Teele is professor and chairman of the Department of Sociology at Boston University. He received the A.B. degree at Virginia Union University and the Ph.D. degree in sociology at New York University. Dr. Teele was staff sociologist at the Judge Baker Guidance Center and a member of the Department of Psychiatry at Children's Hospital in Boston when the study reported on here was initiated. Subsequently, he was an associate professor of sociology, Department of Maternal and Child Health at the Harvard School of Public Health, before joining the faculty of Boston University. In 1970, he was a forum member and consultant to the White House Conference on Children. He has served on review committees at the National Center for Health Services Research and at the National Institute of Mental Health (Life Course Review Committee). In addition to serving as associate editor of the *Journal of Health and Social Behavior,* he has numerous publications relating to the field of deviant behavior, mental health, and education, including *Evaluating School Busing* (Praeger) and *Juvenile Delinquency: A Reader* (Peacock).